CASE STUDIES ON PROJECT MANAGEMENT IN PRACTICE

ELGAR CASES IN BUSINESS AND MANAGEMENT

Elgar Cases in Business and Management offer an instrumental resource to fulfil the needs of instructors in courses across the business curriculum. Spanning numerous discrete fields, Elgar Cases cover state-of-the-art developments in real-world business endeavours, providing expert analysis with an international focus. Casebooks are edited by leading instructors, who bring together experienced and knowledgeable case writers to illustrate and analyse contemporary business scenarios. Each case offers a strong foundation for constructive discussion and includes learning objectives and summary questions to guide classroom discussion. Teaching notes for each case provide opportunities for instructors to further develop understanding and promote class engagement. An invaluable boon to course leaders and students alike, Elgar Cases in Business and Management combine practicality, student engagement and international expertise to bring business and management alive!

For a full list of Edward Elgar published titles, including the titles in this series, visit our website at www.e-elgar.com.

CASE STUDIES ON PROJECT MANAGEMENT IN PRACTICE

Edited by

ALEJANDRO ROMERO-TORRES
Full Professor, Department of Business and Management, Université du Québec à Montréal, Canada

SHANKAR SANKARAN
Professor, School of the Built Environment, Faculty of Design and Society, University of Technology Sydney, Australia

JOSEPH GRIFFIN
Teaching Professor, College of Professional Studies, Northeastern University, USA

ELGAR CASES IN BUSINESS AND MANAGEMENT

EE Edward Elgar
PUBLISHING

Cheltenham, UK • Northampton, MA, USA

Published by

Edward Elgar Publishing Limited
The Lypiatts
15 Lansdown Road
Cheltenham
Glos GL50 2JA
UK

Edward Elgar Publishing, Inc.
William Pratt House
9 Dewey Court
Northampton
Massachusetts 01060
USA

Authorised representative in the EU for GPSR queries only: Easy Access System Europe - Mustamäe tee 50, 10621 Tallinn, Estonia, gpsr.requests@easproject.com

A catalogue record for this book is available from the British Library

Library of Congress Control Number: 2025944014

This book is available electronically in the **Elgar**online Business subject collection
https://doi.org/10.4337/9781035311279

MIX
Paper | Supporting responsible forestry
FSC® C013604

ISBN 978 1 0353 1126 2 (cased)
ISBN 978 1 0353 1127 9 (eBook)
ISBN 978 1 0353 7393 2 (ePub)

Printed and bound by CPI Group (UK) Ltd, Croydon, CR0 4YY

CONTENTS

CONTRIBUTORS

Elizabeth Arteaga-García, ***Universidad Espíritu Santo, Equador***

Ma. Elizabeth Arteaga-García is a doctoral candidate in Administration and Management of Organizations at Universidad Espíritu Santo, with a solid academic and professional background in project management. She holds master's degrees in Project Management from BES La Salle (Universidad Ramón Llull, Spain) and Business Administration from Université du Québec à Montréal (Canada) and ESPAE ESPOL (Ecuador). Elizabeth is a PMP-certified professional, currently serving as the quality and accreditation leader and director of master's programs in Operations and Technology at UEES. She has been recognized for her academic contributions, including several publications, awards, and editorial roles in prominent scholarly journals.

Monique Aubry, ***Department of Business and Management, Université du Québec à Montréal, Canada***

Monique Aubry, PhD, is associated professor at the School of Business and Management, (UQAM). Now retired from full professorship, she pursues her research on the development of megaprojects and organizing for projects. She acts as external adviser on the management of public projects for several ministries and public organisms in Quebec. She is a member of the Project Management Research Chair and of the UQAM's Health and Society Institute. In 2020, she was awarded the PMI Research Achievement Award. In 2012, she received the IPMA Research Award for her research on Project Management Offices.

André B. Barcaui, ***Federal University of Rio de Janeiro and Visiting Professor at the Getulio Vargas Foundation, Brazil***

André B. Barcaui is a seasoned educator and consultant from Rio de Janeiro, Brazil, with a rich academic background, including a DSc. in Business Management, and two postdoctoral degrees in Organizational Behavior and Artificial Intelligence. He also has a degree in Information Technology and Psychology. Professor, consultant, and author, he specializes in combining psychological insights with his IT and AI expertise to improve organizational and project management practices.

Shawn D. Belling, ***University of Wisconsin, United States***

Shawn D. Belling, EdD, PMP, PMI-ACP, CSP, RS@SP, teaches at University of Wisconsin – Madison and UW-Platteville – and University of Southern California. His academic interests are project management, organizational change, IT strategy, and product development. He released the books *Succeeding with Agile Hybrids* in 2020 and *Remotely Possible* in 2021. He holds PMP and ACP certifications from PMI and is a certified scrum professional and registered Scrum@Scale practitioner. He earned his bachelor of science from UW Whitewater, and master of science in Project Management from UW Platteville. He also earned a graduate diploma in Organizational Change Leadership from UW Platteville and doctorate of education in Leadership at the University of the Cumberlands.

Simona Bonghez, ***National University of Political Studies and Public Administration and Colors in Projects, Romania***

Simona Bonghez, PhD, PMP, is a seasoned management consultant, trainer, and speaker, with over 25 years' experience in project management. As the managing partner of Colors in Projects and a lecturer at the National University of Political Studies and Public Administration (NUPSPA) in Bucharest, she has made significant contributions to the fields of agile transformation, project management, and game-based design in education. Known for her engaging teaching style and her ability to connect theoretical concepts with practical applications, she continues to inspire professionals and students alike in navigating the complexities of modern project management.

Jessica Borg, ***School of Management at RMIT University, Australia***

Dr Jessica Borg is a lecturer in the School of Management at RMIT University, Australia. She is passionate about research that makes an impact on the working lives of professionals in today's complex work environments, with a particular focus on research in project-based workplaces and the built environment industry. Dr Borg is best known for her research on the work readiness and career readiness of project management professionals. She continues to research in the areas of workplace transitions, early career work readiness, career management, and professional skill development within project-based contexts.

Paul R. Bruno, ***Fiala Project Resources, United States***

Paul R. Bruno has spent 25 years researching, writing, and studying early Jeep history. After visiting key sites in the story, and years of research, he wrote *Project Management in History: The First Jeep.* After additional research he completed *The Original Jeeps* and *The Original Jeeps in Pictures.* Paul has more than 30 years' experience in the fields of project management and information technology. He holds bachelor's degrees in Management and Computer Software as well as master's degrees in Business Administration and History.

John H. Cable, ***United States***

John Cable, MArch, R.A. PMP, a distinguished academic leader and licensed architect with over 40 years' experience, has made significant contributions to project management education and research. As a professor at the University of Maryland's A. James Clark School of Engineering, he founded the graduate program in Project Management, two undergraduate minors, and the Center for Excellence in Project Management. He has taught courses on Project Management Fundamentals and Managing Projects in a Dynamic Environment, while leading seminars and workshops worldwide. His academic excellence earned him the Lilly Fellowship for innovation in teaching (2013) and recognition by the National Academy of Engineering's Frontiers of Engineering Education (2014). Previously, he served as chair of PMI's Global Accreditation Center (GAC) and contributed to NASA and the National Academy of Sciences on project management research. As a founder and former board chair of the GAC, he continues to serve the organization by leading on-site audit teams.

José Miguel Cevallos Chavez, ***Universidad Espíritu Santo, Equador***

José Miguel Cevallos Chávez is a seasoned professional with extensive experience in public administration, project management, and leadership of multidisciplinary teams in infrastructure, telecommunications, and energy sectors. He is the general manager of EP Aguas de Manta, overseeing significant projects financed by international organizations including the World Bank. Miguel holds a master's in Project Management from Universidad Espíritu Santo and has a strong command of project management methodologies, including Microsoft Project. Fluent in English and Spanish, he has also contributed significantly to Ecuador's telecommunications engineering and public service enhancement.

Caroline Coulombe, ***Department of Business and Management, Université du Québec à Montréal, Canada***

Caroline Coulombe has been a professor at ESG UQAM since 2013, with a PhD in management from a joint program between HEC Montréal (Canada) and EM Lyon (France), top business schools that blend North American positivist and European critical perspectives. She also holds a master's in Industrial Psychology from New York University (NYU). Specializing in organizational behaviour for over 15 years, her research and teaching focus on competency profiles, leadership, management practices, crisis management, and communication within organizations.

Issam El-Asbi, ***AIDIGITS Group, Greece***

Issam El-Asbi is the CEO of AIDIGITS Group (several BIM and digital transformation services providers), the academic director of AIDIGITS Digital Transformation Academies, and the director of the Global BIM Management for Infrastructures Master Program at Zigurat Institute of Technology. Before moving to consultancy, Issam worked with contractors as BIM Director for major projects in the Middle East and has been a champion for building BIM capabilities in the built environment. He has hands-on experience from actual implementation of BIM and digital activities and workflows on-site and off-site for over 25 years.

Sanaa El Boukri, ***Department of Business and Management, Université du Québec à Montréal, Canada***

Sanaa El Boukri, PhD, is professor in Project Management at the School of Business and Management (UQAM). She teaches in the master's program in Project Management. Her research focuses on the social complexity of major projects, project development, and process studies. She is a member of the Project Management Research Chair and the Laboratory for Transferring Innovative Practices in a Project Context (UQAM). She has published in several journals (including *Project Management Journal* and *International Journal of Project Management*). With her co-authors, she received the *PMJ*'s best paper award (2022).

Joseph Griffin, ***College of Professional Studies, Northeastern University, United States***

Joseph Griffin is the senior associate dean of Academic Affairs at Northeastern University's College of Professional Studies, where he also serves as a teaching professor in Project Management. Prior to Northeastern, he worked in construction and land development, and he currently holds a general contractor builder license. Dr Griffin authored the textbook *Residential Construction Management: Managing According to the Project Lifecycle* and numerous articles and papers related to project management. He earned a doctorate of ministry in Workplace Ethics & Leadership from Gordon-Conwell Theological Seminary, an MBA from Lenoir-Rhyne University, and a master's in Project Management from Western Carolina University.

Jonathan Harvey, ***Université du Québec à RImouski, Canada***

Jonathan Harvey is a professor of project management at UQAR. He holds a PhD in Management from ESG-UQAM, where his dissertation explored the interplay between practical wisdom and adaptive intelligence in crisis decision-making. His research examines ethical decision-making in NGOs, collaborative approaches to governance, and the dynamics of complexity and paradox in major public infrastructure projects.

Jose Rodrigo Juarez Cornelio, ***School of Civil Engineering, University of Leeds, United Kingdom***

Jose Rodrigo Juarez Cornelio is a lecturer in Project Management at the School of Civil Engineering at the University of Leeds. He holds a PhD in Project Management from the School of Civil Engineering at the University of Leeds. He has published his work on the termination of infrastructure megaprojects in the *International Journal of Project Management*, and presented in multiple international conferences, such as EURAM, BAM, EGOS, IRNOP, the International Megaprojects workshop, and to the World Bank.

Ulrik Bak Kirk, ***Department of Public Health, Aarhus University, Denmark***

Ulrik Bak Kirk is a chief consultant and PhD faculty fellow at Aarhus University, where he combines his extensive experience in digital public health research and innovation with his skills in agile change management, strategic communication, and policy. He is passionate about tackling complex global health challenges, such as endometriosis, harnessing digital opportunities, through creative and citizen science approaches while engaging multi-level stakeholders. He currently leads and coordinates the EU-funded H2020 FEMaLe Project as a certified half double practitioner.

Mohamed Laye, ***Division of Major Road Works, AGEROUTE, Senegal***

Mohamed Laye is a design engineer in Civil Engineering, graduating from the Polytechnic School of Thiès in 1997. He earned an International MBA in Management from University Paris Dauphine – IAE Paris Sorbonne – CESAG in 2018 and an Executive Doctorate in Business Administration (EDBA) in Management Science from the Business Science Institute of Luxembourg in 2021. He started his career at the Compagnie Sahélienne d'Entreprises, where he was a materials engineer, site manager and then director for road projects in six West African countries. Since 2016, he has been at the Senegalese Agency for Road Works and Management (AGEROUTE) where he currently holds positions as the major road works division manager and as a project implementation unit coordinator.

Bethan Morgan, ***Digital Outlook, United Kingdom***

Bethan Morgan combines extensive management experience in private and public sector bodies with substantial expertise in the teaching and research of digital transformation. She is a founding partner at Digital Outlook. Her current interests include leadership for change, particularly in the construction industry. Her work focuses on the socio-technical aspects of digitalization in organizations, ecosystems, and industries. Her interest in executive education is long-standing and has led to her authoring and teaching using the Harvard Teaching Case method. Having participated in teaching case regularly during her MBA (graduated *cum laude*), she has become a qualified instructor and uses this pedagogy extensively with international groups of executives.

Liv Juul Nielsen, ***Department of Public Health, Aarhus University, Denmark***

Liv Juul Nielsen holds a bachelor's degree in Nursing from Aarhus University College and a master's degree in Public Health (MScPH) from Aalborg University. She works as a research assistant in the FEMaLe Project, leading a work package about monitoring and assessing impact. She also holds a Project Management degree from Aarhus University and is certified at the Half Double foundation level. Besides project management, she works with qualitative interviews and has been studying women's experience with endometriosis during adolescence.

Eleni Papadonikolaki, ***Delft University of Technology, Netherlands***

Eleni Papadonikolaki, ARB, MAPM, SFHEA, is an associate professor in the Management of Engineering Projects and head of the Integral Design & Management section at the Faculty of Civil Engineering and Geosciences, Delft University of Technology (TU Delft). Eleni works with industry as an executive trainer and a management consultant and is a founding partner at Digital Outlook. Her research is on the intersection of digitalization and project studies. She is passionate about collaborative and industry-relevant research and, through it, helping engineering project teams to manage the interfaces between digital technology and projects.

Alejandro Romero-Torres, ***Department of Business and Management, Université du Québec à Montréal, Canada***

Alejandro Romero-Torres is a full professor at School of Management (ESG) at University of Quebec in Montreal (UQAM), holder of the chair in Project Management, ESG UQAM, director of the Lab for Innovative Practices in Project Context, and director of the Observatory of Public Projects. His main research expertise is the governance and management of infrastructure and digital projects, including issues related to stakeholders' engagement, decision-making, and value creation. He works closely with public organizations in Quebec to sustain project performance. He is also chair of directors for the Global Center Accreditation (GAC) of the Project Management Institute. He has a doctorate and master's degree in Technology Management from Polytechnique de Montreal (Canada) and a bachelor's degree in Information Technology Engineering from Anahuac University (Mexico).

Dorit Rotem, ***Israel***

Dorit Rotem has over 30 years' experience in a variety of positions and roles in the field of information systems. Currently, she is a strategic consultant for senior management in this field. Previously she served as chief information officer (CIO) in the food industry. She also served as delivery excellence, country leader, Israel at IBM, and for many years as a project manager at several companies in a variety of industries: telecom, health, and IS/IT services in banking. She is also a graduate of the Technion in Israel (Industrial and Management Engineering), having earned both a BSc and MSc from this prestigious university, which boasts several Nobel laureates. In 2022, she completed her doctorate (DBA) at SKEMA. She subsequently adapted her thesis into an article, which was published following peer review in the *Business and Economic Research Journal.*

Shankar Sankaran, *University of Technology Sydney, Australia*

Shankar Sankaran, PhD PMP, is a professor of Organizational Project Management at the University of Technology Sydney, Australia, teaching on a PMI-GAC-accredited Master of Project Management Course since 2006. He has taught systems thinking to managers since 2009 on that course. Shankar served on the PMI GAC board from 2018 to 2023. He has published articles and chapters on systems theories and praxis and their application and on project governance. He is also a past president of the International Society for the Systems Sciences, where he met prominent systems thinking scholars whose work influenced his teaching and research.

Per Svejvig, *Department of Management, Aarhus Business School, Denmark*

Per Svejvig is an associate professor in the Department of Management, Aarhus University, and Head of the Project Organizing and Management Research Group. His research interests encompass project management, rethinking project management, benefit realization management, project value creation, and virtual project management. He has published in prestigious journals, including the *International Journal of Project Management.* With a PhD in Enterprise Systems from Aarhus University, he brings over 25 years' business experience and is certified as a senior project manager (IPMA level B).

Nilton Hideki Takagi, *Institute of Computing, Federal University of Mato Grosso, Brazil*

Nilton Takagi is professor at the Computing Institute of the Federal University of Mato Grosso, Brazil, and researcher at the ALGORITMI Center at the University of Minho, Portugal. He has a PhD in Technologies and Information Systems, a master's in Informatics and another in Statistics for Data Science. He has an MBA in Project Management and is a graduate in Computer Science. In private companies and public institutions, he has held positions as PMO director, IT manager, ERP development team manager, and project manager. His current research interests address project management and business process management.

Thiago Meirelles Ventura, *Institute of Computing, Federal University of Mato Grosso, Brazil*

Thiago Ventura is professor at the Computing Institute of the Federal University of Mato Grosso, Brazil (UFMT) and worked as a project manager at the Information Technology Center (NUTI) at the same university. He has a PhD in Environment Physics, an MBA in Project Management, and a bachelor's in Computer Science. He is currently director of the Project Management Office at UFMT, being responsible for managing the institution's strategic project portfolio.

FOREWORD

John H. Cable, MArch, R.A. PMP

I am pleased to write the foreword to this collection of project management case studies. Why? As a lifelong project manager, I understand fully the power of stories as a means to convey ideas and culture. As young practitioners we often learned at the elbows of our mentors from the stories told over lunch and after work. We learn from the experience of others, and stories bridge the gap between theory and practice.

Early in my teaching career I had a student tell me that she was going to miss probably three classes because her company was preparing a client for court, and they were working long days, seven days a week. This was before our current learning management systems and recording classes for use online. I told her I would get her copies of my lecture slides and asked if she had a friend who would share their class notes. She said she did, "But, sir, you don't understand. What's important in your class, it's the stories you tell about actual cases to illustrate a concept when we ask you to explain something!" Case studies are stories.

The Harvard Business School pioneered the use of case studies in 1921 and has written volumes on the effectiveness of the method.

> Cases expose students to real business dilemmas and decisions. Cases teach students to size up business problems quickly while considering the broader organizational, industry, and societal context. Students recall concepts better when they are set in a case, much as people remember words better when used in context. Cases teach students how to apply theory in practice and how to induce theory from practice. The case method cultivates the capacity for critical analysis, judgement, decision-making, and action.[1]

Case Studies on Project Management in Practice provides relevant and timely case studies for both teaching and professional development from a global multi-industry perspective. The 16 cases organized in the PMI Talent Triangle® ways of working (6), power skills (5), and business acumen (5) – were prepared by faculty from 11 different countries, providing a rich resource for educators and practitioners.

The six **ways of working** cases look at:

1. A municipal water company and understanding the importance of applying scope management processes.
2. 'Planning is everything', applicable to a multinational information technology company signing a contract with a large public energy company being privatized to revamp its entire IT infrastructure. The contract was hastily negotiated with a poorly defined scope and consequently led to schedule and cost problems.

3. A property and casualty insurance company that examines the applicability and effectiveness of different project and program management methodologies.
4. 'The first Jeep', a case study on the American Bantam Car Company that dared to meet the challenge to develop a lightweight all-around vehicle and build the prototype in the surely impossible timeframe of 49 days.
5. A food company that is purchased from a large corporate food organization by a private person with the intention of becoming an innovative boutique leader in a niche market. Previously all IT services were provided by corporate and now it must build its own IT systems from scratch.
6. Case studies in Brazil that exemplify the information systems and technology center of a public university's involvement in government-to-government projects. A key aspect is the active management of success criteria.

The five **power skills** cases are:

1. 'Navigating complexity: integrating collaboration in public infrastructure projects' is a case of a large government organization needing to overhaul its construction processes amid industry-wide challenges such as labor shortages and declining productivity.
2. 'Scrum team tales' comprises series of short scenarios, each presenting a unique challenge encountered by a scrum team. the focus revolves around the roles of scrum master, product owner, and agile coach in addressing these specific situations.
3. 'Unraveling the ethical knot: a case study on deteriorating team dynamics' focuses on a real project team operating within a large organization. The team comprises diverse members from different departments, each with varying levels of experience and expertise.
4. 'Leveraging work readiness to develop a professional identity' is designed to enable students to become work-ready project managers who possess the attributes that allow them to thrive in their early careers.
5. 'Half Double methodology' presents a large EU-funded research project that has been running smoothly up to the halfway point but is starting to experience problems with lack of motivation and suboptimal delivery of services.

The five **business acumen** cases are:

1. The case of implementing a project management office in healthcare is oriented toward the analysis of social and political aspects that might lead to PMO implementation failure.
2. 'Making the decision of project termination during the delivery stage' presents a high-speed rail project in Peru that is on time at the one-third point but, due to competition for funds from other high-impact projects, the government is considering terminating the project.
3. 'Digital innovation strategy at a construction company's project business' explores how a significant construction company operating in over 40 countries with over 100,000 employees approaches digital innovation and transformation.

4. 'Achieving performance in major public infrastructure projects' is about diagnosing the problems with major road infrastructure projects, including the roles of all the stakeholders, to improve project performance.
5. The final chapter is a case using systems thinking to diagnose a complex contemporary real-life issue and developing a project scope to address the situation.

Relative to traditional lecturing, the conclusion is unequivocal: active learning formats such as using case studies are far more effective. The content is much stickier. The use of case studies engages the learner in active learning not only from the case itself but also from the experiences of fellow students. I am certain you will find these cases interesting and informative. Even though many may not be from your industry, there is much that can be learned from them that applies to yours.

NOTE

1. Nohria, Nitin (2021, December 21). What the case study method really teaches. *Harvard Business Review.*

INTRODUCTION TO *CASE STUDIES ON PROJECT MANAGEMENT IN PRACTICE*

Alejandro Romero-Torres

In today's rapidly evolving world, projects have become central to economic growth, organizational success, and societal transformation. Approximately a third of the gross domestic product (GDP) in developed countries is generated through projects (Schoper et al., 2018), highlighting their significant economic contribution. This phenomenon transcends regional boundaries, as organizations and governments worldwide increasingly rely on projects to drive innovation, infrastructure development, and service delivery. Scholars have coined the term "projectification of society" to describe this shift, where projects dominate not only industrial and technological sectors but also public administration, healthcare, and education (Lundin et al., 2015). Beyond their economic impact, projects are also essential for addressing global challenges, such as climate change, social inequality, and resource scarcity, by enabling focused efforts on complex, multi-stakeholder initiatives (Whyte & Mottee, 2022).

A project is commonly defined as "a temporary endeavor undertaken to create a unique product, service, or result" (PMI, 2021, p. 245). Three key characteristics are emphasized: temporariness, uniqueness, and a clear focus on delivering a specific outcome. Projects can range from straightforward tasks with clear objectives and well-understood methods to highly complex and ambiguous undertakings. While traditionally associated with engineering and construction, projects today span a wide range of domains, including business transformation, technological innovation, social change, and sustainable development.

At the organizational level, projects are now the preferred mechanism for executing strategies, driving innovation, and ensuring long-term competitiveness in an environment marked by volatility, uncertainty, complexity, and ambiguity (VUCA). They act as structured responses to dynamic environments, offering flexibility and targeted problem-solving approaches to achieve organizational objectives. However, alongside this growing reliance on projects, their complexity continues to increase, driven by factors such as globalization, digital transformation, and sustainability imperatives. Projects are no longer isolated initiatives but are interconnected with stakeholders, technologies, and regulatory frameworks. This interconnectedness raises the stakes, as project failures can have cascading effects on organizations, industries, and even national economies (Schoper et al., 2018). As projects continue to grow in both scale and significance, they are also shaping the way professionals work, develop competencies, and collaborate, making project management not only a professional discipline but also a critical societal capability for the twenty-first century (Ribeiro et al., 2021).

PROJECT MANAGEMENT

Rooted in management science and organizational theory, project management combines knowledge, skills, tools, and techniques to effectively balance resources, time, scope, quality, costs, and risks (Morris, 2013). Effective project management serves as a critical enabler of strategic execution, ensuring that initiatives are delivered on time, within budget, and aligned with overarching business objectives. In a world characterized by rapid technological advancements, shifting market demands, and increased global interconnectivity, the ability to manage projects effectively has become not just a competitive advantage but a fundamental necessity.

Over the past six decades, project management has evolved from its origins in large-scale US military and aerospace initiatives of the 1950s into a globally recognized discipline with standardized methodologies, professional certifications, and advanced academic programs (Burke & Barron, 2014). Today, project management stands as one of the fastest-growing academic and professional fields, drawing increasing attention from researchers and practitioners alike (Padalkar & Gopinath, 2018). This growing prominence is reflected in the integration of project management content into traditional university programs and the creation of specialized undergraduate and graduate degrees dedicated entirely to the discipline. While this trend is well-established in North America and Europe, it is also gaining significant momentum in emerging regions in Asia, Latin America, and Africa. Universities across these regions are actively developing tailored programs and certification pathways to equip future project managers with the skills needed to navigate complex and dynamic environments.

To support academic excellence and ensure consistent quality in project management education, the Project Management Institute (PMI) introduced a certification program for university curricula in the 1980s. Building on this initiative, PMI established the Global Accreditation Center (GAC) in 2001 as an independent academic accreditation body responsible for formalizing standards for project, program, and portfolio management education at the undergraduate, postgraduate, and doctoral levels. In 2025, over 200 academic programs worldwide hold PMI GAC accreditation, fostering collaboration, knowledge sharing, and continuous improvement in project management education. In parallel, other prominent associations, such as the International Project Management Association (IPMA) and the Association for Project Management (APM), also play a vital role in bridging the gap between theory and practice. Through partnerships with academic institutions, these organizations contribute to refining teaching methodologies, aligning curricula with industry needs, and promoting research that addresses real-world project management challenges.

PROJECT SUCCESS

Despite project success being a central theme in both professional practice and academic research, there remains no universally accepted definition of what constitutes project success. Historically, success was primarily evaluated through the "golden triangle" of time, cost, and quality, representing the fundamental dimensions of project performance (Morris, 2013). A project was considered successful if it met deadlines, stayed within budget, and delivered outputs that adhered to predefined quality standards. However, as projects have grown in scope, complexity, and interdependence, this narrow perspective has become insufficient to capture the broader dimensions of success in today's dynamic and multifaceted project environments.

Contemporary perspectives on project success have evolved to encompass dimensions beyond technical performance, including stakeholder satisfaction, innovation, and long-term value creation (Morris, 2013). Projects are no longer viewed as isolated endeavors but as integral components of larger organizational and societal systems, requiring alignment with strategic objectives and adaptability to diverse stakeholder expectations. This shift has given rise to a multidimensional understanding of success, balancing both tangible deliverables and intangible benefits. Recent developments in project management research, along with contributions from professional associations, emphasize value creation as a critical measure of success. Notably, in 2024, the PMI incorporated the concept of value into its project success framework, defining success as the "delivery of value that justifies the effort and expense." Projects are now expected not only to meet their immediate objectives but also to drive long-term organizational growth, competitive advantage, and societal advancement (Whyte & Mottee, 2022). A successful project not only satisfies client requirements but also addresses the broader needs of stakeholders, including team members, end users, and the wider community.

Despite significant advancements in understanding project success, persistent challenges remain. Research indicates that approximately 55 percent of projects still fail to achieve their intended outcomes, often due to unclear objectives, inadequate communication, or misalignment with organizational goals (Burrell, 2018). These findings highlight the inherent complexity of managing projects and the need for a diverse set of competencies to ensure success. Technical expertise, strong leadership, effective stakeholder engagement, and adaptability are all critical capabilities that project managers must mobilize to navigate the multifaceted nature of modern projects and deliver sustainable value.

PROJECT MANAGER COMPETENCIES

The success of a project is significantly influenced by the competencies of the project manager. Indeed, project managers with well-developed skills and abilities contribute more effectively to achieving project goals and overcoming challenges (Müller & Jugdev, 2012). Unlike general managers, project managers operate within temporary and unique environments, requiring a blend of specialized project management expertise and general business acumen. Effective project managers must navigate diverse expectations, align objectives with organizational goals, and address unforeseen challenges with agility.

A competency is commonly defined as a combination of knowledge, skills, and attitudes that enable an individual to perform a job effectively (Moradi et al., 2020). Dillon and Taylor (2015) distinguish between attribute-based competencies, which are the knowledge, attitudes, and skills required for effective performance, and performance-based competencies, which involve the practical application of these attributes in achieving desired outcomes. Theories of competency development suggest that these attributes are not innate but can be learned, refined, and adapted over time.

Project managers require a broad range of competencies to effectively respect project constraints, meet stakeholder expectations, lead teams, and navigate organizational dynamics (Müller & Jugdev, 2012). Project managers require a balanced combination of technical competencies (hard skills) and non-technical competencies (soft skills) to ensure project success. Hard skills encompass the knowledge, methodologies, tools, and techniques essential for planning, executing, and controlling projects. These include risk management, budgeting, scheduling, and proficiency with project management software and methodologies. Conversely, soft skills are centered on interpersonal abilities, such as communication, leadership, conflict resolution, motivation, emotional intelligence, and team building. While hard skills ensure effective project structuring, organization and execution, soft skills enable project managers to navigate complex social dynamics, align stakeholders, and foster team cohesion. Research indicates that technical skills are often more prevalent among project managers, leading to an imbalance in skill application. Effective project managers integrate these two skills to maintain equilibrium among the key project constraints – time, cost, and quality – and deliver sustainable outcomes.

Professional associations have played a pivotal role in structuring project manager competencies through well-established frameworks. The IPMA introduced the Individual Competence Baseline (ICB) in 2006, emphasizing a holistic approach to project management by categorizing competencies into technical, behavioral, and contextual dimensions. Behavioral competencies, such as leadership, conflict management, motivation, and results orientation, are particularly highlighted as essential for effective project delivery. Similarly, the PMI developed the Project Management Competency Development Framework (PMCD) in 2002, identifying three core dimensions: project management knowledge, project management performance, and personal competency, which includes critical attributes like leadership, communication, and cognitive skills.

In 2015, the PMI introduced the Talent Triangle® to address the evolving skill sets required for project management professionals in increasingly complex and dynamic environments. In 2022, the PMI updated the PMI Talent Triangle® and identified three critical competency areas:

- **Ways of working** (technical project management competencies) focus on the knowledge and skills necessary to effectively deliver project outcomes. This includes planning, scheduling, and risk management. It acknowledges various methodologies, tools, and techniques for managing projects, such as waterfall, agile, and hybrid approaches.
- **Power skills** (leadership competencies) emphasize the ability to guide, motivate, and direct teams, as well as engage stakeholders. These competencies include emotional intelligence, team building, and conflict resolution. They are typically acquired over time and through experience and must be adapted to the specific context and stakeholders of each project.

- **Business acumen** (strategic and business management) highlights the importance of aligning projects with organizational goals, understanding market conditions, and driving business value. These competencies are crucial for ensuring long-term project success. Project managers utilize them to define the value to be delivered, ensure alignment with the expected value definition throughout execution, and ultimately create and deliver value to all project stakeholders.

OBJECTIVES OF THIS BOOK

This book aims to support project management learning and competency development by offering a carefully curated collection of detailed case studies that illustrate how projects, programs, and portfolios are managed in real-world contexts. By presenting case studies from different regions, industries, and organizational settings, this book addresses a growing need for relevant, timely, and diverse teaching and professional development resources. The collaborative nature of this work brings together contributions from project management researchers, educators, and practitioners worldwide, offering unique insights into a variety of project management challenges, strategies, and success factors. These case studies highlight the complexities of modern projects and showcase how project managers must integrate technical project management skills, interpersonal leadership competencies, and strategic business acumen to deliver value effectively.

The use of case studies as an active learning tool is central to this book. Active learning, through case study analysis, promotes critical thinking, problem-solving, and reflective practice, enabling learners to engage deeply with real-world project scenarios (Ellet, 2018). This approach supports the development of essential competencies, aligning with globally recognized frameworks such as the PMI Talent Triangle® and the IPMA Competence Baseline. Through interaction with case materials, readers are encouraged to confront ambiguity, evaluate trade-offs, and make informed decisions – skills that are crucial for navigating the volatility, uncertainty, complexity, and ambiguity of modern project environments.

To provide a structured and meaningful learning experience, this book includes three distinct types of case studies, inspired by Ellet (2018):

- Decision scenario: Readers are placed in the role of decision-makers, tasked with making critical choices or taking decisive actions based on a thorough understanding of a project, program, or portfolio situation.
- Evaluation scenario: Readers are asked to analyze a specific practice, strategy, or approach, identifying its strengths, weaknesses, and potential areas for improvement.
- Problem diagnosis scenario: Readers must identify the root causes of significant project challenges and propose actionable solutions, often requiring both analytical rigor and creative thinking.

These case studies are not merely exercises in theoretical reflection; they are tools designed to bridge theory and practice, helping learners understand the real-world application of project management principles. By combining diverse perspectives and scenarios, the book seeks to equip students, professionals, and educators with the knowledge, skills, and mindset needed to excel in project management roles across different cultural, industrial, and organizational contexts.

STRUCTURE OF THE BOOK

The book is designed to support project management learning and competency development through 16 case studies drawn from a variety of industries and countries, offering readers a rich and diverse learning experience. The book is divided into three main parts, each aligned with the PMI Talent Triangle® framework, focusing on ways of working, power skills, and business acumen. This structure ensures a balanced exploration of the technical, interpersonal, and strategic dimensions of project management competencies.

Part I, Ways of working, includes six case studies that focus on the technical skills, methodologies, and tools essential for effective project delivery. These cases explore topics such as project recovery, agile methodologies, risk management, and success criteria, offering readers insights into structured and methodical approaches to project execution.

Case study 1: Municipal Public Water Company: shaping water – Elizabeth Arteaga and José Miguel Cevallos Chavez explore financial and organizational challenges in a public water company, highlighting project scope definition, stakeholder resistance, and strategic decision-making.
Case study 2: Project recovery: IT in the energy sector – André B. Barcaui illustrates an analysis of a large-scale technology renewal project in the energy sector, addressing planning deficiencies, risk management, and crisis intervention strategies.
Case study 3: Evaluating project management approaches: a property and casualty insurance company – Shawn D. Belling examines the transition from strict scrum to hybrid agile practices in an insurance company to improve agility and value delivery.
Case study 4: The first Jeep – Paul R. Bruno illustrates a historical case of rapid prototyping, innovation, and risk management under extreme time constraints during the creation of the first Jeep.
Case study 5: Navigating the challenges of rapid information systems implementation – Dorit Rotem explores the rapid development and deployment of IT systems in a food company, highlighting challenges in time management and technical readiness.
Case study 6: Avenue to project success: a decision scenario based on the success management approach – Nilton Hideki Takagi and Thiago Meirelles Ventura analyze two government-to-government projects in Brazil, emphasizing success criteria, stakeholder engagement, and project impact.

Part II, Power skills, presents five case studies emphasizing interpersonal and leadership skills, including communication, team dynamics, ethical decision-making, and conflict resolution. These cases highlight the critical role of human interaction in achieving project objectives.

Case study 7: Navigating complexity: integrating collaboration in public infrastructure projects – Caroline Coulombe and Jonathan Harvey examine the integration of collaborative design processes in public infrastructure projects to improve stakeholder alignment and project outcomes.
Case study 8: Scrum team tales: conquering challenges with scrum masters and product owners – Simona Bonghez analyzes recurring challenges in agile scrum teams, focusing on collaboration, role clarity, and conflict resolution.
Case study 9: Unraveling the ethical knot: a case study on deteriorating team dynamics – Simona Bonghez explores ethical dilemmas and leadership challenges within a project team, emphasizing the importance of trust and ethical decision-making.
Case study 10: Leveraging work readiness to develop a professional identity – Jessica Borg illustrates the concept of work readiness and its role in developing a professional identity among project management graduates.
Case study 11: Half Double methodology in a large EU-funded research and innovation project – Liv Juul Nielsen, Ulrik Bak Kirk, and Per Svejvig present the Half Double application in a research project, addressing motivation, morale, and stakeholder satisfaction.

Part III, Business acumen, comprises five case studies that focus on aligning project outcomes with organizational goals, understanding market dynamics, and driving sustainable value creation. These cases illustrate how project managers can integrate strategic insights into their decision-making processes.

Case study 12: Navigating the tides of transformation: Natalia's quest for a project management office – Sanaa El Boukri and Monique Aubry demonstrate how a PMO has been adopted in a healthcare organization, focusing on stakeholder management and organizational design.
Case study 13: Making the decision of project termination during the delivery stage: the Keystone XL Pipeline – Jose Rodrigo Juarez Cornelio describes the complexities of project termination decisions during the delivery stage, considering financial, political, and strategic factors.
Case study 14: Digital innovation strategy at a construction company's project business – Eleni Papadonikolaki, Bethan Morgan, and Issam El-Asbi explore digital innovation strategy in a construction company, focusing on leadership, resource allocation, and strategic priorities.
Case study 15: Achieving performance in major public infrastructure projects: the case of road works in Senegal – Mohamed Laye describes stakeholder roles and performance evaluation in large-scale public infrastructure projects in Senegal.
Case study 16: Developing systems thinking competencies in project managers – Shankar Sankaran highlights the use of simulations to teach systems thinking, enabling project managers to approach complex issues holistically.

Each case study in this book follows a structured format designed to provide a comprehensive understanding of real-world project management scenarios while fostering active learning and critical thinking. The structure begins with an opening section that introduces the main protagonist(s), establishes the project context, and outlines the key problem, decision, or challenge to be addressed. The body of the case study presents a chronological narrative, offering detailed background information, descriptions of the key stakeholders, and an exploration of the specific issues faced during the project life cycle. This section incorporates multiple perspectives to encourage readers to consider diverse viewpoints and alternative solutions. The concluding section synthesizes the main issues discussed, often raising new questions or challenges to provoke further reflection. Each case is accompanied by key takeaways and a set of reflective questions, guiding readers in analyzing the scenario and deriving actionable insights.

In addition, pedagogical notes are provided at the companion website (see https://doi.org/10.4337/9781035311279) to complement each case study as a support resource for instructors and facilitators. These pedagogical tools ensure that each case study can be effectively integrated into classroom instruction, workshops, or professional training programs. They include a case synopsis, offering a brief overview of the scenario, context, and primary issues explored. The target audience is clearly defined, specifying the appropriate academic or professional level for engagement with the case. Learning objectives are explicitly stated, aligning with the knowledge, skills, and attitudes the case aims to develop. A teaching plan outlines recommendations for delivering the case study, including suggested activities, discussion prompts, and facilitation tips. Additionally, the pedagogical notes include a set of assignment questions with possible answers, carefully crafted to encourage reflection, analysis, and critical debate. Supporting materials, such as references for further reading or supplemental resources, are also provided to enrich the learning experience.

REFERENCES

Burke, R., & Barron, S. (2014). *Project management leadership: Building creative teams*. Wiley.

Burrell, D. N. (2018). Project management: Leading, creating, implementing and ensuring success. *Journal of Management and Innovation*, *4*(1), 24–34.

Dillon, L., & Taylor, C. (2015). Competency-based training: A practical guide. *Journal of Workplace Learning*, *27*(5), 335–350.

Ellet, W. (2018). *The case study handbook: A student's guide to analyzing, writing, and presenting case studies* (2nd ed.). Harvard Business Review Press.

Lundin, R. A., Arvidsson, N., Brady, T., Ekstedt, E., Midler, C., & Sydow, J. (2015). *Managing and working in project society: Institutional challenges of temporary organizations*. Cambridge University Press.

Moradi, S., He, L., & Chen, P. (2020). The role of competencies in project management success. *International Journal of Managing Projects in Business*, *13*(5), 1045–1061.

Morris, P. W. G. (2013). *Reconstructing project management*. Wiley-Blackwell.

Müller, R., & Jugdev, K. (2012). Critical success factors in projects: Pinto, Slevin, and Prescott–the elucidation of project success. *International Journal of Managing Projects in Business*, *5*(4), 757–775.

Padalkar, M., & Gopinath, S. (2018). Six decades of project management research: Thematic trends and future opportunities. *International Journal of Project Management*, *34*(7), 1305–1321.

Project Management Institute (PMI). (2021). *A guide to the project management body of knowledge (PMBOK® Guide)* (7th ed.). Project Management Institute.

Ribeiro, A., Amaral, A., & Barros, T. (2021). Project manager competencies in the context of the Industry 4.0. *Procedia Computer Science*, *181*, 803–810.

Schoper, Y., Wald, A., Ingason, H. T., & Friðgeirsson, T. V. (2018). Projectification in Western economies: A comparative study of Germany, Norway, and Iceland. *International Journal of Project Management*, *36*(1), 71–82.
Whyte, J., & Mottee, L. (2022). Rethinking project management: Value creation and impact in complex systems. *Project Management Journal*, *53*(4), 325–340.

PART I
WAYS OF WORKING

1
Municipal Public Water Company: shaping water

Elizabeth Arteaga-García and José Miguel Cevallos Chavez

OPENING PARAGRAPHS

On January 31, 2020, Juan José Macías, general manager of the Municipal Public Water Company (MPWC), provider of drinking water and sanitation services for Ciudad Puerto in Ecuador, urgently called a coordination meeting with the team of company advisors. The numbers presented in the financial sustainability report prepared by Santiago Vinces, general management advisor, did not meet the targets from the end of December 2019. It was not encouraging at the beginning of Juan José's recent appointment. (He had been made general manager of MPWC on January 15, 2020.)

The company's payroll had grown by 20 percent during the second quarter of 2019, and expenses exceeded income by 15 percent, presenting a deficit of $7 million in December 2019. The company's commercial performance was falling short in the areas of collection and portfolio investment recovery, reflecting decreases in the company's income, which delayed the company from achieving financial equilibrium in a reasonable time. The organizational structure was outdated and did not meet the company's operational needs. The MPWC had become an obese and inefficient organization.

The financial and economic situation of the MPWC was presented by Macías on February 17, 2020, to the president of the board of directors (and Mayor of the city), Augusto Herrera, who, after hearing the bad news, requested that, during the next 45 days, Macías structure a sustainability plan for the company. Among its most relevant activities would be a consulting project for the restructuring, strengthening, and modernization of the MPWC. Juan José and his team complied with the structuring of the requested plan, which they called FIRME. A consultancy firm was hired for the restructuring, strengthening, and modernization of the MPWC. However, at the kick-off meeting on May 15, 2020, Macías interrupted the project presentation, emphasizing that the desired scope and deadline were not being met, that the interested parties had not been managed to define the deliverables and scope, and that the consulting firm was unaware of relevant organizational situations such as opposition to the project expressed by the MPWC workers' union, which could seriously affect the execution of elements of the consulting project. The consulting firm argued in its favor that both the scope and the deadline had been agreed upon with the project sponsor, César Toledo, contract manager for the operation of AQUA in Ciudad Puerto, the strategic alliance of the MPWC.

BODY OF THE CASE

Background

On May 24, 2019, Augusto Herrera was sworn in as Mayor of Ciudad Puerto after over 20 years of the city being governed by two traditional and rival political figures. Herrera was a young politician with a mindset of generational change and modernization of the local government and its public services. When he became Mayor of Ciudad Puerto, he also assumed the position of president of the board of directors of the MPWC as established in the creating ordinance of the company.

The MPWC, with an institutional life of more than 70 years, was the second most important public institution in Ciudad Puerto, responsible for providing essential drinking water and sanitation services. Ciudad Puerto was the city with the most significant growth projection in the Manabí province, thanks to its port infrastructure, which made it worthy of the title of Tuna Capital. The natural beauty that attracted tourists to its beaches and ecological reserves energized the local economy, but it was evident that the city lacked comprehensive planning that would allow the municipal government and its public companies to manage their resources effectively.

The search process for a new manager for MPWC began in November 2019, with an evident need for a different leadership style capable of implementing an innovative management model aligned and consistent with Mayor Herrera's ideals. The company was strongly criticized by the opponents of Herrera, who publicly declared that they had robust evidence of public procurement processes of dubious propriety, an unjustified increase in the MPWC payroll producing the rise in spending, the reduced income of the company, and lack of leadership by the general management in the face of citizens' concerns.

Juan José Macías was a civil engineer who, since May 24, 2019, had been working as director of public works of a canton neighboring Ciudad Puerto, and had just served as technical manager of the public company Refinería del Sur. Macías was well recognized in public management and was unanimously chosen from the proposed shortlist to serve as general manager of the MPWC, on January 15, 2020.

The challenge of establishing a radical change in the MPWC was assumed by Macías in an environment of water emergency, declared by the Cantonal Security Board on January 27, 2020, due to an electromechanical failure of the aqueduct operated by Refinería del Sur, which left more than 200,000 people (nearly 50 percent of MPWC's users) without drinking water. On February 29, 2020, the first case of Covid-19 was registered in the country. On March 16, a national emergency due to the pandemic was declared, directly causing an average national fall of 40 percent in monthly income during the March–June period.

The Strategic Alliance

At the beginning of January 2016, the MPWC undertook the search for a strategic ally to assist in improving the provision of public drinking water and sanitation services. This partnership aimed to implement innovative technological processes to strengthen MPWC's management and control of the hydrosanitary infrastructure, including its water collection, distribution, treatment, and disposal systems. These efforts would help reduce technical and commercial water losses and increase the company's income by making billing and collection of water services more efficient, and including a change management component and technology transfer to MPWC officials, with the respective technical training of operational personnel.

On April 16, 2016, Ciudad Puerto suffered one of the most significant catastrophes recorded during the last 100 years. An earthquake of 7.8 on the Richter scale shook the city from its foundations for 50 seconds. The earthquake claimed many lives nationwide, with Ciudad Puerto the second most affected city in terms of human losses after Pedernales. The economic and social losses became incalculable, and the economic and financial situation of public and private companies was severely affected.

On September 18, 2017, after a long process of designing and structuring the strategic alliance process, MPWC entered a contract with the multinational company AQUA, a world leader in water, sanitation, and environmental management operations with a long history of operations in Equador and South America.

The change management of the strategic alliance implementation process was stormy for company officials; there was an adverse impact on those MPWC officials who feared losing their jobs after the arrival of AQUA personnel, meaning that the joint operation did not flow as expected. There were many obstacles in the processes intended to govern the alliance, a product of the uncertainty generated by the arrival of an outsider that, more than an outsider, was an "ally."

The change of municipal administration on May 24, 2019, when Augusto Herrera took office as Mayor of Ciudad Puerto, further deteriorated the relationship between MPWC and AQUA since many citizens viewed the processes of the strategic alliance with suspicion, essentially calling it privatization of public services. This situation affected the perceived legitimacy of Mayor Herrera's mandate, who announced in his inauguration speech the formation of an internal commission that would lead the comprehensive evaluation process of the execution of the strategic alliance contract that the municipal government of Ciudad Puerto maintained up to that point with AQUA.

Water Management in Ciudad Puerto

From a technical point of view, water management in Ciudad Puerto is complex. The intakes from bodies of freshwater and the purification plants are located outside the city, which increases the cost of distribution and the risk of clandestine connections to the main water pipelines, whichcause significant economic losses for MPWC. Due to operational workload, Omar Mendoza, technical manager of MPWC, could rarely be part of the coordination meetings of the general management; however, he was not reluctant to undertake any project that strengthened the company's management processes.

The company lacked transparent processes in its main areas, both in value adders and support enablers, and the high technical and administrative staff turnover made it unable to operate effectively over time. Its payroll grew from administration to administration, and Mayor Herrera's was no particular exception. The human talent manager, Guillermo Roca, joined the company a few months after Macías assumed general management. Like Mendoza, he was not very participatory in the coordination meetings, but did not object to any decision that sought to modernize the company. Diego Vélez, MPWC syndicate attorney, supported Guillermo in the legal issues of human talent management; one of the most critical points was the new draft of the collective contract that had to be signed with the company's workers, in which Vélez had identified severe contradictions to national laws, requiring a rewrite.

The strategic alliance with AQUA had considerably improved the MPWC processes at the commercial level. However, the road had been long and full of obstacles, and the efficiency index in the collection was enhanced due to the implementation of the first intervention in replacing obsolete drinking water meters and the on-site billing process. The company's Commercial Manager, Carla López, considered that the company's few available resources should be invested in replacing obsolete drinking water meters and that any other project should wait.

In the report presented by Santiago Vinces on January 30, 2020, it was evident that all those improvement actions in the commercial area were insufficient to cover the increase in spending that MPWC had sustained over time. Vinces told Macías with a tone of concern, "We are like a ship adrift with a half-broken hull; more water enters us than we can evacuate; we are on the way to sinking."

FIRME Plan

After the meeting on February 17, 2020, with Mayor Herrera, Macías found himself needing to plan the implementation of a new management model and comply with the provisions set by Herrera after 45 days of the permanent session. On March 31 Macías and his team of advisors presented the FIRME plan, focusing on four axes: 1) reform and strengthen the MPWC through a project that would allow restructuring, strengthening, and modernizing the organizational structure of the company; 2) reduce expenses by optimizing resources through efficiency in value-adding processes and continuous improvement; 3) increase income through the design of new services and the systematization of innovation to achieve financial balance in the medium term; and 4) improve the quality of public services by increasing availability and coverage and restoring the reputation of the company.

With the incorporation of Macías into the MPWC in January 2020, some pending issues in the execution of the strategic alliance contract began to be addressed. After an agreement between the MPWC and AQUA, it was concluded that the decline must not continue and that the company needed to take a different path to sustain its operation. On April 3, 2020, César Toledo, the AQUA contract administrator for the operation in Ciudad Puerto, agreed to Mayor Herrera's request to include in the investment component of the Strategic Alliance the contracting of a consulting firm for restructuring, strengthening, and modernization of the MPWC. The outcomes and deadlines for the consultancy were to be established based on the requirements identified during the meeting scheduled for April 6, 2020, with Mayor Herrera. There were no budget restrictions since the amount available for the investment component of the strategic alliance considerably exceeded the first instance for the consultancy's execution.

The Consulting Project

The first axis raised in the FIRME plan presented to Mayor Herrera was related to actions allowing the reform and strengthening of the MPWC. In a video conference on April 6, 2020, Mayor Herrera thanked César Toledo for his acceptance of hiring the consulting study for restructuring, strengthening, and modernization of the MPWC, with emphasis on transforming the organizational structure that currently reflected a heavy and outdated payroll. Juan José Macías and his team had already compiled the list of desired deliverables for the first of the consultancies, which they shared during the meeting, also explaining that this study had to be ready by the first week of August, when the financing request to the state bank was to be made according to the project plans the credit institution had sent to the MPWC.

Immediately after Macías' intervention, Herrera requested that a set of deliverables related to the strategic alliance be added to the desired scope of this consultancy, including the design of a new management model for the alliance with a proposal for an addendum to the contract and the update of legal and operational instruments. This would function as the operations manual and regulations of the strategic alliance. He also requested the inclusion of a change management plan for the implementation of the consultancy deliverables.

These latter requests by Mayor Herrera surprised Toledo, who argued that these products were unnecessary and that, due to the term restrictions with the state bank, it would not be possible to cover the entire desired scope. However, Mayor Herrera firmly reiterated his request.

Before ending the meeting, Santiago Vinces intervened by reading over the agreements that the parties had reached (see Table A1.1) and stating that these agreements would be communicated via email. He recommended defining the scope of the consultancy by holding workshops and work tables between AQUA technicians and MPWC officials who identify themselves as interested, so that acceptance criteria were estimated for each deliverable based on prioritization, consistent with the restrictions of the project. The scope must be defined to satisfy the requirements of all project stakeholders.

On April 7, 2020, Toledo responded with the following to Vinces' email:

> Dear All,
>
> I confirm receipt of the above email. Ratifying AQUA's willingness to be part of the solution to the problems that occur to MPWC and, therefore, to our Strategic Alliance; however, as I expressed during the meeting, we do not consider the group of deliverables for Strategic Alliance necessary. In addition, due to the deadline restriction we have for the execution of the first consultancy (first week of August 2020), all of the desired deliverables likely cannot be developed on time. It should be noted that, although the budget is

not restricted, at AQUA, we will ensure the optimization of the resources assigned for the investment component of the Strategic Alliance.

I take this opportunity to inform you that this morning, I held a meeting with the Consulting Firm that AQUA would be hired to develop the study. In the coming days, we will proceed to convene them for the project's kick-off meeting.

Greetings,

César Toledo

Immediately, Toledo received a response from Macías:

Dear César, Good morning:

Thanks for your quick response. We understand the restriction you mentioned for executing the first consultancy due to the commitment made with the State Bank to submit the financing request and the project by the first week of August 2020. We hope that during the suggested workshops and work tables through Santiago, we can define a scope that satisfies the requirements of the interested parties.

Kind regards,

JJM

Minutes later, Herrera added to the email from Macías to express the following:

Dear All,

I have reviewed the list of deliverables, and I also understand Toledo's approach. However, I insist on my requirement for the deliverables related to the Strategic Alliance, although I recognize that the deadline restriction is predominant due to the commitment we acquired with the State Bank.

I trust your best judgment.

Sincerely,

Augusto Herrera

Mayor of Ciudad Puerto

During the next three weeks, there was no communication from Toledo, even though Macías and Santiago Vinces sent emails at the end of each week insisting on the suggested workshops and work tables. On April 30, 2020, Vinces proceeded to send the list of desired deliverables with the time estimates that had been worked on internally at the MPWC so that these estimates could be taken as a reference when contracting the consultancy. He indicated that deliverables 1, 2, 5, 6, 7, 8, 9, 12, and 13 were strictly necessary for the presentation of the project to the state bank for the management of financing for the severance of MPWC personnel whom the consultancy, as part of its scope, had to identify. An estimated amount of approximately $7 million was necessary to cover the costs of dismissals, which MPWC could not cover with its funds.

On May 4, 2020, César Toledo responded to Macías and Vinces with the following:

Dear Juan José and Santiago,

I now inform you that the consultancy for the restructuring, strengthening, and modernization of the MPWC has been contracted. The contract was signed with the Consulting Firm on April 30, 2020.

The proposed date for the project kick-off meeting is May 15, where the Consulting Firm will present the scope and deadline of the project. I ask you to please confirm your availability for the proposed day from 8:00 to 9:30 in the morning.

Greetings,

César Toledo

Macías confirmed his and Vinces' availability for the project kick-off meeting, with a high degree of uncertainty regarding what they would witness.

The Project Kick-off Meeting

The kick-off meeting for the project began as scheduled. Mariana Marcillo, CEO of the consulting firm, projected the scope and deadline of the project (see Table A1.2). Juan José Macías proceeded to interrupt, however, and loudly recounted the email conversation between Vinces, Toledo, and Herrera during the conceptualization of the consultancy. He emphasized that the desired scope, especially given what was required by Mayor Herrera, and the proposed deadline were unacceptable, and that, to make matters worse, it was intended to move to an execution stage with these premises. Macías ended his speech by saying:

> The fact that the entire desired scope could not be covered due to the deadline restriction we have for presenting the project to the State Bank should have been communicated in advance and with due justification. And surely, in some way, we would have reached an agreement that satisfies the company's interests. I ask you: Have you agreed with our area managers on the content of these deliverables? Have you identified the most influential stakeholders in the execution of this project? Do you know our delicate situation with the MPWC Workers Union that resists this project? Do you know that there is a draft Collective Contract approved by the previous municipal administration that contravenes national laws?

The room was silent. Macías concluded, "You must understand that this project must be presented for approval to the company's board of directors to access public debt with the State Bank, and the President of the board of directors was emphatic in his request."

At the end of this meeting, the parties agreed that Macías would manage and lead this consulting project as project director, and the project charter was signed (see Appendix A1.3). Along with this document, Macías was given the scope and deadline proposal (shown in Table A1.2), which reflected the final delivery of the project by the end of October 2020, ten weeks after the initial commitment to the state bank for the credit application entry.

The MPWC Workers' Union

The MPWC workers' union counted more than 60 percent of the company's payroll among its members, particularly in operational, technical management, and maintenance of its institutional infrastructure. With this enormous mass of workers in its ranks, the union exerted pressure on the rulers in power, even threatening sabotage of the plumbing systems in certain situations.

Elías Almeida served as general secretary of the MPWC union for over seven years. Although he did not have third-level professional training, he worked as an assistant to the company's water quality laboratory. He had political aspirations, and his strong leadership in the union and mobilization of the masses influenced the management of the administrators. Eduardo Avellán represented the union in legal aspects, and, since Almeida was general secretary, Avellán also acted as its principal advisor and delegate to the MPWC's human talent management.

Rumors had reached the union leaders about a restructuring project that the MPWC intended to execute, which would entail the dismissal of a significant number of workers. This situation was beginning to upset the union's members.

The draft collective contract agreed on between the leaders of the union and the previous Mayor had not been signed. This draft was reviewed by Diego Vélez, MPWC's attorney general, who had found contradictions with national laws regarding the allocation of amounts in benefits such as uniforms, food, and so on. Additionally, the involvement "with voice and vote", of a representative of the workers' union on the board of directors of the MPWC was contrary to what the ordinance in creating the company, which stated that there could be the participation of a union delegate, with voice but without vote, in board sessions.

Through its lawyer Eduardo Avellán, the union expressed its opposition to the company's restructuring project in a formal document, arguing that it was not the time to dismiss anyone and that the draft of the collective contract had already been negotiated and agreed upon with the president of the previous board, and that an attempt was being made to ignore the workers' viewpoints.

Juan José Macías did not have a perfect relationship with Elías Almeida, with whom he had had several disputes during the initial stage of the Covid pandemic because a good percentage of the members were older or had health problems that made them members of vulnerable groups and had been told not to report to their jobs to safeguard their health. This raised doubts among the notified workers, leading them to speculate that they were going to lose their jobs; a situation that Almeida, for union-political purposes, did not hesitate to use in his favor given the campaign for the re-election of his position as general secretary of the union.

Almeida had issued a document to the Mayor's Office of Ciudad Puerto, reporting workplace harassment by Macías. After an unannounced technical visit to the pumping station where Almeida carried out his duties, Macías observed that the data on the results of the physical and chemical water quality tests from the previous night had not been collected. Additionally, Almeida was not at his workplace at the due time in the quality laboratory to take over the continuous duty guards of the drinking water quality assurance process and that he was not in the pumping station facilities either. Macías submitted a report to human talent management indicating that Almeida had arrived an hour late for his shift and requesting that the corresponding sanction be applied immediately.

Another situation that further deteriorated the relationship between Macías and the union was the disengagement of four members. These workers had sold items considered scrap without following the due administrative process. This matter reached higher authorities outside the company's jurisdiction, ultimately leading to the four workers facing criminal convictions.

Shaping Water

On the afternoon of May 15, 2020, Macías called a coordination meeting to inform his team of advisors that he had to call a session of the MPWC board of directors on June 30, to comply with the Ordinance of Creation of the MPWC regarding the mid-year review of management indicators. For this board meeting, Macías and his team had to present the FIRME plan, including the consulting project for the restructuring, strengthening, and modernization of the MPWC, of which he would be the project director. While closing the coordination meeting, Macías noted that it would be five months since he took office as general manager of the company, that the planning of the consulting project was just the tip of the iceberg, and that water management in Ciudad Puerto needed the involvement of all MPWC officials.

After the coordination meeting, Macías reviewed the scarce documentation that the consulting firm had provided him. He observed that, beyond the fact that the scope of the project contracted by César Toledo included what was strictly necessary to manage the financing for the state bank, it was worrying that good practices had not been applied in defining the scope. It was noted that no acceptance criteria or restrictions had been established for the project deliverables and that a scope baseline of the project was not evident. On the other hand, there was a group of key project stakeholders who were not in favor of the execution of the consulting project, including the strong opposition to the project expressed by the MPWC workers' union. He wondered how this would affect the development, negotiation, and approval of the project corresponding to the draft collective contract.

Macías, who was trying not to make the same mistakes as César Toledo and the consulting firm, deliberated between skipping the planning processes and proceeding to the execution stage of the project, for the development of the contracted products, as proposed by the consulting firm, or moving to plan during the 45 days that he had for the presentation of the project at the board session convened for June 30. That would mean managing the key stakeholders, especially the reticent and neutral ones, who needed to define a project scope that satisfied the interests of the company, assuming the high risk of losing access to public funds of around $7 million, which was managed with the state bank, due to having to postpone again the delivery of the project. MPWC urgently needed the development and implementation of the deliverables of this project, which would allow it to take the first steps on the path outlined to overcome the alarming economic, financial, and organizational situation that it was going through. Macías thought out loud, "What a task they have given me. *We have to give shape to the water.*"

DISCUSSION QUESTIONS

1. Why did the consulting firm define a list of deliverables that did not meet MPWC expectations? How could Juan José Macías have avoided these inconveniences?
2. What problems might Macías face if he decides to go directly to the project execution stage?
3. Once Macías was declared project manager, should he have held a new kick-off meeting? What would you suggest doing?
4. If you were Macías, what leadership style would you assume to manage reticent and neutral stakeholders in helping to define the scope of this project?

REFERENCES AND FURTHER READING

Elton, C. (2018). Scope patrol: Scope creep is on the rise as stakeholder expectations increase. Here's how to keep projects within bounds. *PM Network, 32*(7), 38–45.

Goleman, D. (2000, March–April). Leadership that gets results. *Harvard Business Review.*

Goleman, D. (2004, January). What makes a leader? *Harvard Business Review.*

Heerkens, G. (2014). The cost of change. *PM Network, 28*(1), 22–23.

Project Management Institute. (2021). *Project management body of knowledge* (7th ed.). Project Management Institute (Chapters 2.1, 2.6, 3.6, 4.4).

Project Management Institute. (2023). *Process groups: A practical guide.* Project Management Institute (Chapters 3, 4, 5.2, 5.3, 5.4, 5.5).

Rockwood, K. (2017). Fork in the road: Not all disagreements are created equal. Project managers must learn when to push ahead and when to push back. *PM Network, 31*(10), 50–55.

APPENDICES

Appendix 1

Table A1.1 Deliverables and schedule desired by MPWC for the restructuring, strengthening, and modernizing project

Group	Item	Deliverable	Finish date
Legal instruments	1	Ordinance to reform the company creation ordinance	April 13, 2020
Legal instruments	2	Internal regulations for human talent	April 13, 2020
Legal instruments	3	Update of the service provision regulations	April 13, 2020
Legal instruments	4	Collective agreement	April 20, 2020
Human talent management administrative documents	5	Functional organic structure	April 20, 2020
Human talent management administrative documents	6	Positional organic structure	May 4, 2020
Human talent management administrative documents	7	Organic status	May 11, 2020
Human talent management administrative documents	8	Positions and functions manual	May 11, 2020
Human talent management administrative documents	9	Salary scale	May 4, 2020
Human talent management administrative documents	10	Survey of critical processes for the management of the company's human talent	April 27, 2020
Human talent management administrative documents	11	EPMA operations staff training plan	April 27, 2020
Human talent management administrative documents	12	Analysis of existing profiles versus those needed	May 25, 2020
Financing	13	State bank financing application form	May 25, 2020
Strategic alliance	14	New alliance management model	May 25, 2020
Strategic alliance	15	Contractual addendum proposal	May 25, 2020
Strategic alliance	16	Operations manual update	May 25, 2020
Strategic alliance	17	Alliance regulation update	May 25, 2020
Change management	18	Change management plan	July 27, 2020

Appendix 2

Table A2.1 Deliverables and schedule proposed by the consulting firm for restructuring, strengthening, and modernizing MPWC

Group	Item	Deliverable	Finish date
Legal instruments	1	Ordinance to reform the company creation ordinance	May 22, 2020
Legal instruments	2	Internal regulations for human talent	May 29, 2020
Legal instruments	4	Collective agreement	June 12, 2020
Human talent management administrative documents	5	Functional organic structure	May 29, 2020
Human talent management administrative documents	6	Positional organic structure	June 26, 2020
Human talent management administrative documents	7	Organic status	July 31, 2020
Human talent management administrative documents	8	Positions and functions manual	September 4, 2020
Human talent management administrative documents	9	Salary scale	September 25, 2020
Human talent management administrative documents	12	Analysis of existing profiles versus those needed	October 16, 2020
Financing	13	State bank financing application form	October 16, 2020

Appendix 3. Project charter

Project

Consulting for the restructuring, strengthening, and modernization of the MPWC

Purpose of the Project

Reform and strengthen the MPWC through a consulting project that allows access to financing from the state bank to restructure, strengthen, and modernize the organization.

Objective of the Project

Develop and update legal instruments and documents for managing MPWC's human talent for the organization's restructuring, strengthening, and modernization through the financing managed before the state bank within five months with a budget of $180,000.00.

High-level Requirements

1. Approvals of legal instruments must be coordinated with the MPWC Attorney General.
2. The MPWC requests the presentation of progress reports biweekly.
3. At least 80% of the work to be carried out during the consultancy must be carried out in Ciudad Puerto.
4. The information and documents generated in the project's development are the exclusive property of MPWC.

Assumptions

1. The MPWC has the current documents in force that will be reviewed and updated during the consultancy development.
2. The company's senior hierarchical-level officials are aware of the project's need and importance.
3. The MPWC has the forms for the State Bank.

Restrictions

1. The budget cannot exceed 5% of what was planned.
2. Strategic and high-level meetings must be held outside MPWC facilities.

High-level Risks

1. Because the documents to be updated may not reflect the company's reality, the Consulting Firm would not have an adequate reference, causing the project to require more significant effort and be delayed in schedule.
2. Due to the resistance to the project evidenced by certain middle management officials in the company, their participation could be limited, causing the project deliverables not to satisfy the expectations and interests of the company, there being rework on the deliverables and delays in the schedule.
3. Because the Consulting Firm does not know the State Bank's project forms, these could be filled out incorrectly, causing non-approval of financing and delays in the project schedule.

List of Key Stakeholders

Juan José Macías, General Manager (internal, supporter)
Santiago Vinces PMP, General Management Advisor (internal, supporter)
Augusto Herrera, Mayor of Ciudad Puerto and President of the Board of Directors (internal, supporter)
Guillermo Roca, MPWC Human Talent Manager (internal, neutral)
Diego Vélez, Attorney General of the MPWC (internal, supporter)
Omar Mendoza, MPWC Technical Manager (internal, neutral)
Carla López, Commercial Manager of the MPWC (internal, reticent)
Elías Almeida, General Secretary of the MPWC Workers Union (internal, reluctant)
Eduardo Avellán, Lawyer of the MPWC Workers Union (internal, reticent)
César Toledo, AQUA Contract Manager for the operation in Ciudad Puerto (internal, neutral)
Mariana Marcillo, CEO of the Consulting Firm (external, supporter)
José García, Undersecretary of the Ministry of Labor (external, neutral)
Xavier Valencia, Regional Manager of the State Bank (external, supporter)
Luis Delgado, Undersecretary National Water Regulation Agency (external, supporter)

Project Director - Authority Level

Juan José Macías - Validation of deliverables, coordination of approval of deliverables with the Client and/or User (MPWC area manager or end user), and evaluation of the impact of change requests for permission by the project sponsor.

Sponsor - Authority Level

César Toledo - Approval of change requests that affect the project's scope, deadline, and budget.

2
Project recovery: IT in the energy sector

André B. Barcaui

OPENING PARAGRAPHS

Brazil EnerGlow Electric[1], established in the industrial heart of Brazil, is one of the giants in the electric energy sector, boasting a significant legacy that spans over five decades of continuous operation in the country. Since its inception, EnerGlow has been a cornerstone in the energy industry, ensuring that millions of homes and businesses receive reliable and quality energy.

In terms of size, EnerGlow is a large-scale company, employing over 10,000 dedicated staff across various roles, from specialized engineers and technicians to administrative and customer support teams. The workforce not only mirrors the extensive network of company operations but also underscores its commitment to excellence and innovation. Over the years, EnerGlow has prioritized continuous training and development of its staff, positioning itself as a preferred employer in the sector.

Guided by its core values and legacy, EnerGlow states that it looks ahead with a clear, compelling vision. EnerGlow envisions a world where clean, reliable energy powers the future, fostering a harmonious balance between human progress and environmental stewardship. This vision is more than just a statement; it is a road map that directs every project, investment, and initiative the company undertakes. With the dedicated efforts of its vast workforce and the trust of millions it serves, EnerGlow is poised to turn this vision into reality, marking another significant point on its illustrious journey.

Considering this setting, the TIR2016 project (technology infrastructure renewal) marked a significant milestone on the company's journey. Recognizing the need for modernization and updating its operations, EnerGlow initiated a competition aimed at incorporating the latest advancements in information technology (IT) into its infrastructure. This contest was incredibly challenging as it involved not only the integration of advanced systems but also their deployment across a vast geographical area, including three of Brazil's most densely populated and industrialized states: Rio de Janeiro, São Paulo, and Minas Gerais.

Beyond the metrics and milestones, EnerGlow stands out for its unwavering commitment to sustainability and corporate responsibility. Amid rising environmental concerns, the company has consistently invested in renewable energy sources and sustainable practices, aiming not just to meet current demands but also to prepare for a greener, more sustainable future.

BODY OF THE CASE

HAL9000's Entry: Contract Awarded

The company awarded the TIR2016 contract to collaborate with EnerGlow was HAL9000 Consultancy[2]. Founded at the dawn of the IT revolution, HAL9000 is a market-leading consultancy known for its comprehensive and deep involvement in the IT sector. With decades of experience, the firm expanded its operations across Brazil, solidifying its presence in diverse sectors including commerce, industry, and services. This wealth of experience and accumulated knowledge over the years has enabled HAL9000 to develop bespoke solutions tailored specifically to their clients' needs, regardless of the market segment.

Employing a team of over 5,000 professionals, including technology specialists, project managers, analysts, and developers, HAL9000 is renowned for its ability to execute large-scale, intricate projects with precision and efficiency. The company's human capital is among its most valued assets; a highly skilled workforce that undergoes continuous training in the latest industry trends and innovations, ensuring clients receive cutting-edge solutions.

Despite its extensive experience and reputation in the market, not all of HAL9000's projects have been without challenges. With its project-management-focused approach, the company has always aimed to establish a high standard in the implementation and integration of systems. However, like any major consultancy, there were times when the results did not fully align with initial expectations. These moments, although rare, served as valuable lessons learned, driving HAL9000 to continuously refine its processes and tools.

In the IT industry, adaptability and continuous learning are crucial. HAL9000, throughout its journey, has demonstrated its ability to evolve and grow from challenges. While it has paved its way with many successes, the obstacles faced have reinforced the company's commitment to re-evaluate, innovate, and improve. These episodes have become an integral part of its development, further solidifying its determination to be an influential and reliable leader in Brazil's technological landscape.

The selection of HAL9000 as a consultancy stood out for various strategic reasons. Firstly, Mark, HAL9000's sales manager, presented a financial proposal that proved to be very attractive to EnerGlow. In December 2015, during the critical phase of the competition, Mark presented a detailed estimate for the project, predicting costs to amount to \$34,600,000. However, he proposed a fixed contract price to EnerGlow of \$41,520,000. This setup provided a projected profit margin of \$6,920,000 for HAL9000, a significant financial advantage that strengthened HAL9000 position in the selection process.

Beyond the economic advantage, Mark also had a delivery time proposal that exceeded EnerGlow's expectations. He confidently estimated that the project, despite its complexity and scope, could be completed within a continuous 15-month execution period. This promise was particularly appealing to EnerGlow, as the company was only willing to wait 18 months at most. HAL9000's ability to offer a shorter deadline was a determining factor for its selection as the main consultancy.

However, it is worth noting a critical aspect in the formation of this contract: the initial project planning did not involve the participation of any team member responsible for its execution. This detail, which might seem minor at first glance, reflects a potential disconnect between sales expectations and operational realities, a phenomenon that would come to have significant repercussions throughout the project's execution. The project's objectives involved the implementation and/or adaptation of the civil infrastructure of 90 EnerGlow network agencies. Of these 90 agencies, 9 were power plants and 81 were satellite agencies, evenly distributed in each state. In practice, each plant connected 9 agencies (Figure A2.1).

In addition to the infrastructure component, the project also envisaged the installation of network equipment, connections between the plants and the agencies, and the implementation of part of an ERP (enterprise resource planning) -type system in the final installation layer. Support was also provided until the end of the project for the EnerGlow team.

The partial acceptance process established for the project between EnerGlow and HAL9000 was meticulous and had distinct features worth highlighting. First, it is crucial to understand the criteria set by EnerGlow to authorize these acceptances. There were essentially two situations in which acceptance could be granted: (1) when a power plant was fully installed and delivered, ready for operation, or (2) if an agency – a smaller unit but essential in the operational ecosystem of EnerGlow – was directly connected to one of these power plants.

Financially, the value associated with each acceptance was structured uniformly, regardless of whether a power plant or an agency was connected to it. The contract set a fixed amount of $41,520,000, which, when evenly distributed over the 90 expected acceptances, resulted in approximately $461,333 per acceptance. This uniform value ensured financial predictability for both parties throughout the project's progress.

However, an essential peculiarity of the agreement was that, if HAL9000 completed the installation of an agency not directly linked to a power plant, this work would not be recognized as an acceptance. This meant that, regardless of the effort and resources invested by the consultancy, the absence of this specific link would result in non-payment.

The project had a bifurcated nature, where each segment had its specifics and challenges. These branches led to two main focus areas, each with its respective challenges and objectives. On one hand was the infrastructure aspect, which addressed the physical and tangible facets of the endeavor. This phase ranged from construction and space adjustments and equipment installation, to ensuring that all facilities met the standards and requirements set by EnerGlow. Given the nature of an energy company, the robustness, safety, and efficiency of the infrastructure were crucial to ensuring uninterrupted and reliable operation.

On the other hand, the information technology component took a more specialized and detailed approach. It included critical tasks such as network configuration, ensuring that all communication between the various units and power plants was smooth and secure. In this same vein, one of the most challenging aspects was the installation and integration of part of an ERP system. This portion would be EnerGlow's operational brain, responsible for managing the organization's logistics, and requiring meticulous implementation to ensure its effectiveness and integrity.

The project's nature directly influenced the configuration of the HAL9000 project team (Figure A2.2), which consisted of an executive project manager (Paul Feder), a civil infrastructure manager (Jack Austin), and an IT manager (Louis Colbert).

Under Austin's role was a person in charge of civil works in each state, and under Colbert were three specialists: network, ERP, and support for the entire system. Most of the members of this team were external contractors. Initial hires included three contractors for the infrastructure part, totaling approximately 150 people, and an IT team with network and systems specialists, amounting to around 50 people.

EnerGlow's organizational structure had a very distinct dynamic compared to HAL9000's project-based formation. While HAL9000 worked with teams dedicated to specific projects, EnerGlow operated in an extremely functional manner, as illustrated in Figure A2.3. Such a configuration was reflected not only in the division of responsibilities but also in how decisions were made and tasks were allocated.

The project contract was initially signed by the CEO of EnerGlow, highlighting its significance and scale. However, there was no team specifically designated to look after the project within the company's structure. The closest and most involved department was engineering, led by Michael Ohm. Even so, it was common to observe the active participation of the operations director, Sarah Grid, and the IT director, Claire Conductor, in the daily development of the project. This continuous interaction from various departments reflected the multifaceted nature of the undertaking.

What stood out throughout the project was the absence of a dedicated EnerGlow team to closely monitor the progress and challenges. The most frequent communication took place between the executive project manager of HAL9000 and the directors of EnerGlow, including the CEO himself. This feature sometimes added complexity to the flow of information and decisions, as different departments would come up with specific demands, but there was no centralized team from EnerGlow managing these interactions.

The planning was meticulously crafted based on the specifications and agreements established between HAL9000's sales manager and EnerGlow at the time of contract formalization. It is noteworthy that the schedule was not merely a simple projection of activities but reflected the understandings and commitments negotiated between the companies, aiming to meet the agreed expectations and deadlines.

In order to optimize time and meet the geographical demands of the project, after the initial preparation of the environment, a simultaneous operation was set up in three main locations: Rio de Janeiro (RJ), São Paulo (SP), and Minas Gerais (MG). In each of these, a dedicated infrastructure team was allocated with the aim of establishing the power plants and their respective agencies. The parallel approach aimed to ensure that progress was consistent and balanced across all regions, capitalizing on the resources and expertise of the infrastructure teams.

At each agency or power plant, once the infrastructure team had finalized the foundational tasks, the pivotal moment for the IT team's involvement arose. This IT brigade, an extension of the HAL9000 contract, bore the hefty task of diving deep into the project's technological aspects. The scope was vast, encompassing not only the intricate layers of network configuration but also the meticulous chore of implementing various systems that would serve as the backbone for daily operations. It cannot be overstated how crucial the preliminary establishment of a robust infrastructure was for the subsequent technological roll-out. The IT team's effectiveness hinged significantly on this groundwork. Any lapses or inadequacies in the foundational infrastructure could compromise the entire technological framework. Therefore, ensuring a solid infrastructure was tantamount to ensuring the efficiency, integrity, and ultimately the success of the technological solutions being introduced by the IT team.

Project Diagnosis: Ten Months Later

Reaching the ten-month mark of the project, it became clear that the situation did not align with the initial expectations set out in the proposal drafted by HAL9000. Optimistic projections and early promises had given way to a starker reality where tangible outcomes fell short of what had been anticipated. As time progressed, instead of edging closer to a successful project culmination, the unfolding scenario was concerning, resembling a looming catastrophe.

Delving deeper into an evaluation, one of the analytical options we can turn to is the knowledge areas of project management. Through this analytical lens, we can dissect the project's nuances, pinpointing critical junctures, communication breakdowns, and potential bottlenecks that contributed to the misalignment between expectations and reality.

Based on this analysis, several revealing facts emerged. These not only shed light on immediate shortcomings but also offered valuable insights regarding the integrity of planning, task execution, and coordination among the teams involved. Understanding each of these aspects was paramount to charting a corrective course and preventing the recurrence of future mistakes.

Project Scope Management

A poorly defined scope was identified at the time of the sale, which seems to have been influenced by the rush to secure a contract due to competition. Intense rivalry and commercial ambition may have led the sales team to expedite the scope definition process without summoning technical professionals to dedicate the time necessary for precise specification drafting. This rushed approach resulted in inaccurate specifications, making the project ambiguous for all involved.

Moreover, a notable lack of acceptance definitions was observed. Without a clear set of criteria to determine when a task or project deliverable is considered complete, there were multiple instances where expectations were unmet, leading to rework and dissatisfaction among stakeholders. This kind of ambiguity, combined with vague specifications, set up significant challenges in project implementation and delivery.

To further complicate matters, the project suffered from weak change control. Without a robust change management process, changes were frequently introduced without an appropriate impact assessment, leading to more uncertainty and deviations from the original plans.

A set of challenges like this, from the ill-defined scope to uncontrolled changes, underscores the importance of establishing solid foundations and clear processes from the outset of any project.

Project Schedule Management

The interplay of these problems had a direct bearing on the project's schedule estimate. An ill-defined scope and inaccurate specifications caused the initial timeline to be underestimated. The urgency prompted by the sales process and the resulting hastened initial procedures set the stage for such miscalculations. These lapses were exacerbated by the lack of thorough validation of the initial estimates, which led to a misalignment between the projected timeline and the actual work required to meet the project's goals.

A significant issue that stemmed from the imprecise specifications was the difficulty in resource allocation. Without a clear understanding of the project's requirements, both human and material resources were often either over-allocated or under-utilized. This inefficiency not only escalated project costs but also led to unnecessary delays. Teams found themselves waiting for resources or scrambling to accommodate unplanned needs, further straining the already tight schedule.

The immediate fallout of this underestimation was the compromise of the project's baseline. In the absence of a clear understanding of all the milestones and deliverables, the baseline became more of a wishful target than a reliable benchmark. This was particularly problematic for stakeholders who had set their expectations based on this flawed baseline, leading to a mismatch between their expectations and the evolving realities of the project.

Project Cost Management

The underestimation of time was just one of the problematic ramifications stemming from the poorly defined scope and planning failures. Another grave consequence was the unrealistic estimation of the project-associated costs. With vague specifications and the absence of clear acceptance definitions, there was an inability to accurately forecast the financial resources needed for each phase. Every unplanned change led to rework, and every extension in the schedule inevitably brought along additional costs that weren't considered in the original estimate.

Some numbers and facts further underscore the severity of the financial issues. Up to that point, HAL9000 had already invested around $38,200,000. Surprisingly, only 20 percent of the project had been implemented, equivalent to 18 agencies and not a single power plant. This disproportion between investment and actual progress was a clear indicator that something was seriously amiss.

Beyond the already mentioned issues of underestimated costs and inappropriate baselines, the company was facing a financial penalty. A fine was looming due to the breach of contractual terms, which could further exacerbate the project's loss. The fine was set at $6,700 per agency or power plant per month. Since no power plant had been installed up to this point, HAL9000 had received no letter of acceptance.

The imbalance in the cost-progress relationship was alarming. With only a 20 percent implementation and such a significant investment, questions began to arise about the feasibility of continuing the project without a serious review and reassessment of all cost-related aspects. The financial situation, combined with other project challenges, not only jeopardized the return on investment but also threatened the company's long-term financial sustainability.

With potential fines on the horizon and other unaccounted-for costs emerging, such as unpaid overtime already amounting to $300,000, the project was in a precarious position. Worst of all, since HAL9000 had not linked any power plants so far (only agencies), the revenue after ten months into the project was zero.

Project Quality Management

Challenges related to project quality arose from several sources, further amplifying the overall complexity of the implementation. Committing to an excess of milestones was one of the first indicators that the project was on a turbulent trajectory. By committing to many deliveries in a short time span, the team was essentially setting a standard that might be unsustainable in the long run and which often led to rushed solutions, rework, and, inevitably, a compromise in overall quality.

The insufficient quality management plan further magnified this issue. Without a robust and well-defined framework to ensure and verify the quality of deliveries, it becomes easy for subtle or even severe issues to slip through the review process. This gap in quality management could result in operational failures, technological incompatibilities, or even safety concerns for the implemented systems.

Another area of concern was the lack of clearly agreed-upon "ground rules" with the client. In any project, defining expectations, responsibilities, and success criteria is vital to align all involved parties. Without this alignment, the risk of misunderstandings and frustrations is high, and can result in deliveries that do not meet client expectations, even if they are technically sound.

The lack of standardization across power plants and agencies introduced yet another problematic variable into the quality equation. Standardization is essential to ensure consistency, efficiency, and predictability of deliveries across all installations. Without it, each installation could have its nuances or peculiarities, making maintenance, system integration, and even team training for the operation and management of the installations more challenging.

Project Resources Management

As mentioned before, resource management was heavily compromised throughout this venture, leading to a series of adverse consequences that affected both technical execution and team well-being. Delayed payments were undoubtedly one of the most impactful problems. Compensation is one of the primary motivational factors for any team and, when compromised, can affect not only morale but also trust in project management and the organization as a whole. Associated with this, the significant volume of overtime hours, which totaled an astonishing unpaid $300,000, exacerbated the situation. By requiring the team to work beyond the norm without proper compensation, the project faced a wave of discontent and demotivation.

This demotivation was further intensified by the poor handling of internal conflicts. In any project, conflicts are inevitable, but how they are managed can make the difference between a cohesive team and a fragmented one. The lack of skill or willingness to effectively resolve these internal tensions only fueled an already strained environment, resulting in widespread stress among team members.

Beyond human challenges, inadequate resource management also manifested in material and financial problems. There was an urgent need to acquire $300,000 in materials for the project's continuation. This gap in acquisition not only compromised schedules and the baseline but also increased pressure on the team, which was already overloaded.

Regarding the HAL9000 organizational chart, after this ten-month period, the two project managers (Jack Austin and Louis Colbert) were dismissed from the company due to poor performance. The executive project manager (Paul Feder) was reallocated to another project. To further complicate the situation, the wear and tear on the EnerGlow project team remained undefined. This not only delayed decision-making and effective communication but also made it difficult for the main project team to align expectations and deliver results that met the client's needs.

Project Communications Management

Communication management is the backbone of any project, providing clarity, direction, and alignment for all involved. In this particular project, however, it was evident that communication was lacking, with consequences that extended to stakeholder management, as previously mentioned.

Initially, the deficient communication plan served as a fundamental barrier. Such a plan is essential to determine who needs to be informed, about what, when, and how. Without an effective plan, crucial messages can be lost or misinterpreted, and stakeholders might be uninformed or feel neglected. The impact of this was seen in the dissatisfaction of EnerGlow's CEO and HAL9000's director, both key stakeholders who expressed discontent.

The absence of a responsibility matrix only further exacerbated the situation. This matrix would clearly set out who is responsible for which tasks and decisions, ensuring there are no ambiguities. Without it, there can be overlaps, omissions, or confusion about who does what, leading to rework and delays.

Weak communication, both formal and informal, between the project teams and the management team was another hindrance. Constant and open communication is essential to ensure everyone is on the same page, to solve problems quickly, and to share vital information. The failure in this regard potentially contributed to the teams' feelings of dissatisfaction.

The constant engagement of HAL9000's board was another concerning symptom. While the board should be informed and involved, frequent engagement might indicate crises, decisions unresolved at lower levels, or a lack of trust in the project teams. This tendency not only overburdened the leadership but also led to more rushed decisions.

Lastly, the poor planning of meetings, a basic communication tool in projects, showcased a lack of structure and organization. Well-planned and effective meetings are vital to align teams, make decisions, and disseminate information. Without them, it is easy for team members to lose focus or be caught off guard by unexpected developments.

Project Stakeholders Management

Stakeholder management often determines the success or failure of a project. In this scenario, the challenges associated with this area were tangible and multifaceted.

The disquiet of EnerGlow's CEO and HAL9000's director already signaled significant concern. These were key stakeholders whose support and trust were crucial for the continuity and financing of the project. The dissatisfaction of these leaders can be symptomatic of communication failures, unmet expectations, or results falling short of the mark. More than that, when figures of such influence express their discontent, it can reverberate throughout the organization, affecting morale, trust, and even the project's dynamics.

The situation here was compounded when it was found that the HAL9000 teams were also entirely dissatisfied. Dissatisfaction at operational levels had various origins: workload overload, lack of resources, and even misalignment regarding the project's objectives. As we know, when teams are discontented, the risk of delays, failures, and rework increases considerably.

The economic situation also proved problematic, with revenue losses on both sides. This not only indicates problems in project execution but also suggests direct impacts on the financial results of the companies involved. A revenue loss can, in the long run, jeopardize the project's viability, as well as affect investor confidence and market perception.

Project Risk Management

In the context of an infrastructure and IT installation project, which covered both network components and system implementation, the analysis and management of risks proved to be notably deficient. This negligence manifested in various ways, severely affecting the progression and outcomes of this complex project.

A clear example of this imprecise risk assessment can be observed in the hardware purchase. The choice of equipment is vital in such projects since they form the physical foundation upon which IT systems operate. An inadequate risk assessment led to the procurement of incompatible, outdated, and insufficient hardware for the system's demands, resulting not just in delays and additional costs but project implementation failures.

Another significant challenge was the pressure and interference exerted by the power plant managers. Many of these managers exhibited a territorial and possessive stance concerning their respective plants and agencies. This attitude not only created day-to-day project hurdles but also profoundly interfered with planning and execution. Each time an advanced construction schedule was established, it usually had to be reviewed and rescheduled due to the demands and interventions of these managers. This repeated need for adjustment deviated the project from its initial path and increased the risks associated with delays, scheduling conflicts, and cost overruns. Furthermore, this unstable scenario made it extremely challenging for the project team to anticipate and prepare for the challenges that would inevitably arise. The sense of ownership these managers had over their plants and agencies also created a significant barrier to information flow. In projects of this magnitude, transparent and timely communication is essential to ensure that all stakeholders are aligned and informed. When this flow is interrupted or filtered, the project team can be left in the dark about critical decisions, last-minute changes, or emerging issues.

Meanwhile, the national regulatory agency's unawareness about the project's progress elevated the risk level even further in terms of communication. The fact that the agency was left in the dark and was about to take measures suggests possible non-compliances, which could result in penalties, fines, or even the project being halted.

What aggravated these and other problems was the total absence of risk management. In IT and infrastructure projects, where the interaction between physical components and digital systems can generate a plethora of unexpected issues, the absence of a risk plan is almost reckless. Without such a plan, the team lacks a predefined strategy to identify, prioritize, and respond to potential problems, leaving the project vulnerable to any adversities that might arise.

Project Procurement Management

Procurement processes are essential in almost any project, especially when multiple entities and variables are involved. In this case study, procurement, or the lack thereof, played a significant role in the challenges faced.

Initially, there was a notable error in planning for third-party resource and material purchases. This mistake might have originated from inadequate estimates, forecasting failures, or simply an insufficient understanding of the project's actual needs. Without an effective procurement strategy, projects can easily deviate from their course, incur additional costs, and face significant delays.

The issue of "unmatched" contracts between HAL9000 and EnerGlow further exacerbated the procurement situation. While HAL9000 operated under a fixed-price contract with EnerGlow, many of HAL9000's contracts with its suppliers were based on time-material terms. This discrepancy in contractual models generated financial and operational risks. With time-material suppliers, costs can fluctuate depending on the time and resources used, making it challenging for HAL9000 to ensure profitability under its fixed-price contract with EnerGlow.

The instability of external partners became another critical issue when two key infrastructure contractors went bankrupt during the project. This was devastating to the project, leading to, for example, delays, additional costs, and the need to swiftly find reliable alternatives.

Beyond these challenges, the project also faced issues with a lack of material procurement. This omission was a consequence of initial planning errors and cash flow issues resulting from other procurement problems. Either way, the lack of essential materials undoubtedly affected the project's progression, leading to potential delays and cost overruns.

Project Integration Management

Integration management is vital for unifying and coordinating the various components of a project, ensuring that all pieces work together harmoniously toward the end goal. However, the lack of a formal project plan was a fundamental oversight. Without a consolidated plan, the direction, objectives, and decision-making criteria became unclear. This may have led to scope deviations, resource wastage, and a lack of alignment among the involved teams. A formal plan not only provides a framework and road map for execution; it also serves as a point of reference for all stakeholders, ensuring everyone is on the same page.

Similarly, change management, when poorly handled, can be a major hindrance to any project. Changes are inevitable in dynamic environments, but it is crucial that they are tracked, evaluated, and implemented in a controlled manner. In this case, poor change management resulted in delays, additional costs, and widespread confusion as teams struggled to adapt to changes without clear guidelines or understanding the full impact of these changes.

In conclusion, the lack of planning and integration between HAL9000 and EnerGlow may have been pivotal in discerning the root cause of the project's problems. Without clear alignment between these entities, there might have been gaps in responsibilities, duplication of efforts, and misunderstandings regarding expectations and objectives. This misalignment not only complicated the project's execution; it is also likely to have strained the relationship between the two organizations.

Some Useful Data

- Total number of people originally working = 200
  - Infrastructure:
    - 50 from infra company A
    - 50 from infra company B
    - 50 from infra company C
  - IT:
    - 50 from company D (network plus systems).
- As two infrastructure companies went bankrupt, we now have:
  - 50 from company C (infrastructure)
  - 50 from company D (IT)
  - Total = 100 people.
- Cost of allocated team (100 people) = US$200,000 per month.
- Cost for each new team (50 people each) = US$100,000 per month.

- Cost of hiring/mobilizing a new team (infrastructure or IT) with 50 people = US$200,000.
- Minimum team for setting up one agency or power plant:
  - 50 infrastructure people
  - 50 IT people.
  - Implementation (infrastructure plus IT) times:[3]
    - Agency set-up = 10 days (5 for infrastructure plus 5 for IT)
    - Power plant set-up = 20 days (10 for infrastructure plus 10 for IT).

The Challenge

Given the complex scenario presented in this case study and the adversities faced throughout the project between EnerGlow and HAL9000, it is essential to reflect on the lessons learned and how they can be applied in future ventures. The experience shared by these companies serves as a warning about the importance of effective communication, meticulous planning, and active involvement of all stakeholders from the earliest phases of a project.

Moreover, this case illustrates the need for a realistic and careful assessment to be made at the time of defining proposals and agreements. Excessive optimism and projections without a solid foundation can generate unrealistic expectations and lead to commitments that do not reflect the team's true delivery capacity. This dissonance between what is promised and what is possible can be the root of frustrations, delays, and, in extreme cases, catastrophic project failures.

In conclusion, after a deep analysis of the challenges faced and the shortcomings identified in the project management between EnerGlow and HAL9000, the director of HAL9000 made a strategic decision. Aware of the complexity and the critical importance of the project, he recognized that to resume and drive the project to a successful conclusion, it would be essential to bring in external expertise. The decision was then made to hire a company specialized in project management, with proven experience in rescuing off-course projects.

In this scenario, imagine yourself and your team as a project management consulting company. Your mission (as well as your competitors') will be to draft a successful recovery plan for this complicated project in crisis. As a consultancy company, you will be tasked with taking the reins of the project, identifying the failures, reassessing the goals, and developing a robust plan to guide the venture to a successful conclusion.

Be ready for this challenge, as the task will not be straightforward. You will inherit the problems, the constraints, and the established expectations. However, with a methodical approach, a focus on the best project management practices, and an unwavering commitment to excellence, your team will have the opportunity to turn a crisis scenario into a success story, reaffirming EnerGlow's trust in HAL9000 and safeguarding the company's reputation.

DISCUSSION QUESTIONS

1. What were the main factors that contributed to the misalignment between the established expectations and the reality faced in the project between EnerGlow and HAL9000?
2. Analyzing the initial proposal from HAL9000's sales manager, what possible red flags could have been identified and might have prevented the challenges faced?
3. Based on the areas of knowledge in project management, what practices could have been implemented to ensure a more aligned and effective execution of the project?
4. How could communication and stakeholder involvement have been improved to ensure a shared vision and more harmonious project execution?
5. How would you structure tools, processes, and artifacts from each area of project management knowledge to assist HAL9000 in its crisis project and deliver the entire scope to EnerGlow?

NOTES

1. We adopted a fictitious name in order to preserve the company's identity.
2. For the same reason, we adopted a fictitious name not only for the company, but also for its employees.
3. Times were already optimized to the maximum. There was no way to improve this time, not even by adding more people.

REFERENCES AND FURTHER READING

Arkhipov, I. (2023). *Information technology essentials: For business analysts and project managers.* Independently published.
Jaques, T. (2014). *Issue and crises management: Exploring Issues, crises, risk and reputation.* Oxford University Press.
Kerzner, H. (2014). *Project recovery case studies and techniques for overcoming project failure.* John Wiley & Sons.
Hayden, J. (2023). *Project management mastery: A comprehensive guide to successfully implementing the core principles of project planning and scope management from concept to completion.* EB Publishing House.
Heagney, J. (2022). *Fundamentals of project management* (6th ed.). HarperCollins Leadership.
Meredith, J., Schafer, S., Mantel, S., & Sutton, M. (2021). *Project management in practice* (7th ed.). John Wiley & Sons.
Nieto-Rodriguez, A. (2021). *Harvard Business Review project management handbook: How to launch, lead and sponsor successful projects.* Harvard Business Review Press.
PMI (2022). *Process groups: A practice guide.* Project Management Institute.
PMI (2021). *PMBOK guide.* Project Management Institute.

APPENDIX

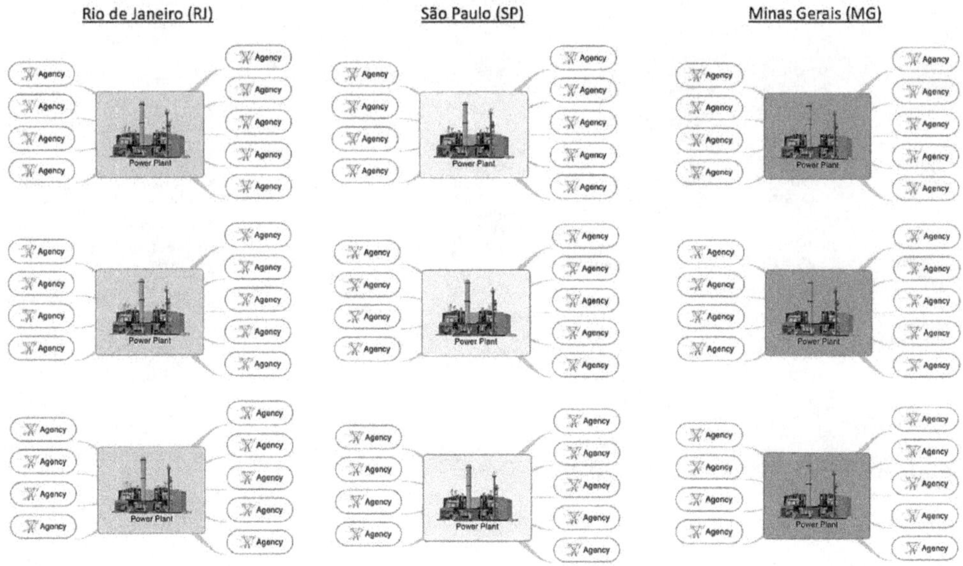

Source: Author.

Figure A2.1 Distribution of power plants and agencies

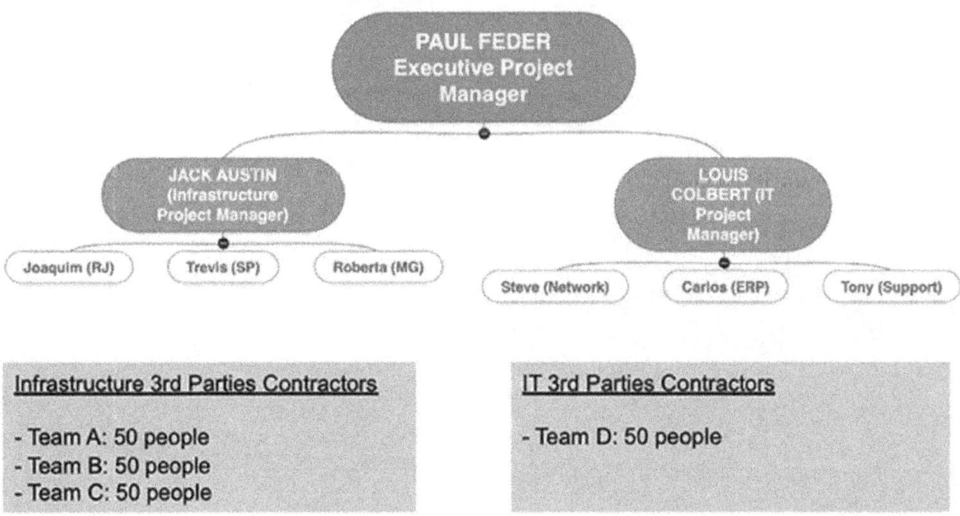

Source: Author.

Figure A2.2 Organization chart for HAL9000 consulting company

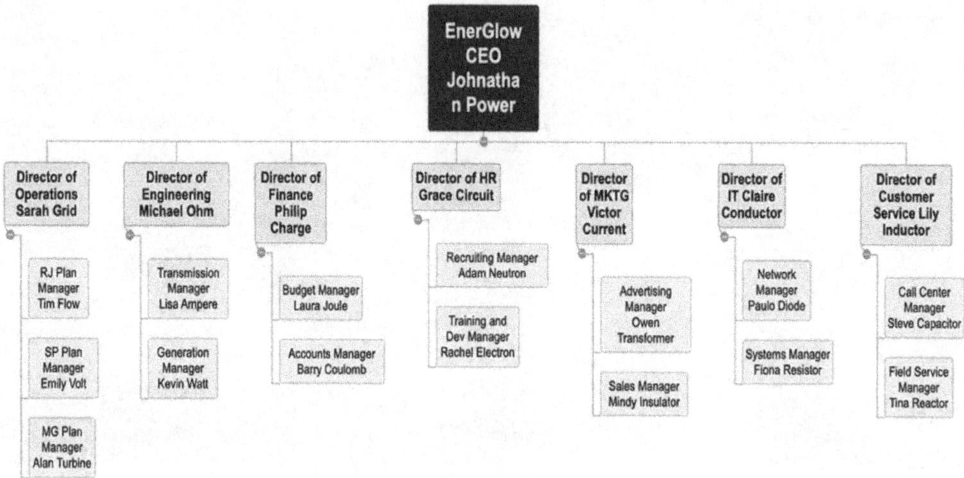

Source: Author.

Figure A2.3 Organization chart for EnerGlow

3 Evaluating project management approaches: a property and casualty insurance company

Shawn D. Belling

OPENING PARAGRAPHS

The case involves a large property and casualty insurance company based in the upper Midwestern region of the United States. The company operates in 29 states, generates over $1.5 billion in revenue, and employs approximately 1,500 people. The company is widely recognized as a desirable employer in its classification and region, well-known for its progressive and employee-friendly work policies and practices. The CEO from 1999 to 2023 was noted for a focus on leveraging technology to move the company ahead of its competitors and brought a deep understanding of technology to the executive leadership. The company prides itself on its internal technology and software development capabilities and often believes it can build any technology solution more effectively than could be obtained through a purchase of technology solutions.

This insurance company had been successful for most of its existence using waterfall project management practices to deliver the technology projects and to develop and deliver new products. It had used waterfall practices successfully for a number of years, but the evolving nature of technology project delivery and the increasing speed of change and competition within the insurance market led the organization to consider other approaches to project delivery, including agile frameworks such as scrum.

BODY OF THE CASE

Adopting Scrum

In 2018, the company decided to adopt scrum practices for technology development and new product development projects. The company invested significant time, money, and energy in this endeavor. It invested in scrum training, adopted a change in culture to embrace this new approach to working, and created new scrum-specific positions within the business and operating units. The company reorganized its business teams and processes to be product-oriented. The organization brought in external resources to help further with scrum training and created many of its own internal resources to assist with the development and adoption of scrum.

After approximately three or so years of experience and implementation, the company determined a need to assess its scrum practices and began doing so within its leadership and practitioner ranks. Initial impressions and perceptions indicate that the adoption and implementation of "strict scrum" across many teams have actually led to less agility in the planning, execution, and delivery of valuable outcomes to the organization – the core goal of scrum development and delivery practices. Current assessments point to other areas for potential examination and refinement to enable the company to continue its evolution as an agile organization focused on effective practices for value delivery for the benefit of its customers and the organization itself.

Accessing Scrum Adoption

Despite initial investments in culture change, scrum training, and scrum-specific roles, the company's scrum implementation has faced challenges and impediments. After about three years, the company realized things were not going quite as had been hoped. The organization found that many of the practitioners, as well as many leaders, had become too concerned with the perfect practice of scrum, to the detriment of a focus on value delivery. It also found that many scrum practices were being incorrectly applied. These included a lack of proper project prioritization and a cultural hesitation to reject additional project requests. These factors led to some business units facing an overburdening backlog and caused some leaders and workers to question the efficiency of the scrum framework. The misapplication of scrum practices and cultural hesitation to say no to project requests led to dysfunctional behaviors that compounded the challenges the company faced.

For example, in order to gain approval for a favored project, a leader or manager would label the project as a "product" and essentially "shop" the project around to the company's various technology teams and their leaders until they found a product owner willing to add it to their backlog, whether it belonged there or not. This practice resulted in some projects being incorrectly defined as "products" and landing in the backlogs of teams that were not the right fit to do the work. It left teams saddled with lengthy backlogs of projects that did not make sense for them and that they were not likely to actually work on in a realistic time frame.

In another example, some teams tended to focus on performing scrum ceremonies without evaluating whether these ceremonies were providing value, and whether they needed to be incrementally improved or modified to do so. Instead, the focus was on the prescriptive: if the scrum framework included a practice or ceremony, then the teams felt obligated to perform it without asking whether they could modify it to make it more effective, and whether the way in which they were using the framework was helping them to deliver value to their customers more efficiently and effectively.

As the company began to have some suboptimal and even negative experiences with the scrum framework, some leaders began to question the move to scrum. Some leaders and workers noted that, for many years, the company's waterfall project management practices had served them well enough. They did not criticize the scrum framework or approach itself, but rather felt that the emphasis had become conformance to scrum protocols versus successful delivery of important projects for the company. In the words of one leader (who recently became the new president), they were not "being agile about agile." The company found itself in the position of grappling with a critical decision: Should it continue with scrum, revert to the previous waterfall project management practices, or explore a hybrid agile approach to project management?

Prioritization

In addition to the struggles with the implementation of the scrum framework, the company realized that it faced challenges with project and work prioritization. In the Midwestern United States, it is a common cultural business practice to say yes to your colleagues when they ask you to take on a project. Due to such cultural norms, saying no to a colleague who asks for a reasonable project to be considered and approved is often difficult, and this in turn frequently results in commitments by teams and individuals to complete more projects than they are realistically capable of delivering during specific time frames. Further, this tendency often leads to the creation of very large backlogs of projects and product initiatives that an organization or team has no hope of actually completing. Further, the company faced challenges with capacity planning and demand and resource management. The company's project and portfolio management office did not have all of the information or the views on how its people were allocated to projects, nor the routine work that would enable them to accurately assess the capacities of teams and individuals and make informed demand management decisions.

What is Working

Despite the challenges with scrum, assessment of the company's situation yielded many elements of its agile practices that were working effectively. The effectiveness of these elements should be considered in the overall context of the evaluation project. The following sub-areas are offered for consideration: people, leadership support, existence of long-lived teams, project visibility, processes and tools, and iterative value delivery.

People

Internal interviews discovered, for example, a unanimous sense that people in the company have embraced agile and are working with great attitudes and the best of intentions. People seem to understand why the company made the move to agile.

Leadership support

Internal interviews with teams and individuals indicated strong support from company leadership for agile. Multiple interviews with leadership demonstrated a belief, and evidence, that the company had completely bought into agile as a way of operating the company. The senior leaders themselves felt that early wins, piloting agile, and promoting the benefits of agile helped during the early phases and enabled additional teams to come in with open minds. In addition, there was a common understanding that this transformation is an ongoing journey, and that latitude must be provided to people and teams.

Long-lived teams

Some of the interview responses indicated that the practice of building teams and then keeping them together for the long term, which is a core scrum tenet, was working well and was appreciated and embraced. Some team members commented that a consistent team makes retrospectives more effective because they are then able to improve their practices over the long term. It can take teams a period of time to develop the trust and honesty necessary for effective retrospectives, so, these long-lived teams are beneficial for this and the associated outcomes. Senior managers reinforced that consistent and focused teams for particular products and projects were working well.

Project visibility

A frequently noted theme throughout the interviews was an appreciation for the visibility and transparency that agile practices have brought to the company product delivery. Agile practices such as sprint and release planning, retrospectives, backlog grooming, and prioritization have helped to highlight pain points and reinforce the need to focus on improvement. The same practices have also highlighted dependencies and constraints, bringing visibility to the impact these have and the impediments that they can present. Conversations conveyed a sense that the transparency and connection throughout business and technical teams was beneficial. Teams noted that they appreciated the transparency and accountability.

Processes and tools

The processes and tools theme can perhaps best be summarized by emphasizing that the company is doing many things right. Positive comments were made on many elements, from the training approach, coaching, the use of retrospectives to identify areas for improvement, managing throughput and bandwidth, and so on. Some people noted that processes were more consistent and contributed to empowering product owners and ensuring connection to strategy. Sprint reviews were cited as helping to generate quality feedback, leading to further improvements in product and process. Visibility to work in progress was cited as supporting the ability to identify and move high-priority items forward, faster. The intentional use of tools and testing as well as a focus on the customer and the customer journey were noted as processes and tools that were working well.

Iterative value delivery

Conversations at all levels supported a sense that delivering in iterative and smaller pieces was working and was valued. Smaller and incremental deliverables and rapid value realization through slivers of value were deemed as positive. The concept of a minimum viable product was understood and is embraced. The focus on value and prioritization inherent in scrum has been perceived as helping to identify priorities for throughput and to allow less important work to drop. The focus on iterative value delivery has enabled identification of important products and high-priority items to move forward incrementally. Interviews noted that customers were becoming more accepting of incremental value delivery, and more mature customers have adopted thinking in these terms and alignment of expectations with scrum delivery practices.

It is worth noting that the good impression of iterative value delivery and prioritization as something working well tended to come more from senior leaders than the product/delivery teams themselves.

What is Not Working

Assessment of the company's situation did, however, yield many elements of their agile practices that were *not* working so effectively. The ineffectiveness of these elements should be considered in the overall context of the evaluation project. The following sub-areas are offered for consideration: a focus on achieving "perfect scrum", a tendency to treat everything as a product, challenges in prioritization and saying no to projects, challenges in handling dependencies across teams and projects, the role of technical and functional managers, team sizing, scrum meetings, and technical debt.

"Perfect scrum"

A common theme is a sense that, if a team is not working to "perfect scrum", it is failing. Teams may become frustrated because they feel they are not executing scrum perfectly when in fact they are still performing and achieving well and delivering value. The "perfect scrum" theme also manifests in examples where teams feel that they must follow a scrum practice or process exactly rather than take the initiative to be more creative or, in fact, be *agile* about how they execute the work. It was felt that strict adherence to strict scrum practice actually gets in the way of ultimate value delivery.

Interviews confirmed that the company was at a point where scrum practices were understood well enough and were in practice widely enough that the company teams could begin to move to the next phase of adoption, where they take some initiative and latitude to be more flexible with scrum and general agile practices and begin to make them their own, using their experience and judgment combined with trust and empowerment from leaders. This also sets the stage for implementing hybrid agile approaches.

"Everything is a product"

Since adopting agile there has been a tendency to treat everything as a "product". There is some sense that "products" are being used as repositories for work rather than being defined as true products and product goals for value delivery, so work simply gets dumped into products. Since the company culture avoids saying no, ideas often go into endless backlogs. Interviews revealed the need to convey that it is perfectly fine to have projects as well as products, and this is where hybrid approaches to project management could be beneficial in reinforcing the understanding that retaining and incorporating some waterfall practices are acceptable.

Interviews revealed a lot of work-in-progress rather than a focus on a vital few projects. Interviews also noted that work was coming into teams from other products, and with competing priorities (external and individual, for example). This is likely in part because people do not feel comfortable saying no, which results in too many active sprint backlog items – ruthless prioritization is not happening.

Prioritizing and refusing

As noted, a theme that came through in interviews is a clear sense that the company needs to do a better job of prioritizing and saying no to various initiatives, features, and other work. This problem is common in many if not most organizations. The ability to "ruthlessly" prioritize and focus on an crucial few products and projects is essential to successful value delivery. Senior leaders had a better impression of their ability to prioritize compared to the individuals and teams. A repeated theme was being unwilling to say no, or scenarios where a product owner did said no, only for the requester to go "shopping" for another product owner or team that would take on their project. This points to the need for prioritization, vetting of ideas, sifting and winnowing "bad" ideas, and focusing on the vital few as critical capabilities for this company to develop.

Another take on prioritization is that the focus on product-owner priorities espoused by scrum means that some items that would be valuable and viable fixes are not prioritized, leading to the accumulation of technical debt (addressed in more detail later).

Dependencies

Interviews with teams and individuals noted that dependencies on specific specialties or competencies caused impediments to delivery and execution. There were instances where people with certain skill sets were spread across too many projects, and instances where a development team or even a single person became a constraint.

Utilization of managers' technical expertise

Interviews indicated that there was some degree of challenge in identifying the best way to leverage technical or functional managers. There was general agreement that there was work to be done to determine how best to leverage the company's experienced and technically adept manager cohort. Some managers are in agile roles but may not necessarily be good fits for these roles. In other cases, there is recognition that these technical managers can be powerful resources and provide great advice on how to accomplish work effectively and efficiently, but some are too involved in deciding how the work gets done. There is some sense that these latter leaders should not be consulted at all (which is not a best practice). Meanwhile, other elements of the interviews conveyed a belief by some teams that they did not have enough say or latitude on what they worked on or how they worked on it.

Clearly, the actual situation lies somewhere in the midst of these various viewpoints. The conclusion is that the experienced technical managers, when used well, are a critical resource that can contribute to the evolution of agile and ensure ongoing improvements in process as well as in value realization and overall organizational agility.

Team size

In this organization some scrum teams have grown significantly past the "7–9 members, plus or minus 2" guidance that scrum practices recommend. This results in meetings and daily stand-ups that are too long and in which many team members feel disconnected from the work of others on the team, among other inefficiencies.

Meetings

Meetings are a common target and scapegoat at any organization. It is important to avoid the generalization of "we have too many meetings" and instead focus on the elements associated with meetings in scrum and agile practices. In scrum, the recommended meetings are intended to create efficiencies and enable teams to focus on their committed work during sprints. For this company, when team members are involved in multiple projects or serve on multiple teams, the scrum meetings take up additional time that could be spent on heads-down value delivery. This issue is connected to some of the other elements identified as not working. There is also a sense that some meetings have too many participants who are not clear about the reason for their participation.

Technical debt

In the context of scrum and most agile development frameworks and practices, "technical debt" refers to the accumulation of unfinished work, bugs, and other incomplete or suboptimal items that are often not fully visible to people outside the team, can impede value delivery, and negatively impact the quality of the product. Company interviews indicate that focus by product owners on prioritized value delivery has the unintended result of reduced attention to technical debt. Items that could be quickly and easily addressed are deprioritized, and some people feel that, in the strict scrum, they do not have the freedom to use their judgment to take the initiative and quickly fix these items. There is also a sense that a holistic view of technical debt is lacking, although one group quantified the debt as "massive." The aforementioned technical managers respect technical debt, but this understanding of the importance of foundational technical excellence through reduction of technical debt may not be shared by product owners.

Opportunities and Process Assets

The organization has in place people and processes that could be assets in any selected approach or decision regarding the future of project management practices in the organization. These include the chief product committees (CPCs), the company's technical and functional managers, and the agile practice and agile coaches.

Chief product committee

The company's CPC was noted as an entity that may not be working as effectively as it could, with some comments noting that the committee could diminish the role of the product owners. However, if the company seeks to scale its scrum practices (assuming it perseveres with scrum), the CPC could evolve to a role in which it serves as a conduit of strategy to product owners as well as ensuring coordination and prioritization across multiple products, product owners, projects, and teams.

Technical/resource managers

As noted earlier, there is a significant opportunity here to leverage and evolve the role of technical or resource managers. Redefinition of their roles along with associated coaching and training can help to ensure that these important leaders and technical resources make important contributions to products and release and sprint planning as well as to the development of people from a technical and functional perspective.

For this company, the role of the highly technical managers needs to be more clearly defined. There are important areas of input from these managers, in which their technical oversight is valuable. It is important that the teams understand that it is fine, if not desirable, to leverage their resource managers. Technical excellence is a constant goal and can be supported by these technical and resource managers – in fact, they are responsible for this. These technical managers can also be very valuable in planning, as their experience and technical expertise helps them see the big picture and ensure that releases will be coherent.

Agile practice and coaching approach

The company has developed a strong and experienced cohort of agile coaches who have contributed significantly to training and adoption throughout the company's scrum practices to date. These coaches will continue to play a critical role as the company evolves and should it choose to keep and scale its scrum practices. Some scrum masters are truly challenging teams to get better, and teams generally lean into opportunities to improve, learn, and try new things in the interest of continuous improvement.

The Situation

As the challenges of the company's situation became more evident, some of the senior leaders engaged the assistance and advice of a professor with whom they had worked on a graduate program. The professor had written a book on agile hybrid project management. The ideas and practices in the book caught the attention of the leaders in the project management office as well as some senior executives. These stakeholders wanted to bring the professor into the company as a consultant to help them transition to a hybrid agile approach to project management. Other stakeholders wanted to return to the "old" way of doing things using waterfall project management practices. Still other stakeholders wanted to continue to make scrum work, since they had invested a lot of time, energy, and money in scrum training and implementation.

Specific Concerns

As the company considers the possibility of engaging the professor as a consultant to help assess and improve the situation, there are specific concerns for the reader to focus on, as outlined in the chapter so far. As you begin to focus on the specifics, note the following concerns and consider how they influence the current situation and would be critical factors in any recommendation, decision, and path forward for the organization:

- The company started its agile transformation over three years ago. Most of the company's project management work and delivery had converted to agile practices, and most teams were using scrum or kanban. The company had previously worked with a consulting firm on agile transformation.
- The company had identified demand management and portfolio management as areas requiring attention within the context of agile transformation, to better enable strategy execution through demand management.
- The company recognized the need to assess where it was in its agile transformation and how it would scale agile practices.
- In some respects, the company felt it had taken the waterfall project practices and just moved them into scrum teams without actually transforming the work.
- The company had set up product teams but found that some teams were acting more as value stream teams, with some teams potentially too large compared to agile best practices.
- The company recognized that prioritization was a potential issue. Staff had a hard time saying no to requests and so needed to assess their portfolios and how these were approved and prioritized.
- Three-plus years into the agile transformation, the company needed to revisit its agile teams and practices, see how things were working, and identify where could they be more efficient.
- A key goal was to assess where the organization was at this point and to ensure it was leveraging overall good project management practices in concert with agile practices – not abandoning one for the other, but rather seeking an appropriate balance.

Scenario Options

This scenario presents the reader with the opportunity to review and process the information provided so far and to make an evaluation. The purpose of the evaluation is to assess the insurance company's options in the scenario described and determine the best course of action for the company to pursue with regard to the structure of its project and program management and delivery practices. At a high level, there are three primary courses of action available to the company. Of course, it is possible to consider elements of each option in the overall evaluation.

Option 1

The company could continue as it is, which would mean continuing to work to improve the application and practices of the scrum framework and the various scrum-oriented team and business structures that it had put in place and had been using for about three years.

Option 2

As a second option, it could call its attempt to implement scrum a failure and revert to using the waterfall project and program management practices that had been in use prior to the implementation of scrum. This would be a major decision, as the company and its staff have invested much time, energy, and money in scrum over the past three years, and many in the business units like aspects of scrum and other agile practices and do not want to revert to waterfall practices.

Option 3

As a third option, the company could consider hybrid project management, using a blend of agile and waterfall practices. This would require the assessment of current scrum and agile practices as well as assessment of past waterfall practices and updated waterfall methods, along with the development of methodologies and frameworks to train and apply this hybrid approach.

Overall, the evaluation must consider the pros and cons, risks, obstacles, resources, stakeholder support, and other factors associated with each option to determine and recommend a course of action.

Scenario Analysis Objectives

- Provide practice recommendations, training recommendations, and recommend immediate and long-terms steps.
- Determine if the business can leverage its considerable investment and the successes it has had in scrum and agile while continuing to transform and evolve its practices to ensure maximum organizational agility and maximize value realization in products and business processes.

- Retain the existing flexibility in product and project management and delivery approaches that is key to the company's continued growth and evolution.
- Reinforce the connection between top-level, cross-functional strategies and executive and senior level leadership responsibility for delivery of projects and products to support these strategies.

Stakeholders

The stakeholders in this scenario can be broadly defined, as with most projects and their related decisions. In this case, the external customers of the insurance company will certainly be stakeholders, given that the project management practices used by the company will influence the outcomes of projects that in turn result in or affect the products and services used by the customers. The primary stakeholder groups in this scenario, however, are internal to the company. These include executive leadership and senior leadership groups. The primary stakeholders are members of four business units within the insurance company: a business consulting unit, information technology, marketing, and an analytics department. The majority of the stakeholders within these four business areas are practitioners, as opposed to leaders of the business units.

As highlighted elsewhere in this case study, it is important to note that the stakeholder groups had varying experiences and attitudes towards the adoption of scrum and agile practices. One influential line of business, for example, did not appreciate what its leaders perceived as a lack of management control or responsibility in assigning work to teams and team members to projects. They also struggled with capacity and resource allocation issues in the scrum and agile framework.

A survey used to assess the stakeholders in the four business units provided the following breakdowns and characteristics of this stakeholder group. The survey yielded 202 responses from practitioners and leaders in a business consulting unit, information technology, marketing, and the analytics unit. Figure 3.1 shows the breakdown of participants by business unit membership.

The majority of survey participants were practitioners (82 percent), had participated in scrum and/or kanban training (84 percent), and were actively working in a scrum or kanban

Source: Author.

Figure 3.1 Agile practices survey participants – business unit membership

team (83 percent). The majority of participants indicating scrum or kanban training participation were trained in scrum (69 percent). Figure 3.2 shows the breakdown of the organization's training participation.

The majority of survey participants working on agile teams identified as development team members (73 percent). Figure 3.3 shows the breakdown of the agile roles.

Constraints

The most relevant constraints to consider in this scenario are the usual ones associated with resource availability. The organization must continue to deliver on strategic projects, tactical projects, and ongoing operations while undergoing this process evaluation and ultimately implementing whatever decision is made. Like many, if not most, organizations in this situation, it is resource-constrained in its technology teams as well as its functional business units. The organization finds that there are always more projects demanded than there are resources to deliver, and the necessities of operating a property and casualty insurance company and meeting the needs of customers demand that significant resources be allocated to keeping existing systems and processes functioning.

Associated with this constraint are the organization's struggles with visibility regarding its resource allocation and demand management. On one hand, the organization's business systems and project management tools enable the assignment of resources to projects and the

Source: Author.

Figure 3.2 Agile practices survey participants - scrum and kanban training

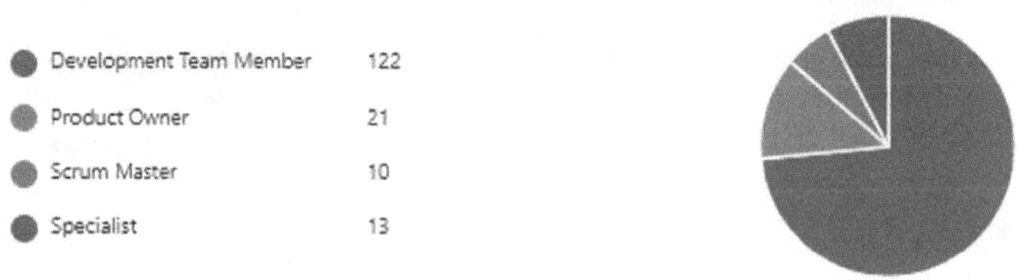

Source: Author.

Figure 3.3 Agile practices survey participants - breakdown by role

tracking of the projects. On the other hand, the organization is aware that it does not have a "single source of truth" to provide it with real-time visibility of the percentage of people's time allocated to a project versus actual time spent on the projects and their associated tasks.

Property and casualty insurance companies in the United States are highly regulated. Each state has its own set of regulatory requirements that must be met for an insurance company to do business in that state. Therefore, regulatory concerns have some influence and pose certain constraints – not in any way associated with the selection of the project management methodology, but in the way they affect and influence the overall project delivery environment. Therefore, they should be considered when evaluating and recommending a project management methodology option.

Other constraints center on the culture, aptitude for change, and acceptance of change in project management approaches of each of the business units in the organization. One of the lines of business in this company is particularly large and influential. At the same time, this business unit has struggled with dysfunctional product leadership and internalizing some aspects of agile delivery. Some of the leaders in this unit have advocated for the return to waterfall practices. Some of the same leaders also struggle with agile concepts such as dedicated teams and the changing role of functional managers in agile practices.

DISCUSSION QUESTIONS

While reviewing and analyzing this case study, consider the following questions as part of your own analysis, as well as questions to synthesize into potential group discussions around making and supporting a recommendation:

1. What are the pros and cons of selecting each of the proposed methodology options?
2. What are potentially the most significant impediments associated with the selection of each option?
3. Why might you ultimately choose and recommend a particular option?
4. What data, whether qualitative or quantitative, would influence your decision and recommendation?
5. How might this organization ensure that it does not experience similar dissatisfaction with its selected approach and the outcomes after a few years?
6. How should the organization handle the organizational change management elements associated with the recommended approach?
7. How might the organization approach the training requirements and challenges associated with the recommended approach?

REFERENCES AND FURTHER READING

Anonymized survey data (2022). Qualitative and quantitative data collected in collaboration with a client in property and casualty insurance for the purpose of assessing the state of agile practices.

Belling, S. D. (2016, May 19). Agile vs. waterfall: Understanding the best project management approach for your business. *CEOWorld Magazine*. https://ceoworld.biz/2016/05/19/agile-waterfall-understanding-best-project-management-approach-business

Belling, S. D. (2020). *Succeeding with agile hybrids: Project delivery using hybrid methodologies*. Apress.

Collyer, S., Warren, C., Hemsley, B., & Steves, C. (2010). Aim, fire, aim: Project planning styles in dynamic environments. *Project Management Journal, 41*(4), 108–121. https://doi.org/10.1002/pmj.20199

Darwish, N. R., & Megahed, S. (2016). Requirements engineering in scrum framework. *International Journal of Computer Applications, 149*(8), 24–29.

Hiatt, J. M. (2006). *ADKAR: A model for change in business, government, and our community*. Prosci, Inc.

Nieto-Rodriguez, A. (2023, October). It's time to end the battle between waterfall and agile. *Harvard Business Review*. https://hbr.org/2023/10/its-time-to-end-the-battle-between-waterfall-and-agile

Pawar, R. P., & Mahajan, K. N. (2017). Implementation of change management in software development by using scrum framework. *International Journal of Advanced Research in Computer Science and Software Engineering, 7*(7), 400–404. https://www.researchgate.net/profile/KirtiMahajan/publication/326077606_Implementation_of_Change_Management_in_Software_Development_by_using_Scrum_Framework/links/5f73b931458515b7cf589bd8/Implementation-of-Change-Management-in-Software-Development-by-using-Scrum-Framework.pdf

Rigby, D., Elk, S., & Berez, S. (2020, May). The agile C-suite. *Harvard Business Review*. https://hbr.org/2020/05/the-agile-c-suite

Schwaber, K. and Sutherland, J. (2020). *The Scrum Guide*. https://scrumguides.org/docs/scrumguide/v2020/2020-Scrum-Guide-US.pdf

4
The first Jeep

Paul R. Bruno

OPENING PARAGRAPHS

The objective of this case study is to examine the elements of prudent project management from an on-the-ground, sleeves-rolled-up perspective as applied to the creation of the first Jeep, one of the great accomplishments in world history. Specifically, the case will provide:

- a thorough understanding of the events that led to the creation of the first Jeep
- greater understanding of the ways of working on projects, including in the areas of methodology (waterfall and agile), linking strategy to projects, stakeholder analysis, how projects originate, requirements gathering, bid/contract process, practical issues in completing project tasks including team dynamics, the role of testing in projects, risk management and how power and politics influence projects
- a more robust appreciation of how projects can impact and operate at the strategic, operational and tactical levels
- greater appreciation of the dynamics and challenges of stakeholders working together
- an understanding that, while the Army represented one main stakeholder, inside the Army were individual stakeholders each with their own objectives and agenda impacting the project
- awareness that, during the life of a project, the unexpected, the arbitrary and serendipity, which are largely out of the project manager's control, can have a massive impact on the success or failure of the endeavor.

The project deliverable turned out to be a revolutionary new vehicle to replace the mule in the United States Army's arsenal and move troops and small payloads. It was created against this strategic backdrop: rapid German and Japanese military successes; the operational challenge of a weakened US Army constrained by the peace decade of the 1920s; budget cuts during the Great Depression of the 1930s; and the seemingly insurmountable tactical risk in developing a four-wheel-drive front-axle vehicle that would have to meet a certain as-yet-undetermined weight requirement—none of which had ever existed before.

The lack of mobility among multiple platoons using arms became an issue that had vexed the Army since the end of the First World War, and which had now become urgent. Solving the issue defined the purpose of the project. The objective of creating a revolutionary new vehicle in an amazingly brief time frame presented a challenge that many at the time believed impossible to overcome. However, given the unthinkable risk being faced, i.e., the extinguishing of freedom around the world, the US Army could not and must not fail. Given the enormous operational risks and budget and time constraints, failure to invent the vehicle would leave the army hopelessly behind the Germans in mechanized warfare. Worse yet, the rest of the free world would stand on the brink.

Stakeholders included the infantry, cavalry, ordnance, field artillery and quartermaster corps (QMC) branches of the Army, and the individuals who comprised the American Bantam Car Company, a small, now bankrupt manufacturer located in a town north of Pittsburgh in Pennsylvania. As stated, if the Army and Bantam failed in this effort, defeating Germany and Japan would prove vastly more difficult or possibly unachievable.

BODY OF THE CASE

Stakeholder: the United States Army

The US Army found itself significantly unprepared for war in 1940. It especially lacked the most important technological advances of the interwar period: tanks, air power, mechanization and mobility. This hole in the armor, as it were, came from a conservative domestic fiscal policy in the 1920s, actions taken on the international scene in response to the devastation of the First World War, and the political and financial upheavals triggered by the global economic calamity of the 1930s known as the Great Depression (see Figure 4.1).

In the summer of 1914, the nations of Europe had blundered their way into a cataclysmic war that claimed around 25 million casualties and billions of dollars by the time the armistice was signed in November 1918. The major belligerent powers met in Versailles, France, in 1919 to draw up a peace treaty. The victors, however, had competing aims and goals, which resulted in a compromise that satisfied no one but nonetheless punished Germany severely. The perception in Germany of the treaty's "unfairness" was a salient issue, which the Nazis could (and would) exploit during their rise to power in the early 1930s.

On the other side of the Atlantic, the United States had a history of maintaining a weak military other than in times of conflict. The US rapidly demobilized after the First World War, quickly leaving a very small army. This tradition, along with domestic and international policy decisions made by three successive Republican administrations, left the US Army seriously depleted by the end of the 1920s.

Fiscal policy limited domestic federal government spending that weakened the Army further after demobilization. It left the military starved for funds during the "roaring twenties". International relations that pursued a fervent desire for "peace" among the nations of the world dominated US and European foreign affairs during the age of prohibition. This peace movement saw its expression in a number of treaties, including the Washington Naval Treaty

Source: Encyclopaedia Britannica.

Figure 4.1 An unemployed man selling apples at the height of the Great Depression

of 1922, the Locarno Treaty signed in 1926 and the Kellogg-Briand Pact of 1928. Each of these sought to limit military power among the signatory nations and had a direct and negative impact on US Army preparedness.

On the international scene, an ominous sign of things to come could be seen in 1922. In Italy, Benito Mussolini took advantage of the chaos in post-war Europe to establish the first fascist dictatorship on the continent. By the end of the 1920s, economic events had overwhelmed the international idealism of the "roaring" decade when the worldwide Great Depression struck in late 1929. Throughout the 1930s, a policy of appeasement towards Germany, embodied in the 1938 Munich Agreement, limited the West's response to Hitler's aggression. In April 1940, Hitler turned his armies against the West. By mid-June, they had produced sudden and shocking defeats of Denmark, Norway, Luxembourg, Belgium, the Netherlands and France. They deployed an entirely new type of warfare, which they had debuted in Poland, called Blitzkrieg (lightning war). This major change in tactics from the First World War relied on the use of mobile vehicles and tanks in formation to blast through enemy lines, as well as the use of ground and air power together to produce quick victories with minimal casualties on the German side.

The US Army, suffering from fiscal starvation and the impacts of the peace movement of the 1920s and the Depression of the 1930s, found itself completely ill-equipped for this new type of warfare. Germany's overwhelming display of tanks, air power, mobility and mechanization led to the issuance of directives by the Army on August 20, 1940, that would guide research priorities moving forward. One recommendation—to further the development of "reconnaissance vehicles"—belatedly provided the justification for the first Jeep project, which had begun in June 1940.

Stakeholder: American Bantam Car Company

The American Bantam Car Company of Butler, Pennsylvania—a forgotten manufacturer of small cars in the late 1930s—traces its lineage to Sir Herbert Austin, a British automobile magnate. Born in England in 1866 to a farming family, Austin migrated with his uncle to Australia in 1884 and during his youth displayed an aptitude for mechanics and engineering.

Eventually taking an interest in automobiles, by 1901, Austin had designed his first car and continued to improve his designs over the next 13 years. By the time of the First World War in 1914, the Austin Motor Car Company of Birmingham, England, was building and shipping about a thousand units a year of four-cylinder vehicles. The war years saw Austin put his mechanical talents to use producing munitions, which resulted in a knighthood. He returned to the automobile industry after the war, specializing in small cars, first the Austin Twenty, and later the phenomenally successful Austin Seven. The Seven proved immensely popular in Europe, which had high gasoline prices, short driving distances and an exponential increase in passable roads.

In 1929, Austin decided to build his small cars in the United States. He located his company in the small city of Butler, Pennsylvania which had an idle automobile factory. Naming the firm American Austin, he would eventually have vehicles to sell and a distribution network, but the Depression would doom his efforts. The United States' only small car manufacturer sold a paltry 8,558 units in 1930 and 1,279 in 1931. As 1932 dawned, bankruptcy appeared the inevitable end to Sir Herbert's dream of small cars in America.

Roy S. Evans, meanwhile, had been born in the small rural community of from Bartow, Georgia in 1900. Early on, he displayed an aptitude for risk taking and entrepreneurship. He started a taxi service in his hometown at the age of 14, operated a "news butch" venture on passenger trains, and eventually became a clerk for the Central Bank of Georgia. He raced motorcycles for a short time, then sold his two-wheeler and, with the proceeds, bought a Model T Ford, rebuilt it and fell in love with automobiles. He became a used car salesman, and, with excellent salesmanship and indefatigable energy, by 1932 he had built the largest used car dealership network in the South. Evans signed on early to sell the American Austin line and became the firm's biggest customer, accounting for 80 percent of sales.

With American Austin on the ropes in 1932, Evans personally began efforts to save the company. His work appeared to pay off as sales rebounded to 3,846 in 1932 and an astonishing 4,726 in 1933. Alas the Austin miracle would not last. Purchases plummeted again in 1934 and American Austin declared bankruptcy in June.

Evans would not give up on these small cars, however, and arranged to purchase the entire Butler factory for $5,000 on an asset valued at $10 million in 1936. He renamed the company American Bantam because 'Bantam' had become associated with the Austin vehicles, probably a reference to the miniature chickens of the same name, as the public viewed the cars as "miniatures". By 1938, Evans had updated the Austin's designs; however, as for Sir Herbert, "timing was everything". A lack of demand, exacerbated by a recession inside the Great Depression, doomed sales to an anemic 2,000 in 1938 and a dismal 1,225 in 1939. Sales continued to plummet towards only 800 units in 1940. By June that year, American Bantam had suffered the same fate as American Austin—bankruptcy.

Genesis of the Project

After the First World War, mobility on the battlefield and how to achieve it constituted the critical problem confronting American military leaders. The lack of funding hamstrung the armed services in all areas of research and development through the two decades following the war. That funding obstacle hindered the invention of mobile vehicles needed to replace the all-too-slow, cumbersome and always-vulnerable animal-based transportation. The motorcycle with sidecar proved dangerous to ride and performed poorly in cross-country conditions. As the 1930s ended, the need crystallized into the desire for a light, highly mobile car that operated effectively in any conditions.

During the 1930s, the Infantry focused its mobility efforts on weapons-hauling. The Cavalry, in contrast, needed a vehicle that could act in a reconnaissance role and that could go anywhere, gather information and return safely. Both Infantry and Cavalry realized they needed a truck, with a low silhouette, that could carry a small crew of one to two soldiers along with their weapons and ammunition.

The Infantry's efforts to find a suitable weapons-mover culminated in two major initiatives, one for the Howie Machine Gun Carrier, and another focused on vehicle testing in the late 1930s. The Howie Machine Gun Carrier would prove unusable.

As 1938 dawned, the Infantry still wrestled with the issue of finding a lightweight weapons carrier. The intrepid staff at Fort Benning, Georgia, who had built the Howie Carrier, evaluated an assortment of trucks, tractors and cars. These tests narrowed the field to a commercially available vehicle, the Marmon-Herrington half-ton 4x4 truck (Figure 4.2). The Infantry then ordered a number of these trucks for further evaluation from the Quartermaster Corp (QMC), the Army's procurement branch.

The Quartermaster, however, for reasons lost in history, failed in its assignment. This created resentment at the Office of the Infantry, and that animus would greatly impact the course of the creation of the first Jeep. The Infantry's testing, however, had proved that the best solution was a lightweight military vehicle with a low silhouette, a weight of half a ton or less and four-wheel drive.

General Requirements

Francis H. Fenn rose to the position of President of the American Bantam Car Company in 1939. In an attempt to save the bankrupt firm, he hired Charles "Harry" Payne in February 1940 to obtain aviation parts contracts with the army. After traversing Washington, DC for months, Payne, instead of procuring aviation parts, aroused interest within the military for Bantam to manufacture a lightweight, high-powered, low-silhouette vehicle.

Source: Public Domain.

Figure 4.2 A half-ton Marmon-Herrington 4x4

Stationed at Fort Benning during the late 1930s, Colonel Ingomar M. Oseth knew of the Infantry's tests to find a suitable cross-country weapons carrier. While at the Georgia post, he had also acquired specialized knowledge related to off-road weapons vehicles. Oseth eventually came to work in the Chief of Infantry's office in Washington, reporting directly to the branch's commander, General Lynch.

Lynch assigned his vehicle expert to the Quartermaster Corp's Technical Committee. This group, comprised of members from the various branches of the Army, advised the procurement arm on items to be purchased for military use. The Technical Committee had a subcommittee on motor transport, and Lynch assigned his expert on mobile weapons to that committee.

In May 1940, Oseth attended a key meeting of the motor transport subcommittee at Camp Holabird, the Army's main depot for procuring vehicles, located near Baltimore, Maryland. The main focus of discussion at that summit centered on the Army's lack of mobility and a vehicle suitable for cross-country movement. When the conference ended, the participants realized the United States Army had no vehicle in its arsenal to meet their mobility needs, and no plan on how to procure such a vehicle.

When he returned to his office from the three-day session at Holabird, Oseth was surprised to find Bantam's representative Harry Payne sitting in the window behind his chair. After a brief discussion, the two embarked on a journey to draw up a memo that would encapsulate the characteristics of a suitable light mobile weapons carrier. On June 6, 1940, the Infantry issued a document that outlined eight general requirements for the vehicle:

- Minimum height: 36 inches.
- Maximum weight, without payload: 750–1,000 pounds.
- Adequate cross-country ability, and grade ability equal to that of a standard cargo vehicle.
- Caliber .30 machine gun mount, either integral with the body of the vehicle or detachable.
- Capacity: a crew of at least two men, one machine gun with accessories and 3,000 rounds of ammunition or equivalent weight.
- Armored face shield for the driver.
- Four-wheel drive (except where tricycles are considered).
- Ground clearance: maximum possible consistent with the desired silhouette.

Oseth had insisted on the requirement for an "armored face shield for the driver" because the Ordnance branch spearheaded the procurement of any armored vehicle. The Infantry, still angry from the year before at the QMC's failure to obtain the Marmon-Herrington for its use, wanted to steer the project away from the Army's procurement branch. Later on, Oseth called his inclusion of the armored shield a "lawyer's trick". Nevertheless, his tactic succeeded. It meant that the Ordnance branch, though ill-equipped to procure a vehicle outlined in the June 6 memo, took initial charge of the project.

Specific Requirements

Before the June 6 memo went to the Adjutant General (AG) for approval, the Infantry routed it to the Cavalry branch in order to gain its support for the eight general specifications. The AG forwarded the memo to the Quartermaster General, in defiance of Oseth's "lawyer's trick" and upsetting the Chief of Ordnance, who sought "comment and recommendations" on June 14, 1940.

By the next day, the War Department General Staff, Supply Division, became aware of the efforts being made and ordered immediate action. The Ordnance Chief quickly called a meeting of his technical committee for June 17, 1940. Afterwards, having no real idea on how to proceed, Ordnance authorized a trip to Butler to discuss the vehicle with Bantam officials. The goal of the visit was to gain sufficient understanding of the new car to develop specific requirements that a manufacturer could build to.

With the Army on its way to him, Francis Fenn brought his plant manager Harold Crist into the effort. Crist served Bantam in that capacity from 1937 to 1942. His career consisted of work as a draftsman, a supervisor, a designer and a master machinist. He possessed extensive knowledge of cars from the ground up.

The Army visited the Bantam plant on June 19–20, 1940. Over the course of the two days, the Army and Bantam fleshed out the initial details of the vehicle. Those specifics included a concept drawing (Figure 4.3) created at the end of the first day. An engineer from Spicer Automotive of Toledo, Ohio, experts in axle manufacturing, joined on the second day. They discussed the development of a 4x4 front axle, a risky but essential requirement.

The members of the Ordnance Technical Subcommittee now had a more definitive idea of what the new truck would consist of. These concepts now needed formalizing into a detailed specification. That document would result from 12 days of frantic effort interfacing with the very department the Infantry had wanted to avoid—the Office of the Quartermaster General!

After returning from Butler on June 22, 1940, the Ordnance team met and developed a more detailed set of requirements than the original June 6 memo had contained. This new memo included a recommendation that, "since this vehicle is a commercial wheeled type without armor protection, the Quartermaster General be charged with its development and procurement". Oseth's "lawyer's trick" to keep the vehicle's development with Ordnance had failed. The QMC appointed the talented Colonel Edwin S. Van Deusen to oversee the development of the specification. The Quartermaster Corp also assigned its top engineers to work on the document.

Having learned their lesson that a lack of stakeholder input had doomed the Marmon-Harrington procurement, the QMC engineers consulted regularly with the Infantry, Cavalry and Harold Crist of Bantam. The Quartermaster wanted to ensure that those who would be using it ultimately received the vehicle they wanted. Infantry Colonel Oseth's gambit had failed tactically but succeeded strategically because, in the end, the QMC involved all interested parties in the specification's development.

The Quartermaster Corp finalized a detailed specification on July 2, 1940, known as ES-475, and a drawing, QM-08370-Z, from which a manufacturer could build a vehicle. The

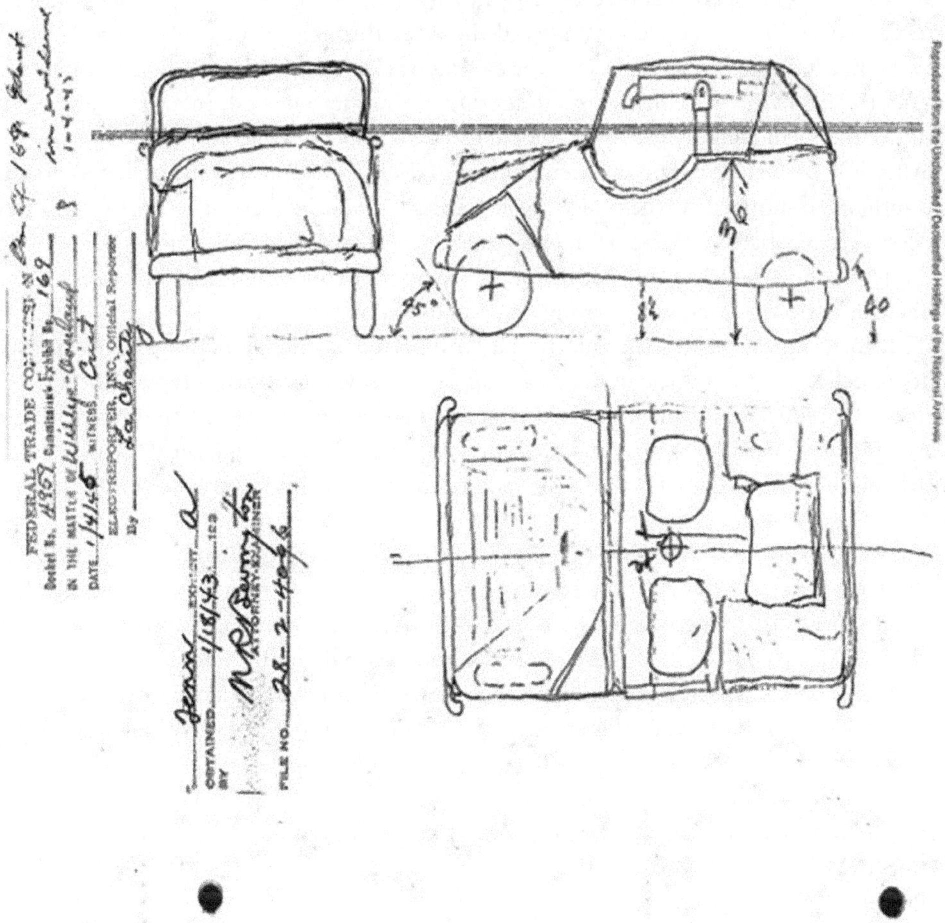

Source: United States National Archives, College Park, MA.

Figure 4.3 Jeep concept drawing, June 19, 1940

final document specified that the car weigh no more than 1,200 pounds (a quarter-ton). The designers arbitrarily arrived at the weight by choosing what was exactly between a half-ton truck (2,000 pounds) and a motorcycle with sidecar (500 pounds). Based upon that unscientific metric, the QMC assigned the name "¼-ton 4x4" to the vehicle. This subjectively determined weight would become a major risk to the development and acceptance of the new truck.

Bid and Contract

The official transfer of the procurement into the auspices of the QMC occurred on June 27, 1940. The orders accomplishing this action emanated from the highest level, the Chief of Staff.

The memorandum that officially recognizes and organizes the undertaking acted as a de facto project charter. This directive summarized the work through to the end of June 1940 and would guide it through its completion. The parameters included time (by August maneuvers), budget ($175,000 for 70 vehicles), resources (Quartermaster General, Infantry, Cavalry and Field Artillery) and quality (the requirement of an extensive service test).

After July 2, the Quartermaster General had to decide what process to employ to procure the authorized number of trucks. This would entail either a request for proposal (RFP)/bid process or a negotiated contract with one vendor. After the Butler conference, Fenn assumed the latter method would prevail, with Bantam. On July 9, Bantam salesman Payne sent a letter to the Quartermaster General detailing a sole source contract.

To help decide the matter, the Quartermaster inquired of the Infantry regarding the feasibility of delivering the vehicle in time for August maneuvers. Infantry's reply indicated that October 15, 1940, would suffice for the delivery of the new car. On July 10, the Quartermaster Corp opted for the RFP/bid option, which stipulated a build time requirement of 49 days (the third and final high risk). It sent the specifications to 135 manufacturers in order to solicit bids.

The rejection of their offer and the need to participate in an RFP/bidding process caught Fenn, Payne and Crist completely by surprise. Bankrupt American Bantam did not have an engineering department and would have to immediately create one to contend for the contract. That would bring into the effort automotive engineering veteran Karl K. Probst. The Detroit-based expert, at 60 and having 37 years' industry experience by this time, was the seasoned veteran of the Bantam team. A mechanical engineering graduate of Ohio State University, he had worked for a number of years for various companies. He moved to Detroit in 1933 and established a consulting office. Over the next seven years he would work with almost all the major firms in the car business including Packard, Ford, Chrysler and General Motors (GM).

Probst had heard about the project soon after the RFP had been mailed out. Having to work on a contingency basis made him initially reluctant to join the project, but he eventually signed on after some persuasion by officials at the highest levels of the federal government.

Fenn called Probst on Wednesday, July 17. They engaged in a detailed discussion about the challenges inherent in what the Army proposed—especially the front axle, the quarter-ton weight requirement and the 49-day build schedule. At the end of their discussion, Probst immediately left for Butler. He stopped at Spicer Axle in Toledo that afternoon to discuss the critical axle component with key staff.

Driving overnight, the seasoned automotive designer arrived in Butler on July 18. Fenn immediately introduced him to Harold Crist, who he described as a "human dynamo". Crist presented Probst with tentative specifications, and helped him develop a vision for the vehicle. With their proposal due on July 22, Probst began drafting the car design at 1:00 p.m. that same day.

Probst worked throughout the rest of the 18th, slept and then put in a full day on the 19th, to complete the bulk of his responsibilities. He then took a break to watch the latest Hedy Lamarr movie. The team completed a chassis parts list overnight on the 20th and, during the remainder of that day, calculated estimated costs. They typed up the bid forms on Sunday, July 21, and Fenn and Probst then headed to Baltimore for an evening meeting with Harry Payne.

While reviewing the bid documents on the evening of the 21st, Payne found a major issue. Fenn and Probst had specified the vehicle weight at 1,850 pounds. Payne asked them, "Don't you fellows know you can't get accepted at that weight? They never expect you to make the weight in the specifications, but you've got to bid it at the 1,300-pound figure. We'll get it revised after we get the contract."

Payne arranged to have new blank forms delivered from Holabird and engaged the hotel manager's stenographer to retype the forms. She arrived at 3:30 a.m. on the 22nd, and retyped all the forms with a new weight of 1,273 pounds. While Crist and Probst had no idea if they could build the vehicle in 49 days, Fenn and Payne decided to state that they could. The intrepid stenographer finished just in time for Fenn, Probst and Payne to make it to Camp Holabird by 8:30 a.m. on Monday, July 22.

The Bantam team arrived to the greetings of competitors, Ford, Crosley and Willys-Overland. Totaling just four contenders, the group made for an unusually low turnout in view of a bid sent to 135 manufacturers. Major Herbert Lawes, the officer in charge of vehicle procurement, called for bids at 10:00 a.m.

In the end, Ford and Crosley declined to submit, arguing the impossibility of building the prototype in 49 days. Willys offered a hastily prepared handwritten document that specified a build-time and costs only, no plans, weights or specifications. Fenn, Payne and Probst tendered their comprehensive proposal. The choice would come down to Bantam or Willys.

Major Lawes retired to his office to review the two bids. As Probst later recalled:

> Major Lawes, the purchasing and contracting officer for Holabird, called us into his office at 10:30 with the Willys people. He started by saying, "Willys has the low bid," and paused. The bottom dropped out of me. Frank turned white. Payne cracked his knuckles. "However," Major Lawes continued, "our requirements are forty-nine days delivery for the pilot car. Bantam has bid forty-nine days; Willys has bid seventy-five days. The contract will be awarded to the company that commits to our delivery requirement—Bantam."

While the Quartermaster Corp drew up a contract, the Bantam team returned to Butler. They began preparations to attempt to build a revolutionary new vehicle in a predetermined time frame of a mere 49 days. Many experts in the automobile industry agreed with Ford and Crosley that it would be impossible. A technical analysis of the winning bid was quickly completed by July 25, 1940. The Army sent official notification of the award to Bantam on the same day.

The contract became final on August 5, and that document provided the last piece of information the squad in Butler would receive in order to build the quarter-ton 4x4 prototype. It included changes and additional information as reported in the technical analysis. The agreement specified the number of vehicles ordered (70), dependent upon the successful deliverance of the prototype in 49 days and its acceptance after testing. The cost would be $173,000, just within the Army's $175,000 budget for procuring the vehicles. The Bantam team would have until September 23, 1940, at 5:00 p.m. to build and deliver the new car.

Build

After the June conference, Frank Fenn had begun preparing his firm to build the vehicle. The Army designated the first car a pilot model or prototype. After Bantam won the contract in July, Probst began building the additional engineering capacity that was needed.

Bantam had two experienced hands to guide the engineering and hands-on building of the pilot model—Probst and Crist. In order to build the vehicle from the ground up in 49 days, Crist, the factory manager, had to quickly acquire additional experienced staff, although he wanted to keep the core team small. He hired Chester Hempfling a "can-do, jack-of-all-trades" automotive man, and Ralph Turner, a mechanically gifted individual. This hands-on team impressed Probst, "He (Crist) and his four key men could produce tools and parts—some with no drawings. We needed that ability for sure."

While this crew had vast amounts of automotive experience, no one had ever attempted anything of this magnitude—build a revolutionary new vehicle with strict requirements in an unimaginable time frame. The legion of experts in Detroit put the odds at 5:1 against Bantam.

Probst laid out the general game plan for completing the vehicle. The car's construction would be a design-build iterative process with reworking the norm. Probst acted as project manager and lead designer. Crist led the build team as a hands-on boss. Turner took responsibility for the chassis and the engine. Hempfling had charge of fabricating the sheet metal parts. Fenn provided on-site executive support.

The two main risks that the team needed to overcome concerned the front axle and the vehicle's weight. After joining the Bantam team in July 1940, Probst immediately recommended that they should ignore the 1,300-pound weight requirement. He reasoned that, eventually, the Army would adjust that requirement upward. Probst told Fenn during their first conversation on July 17, "Well, we can produce drawings faster than our competitors. Of course, we can't make that weight, but neither can anyone else."

Nonetheless, they still need to resolve the front axle situation. Fenn and Crist had already met with engineers from Spicer Axle, on June 20, 1940, during the two-day Ordnance Committee visit. The Toledo firm eventually modified a Studebaker axle to meet specifications. This key component arrived in Butler on September 15, 1940, eight days before the delivery deadline.

The team completed the vehicle on September 21, 1940. Ten minutes after completion, they rolled it out and gathered in and around it for a photograph. After taking the now-iconic picture, the team had to decide what to call it. After some discussion, they agreed upon Bantam Reconnaissance Car or BRC.

The team had one day to assess the vehicle and resolve any further issues that they could before delivering the pilot model to Camp Holabird no later than 5:00 p.m. on September 23. For a revolutionary new vehicle that was to face, as Probst described, "the most grueling proving test imaginable", two days of checkout amounts to no time at all.

Early on Monday, September 23, 1940, the team set out for the Army's vehicle procurement depot. The honor of driving the BRC to the base went to Ralph Turner. Fenn, Crist and Probst followed in Crist's car. A group of soldiers, officers and civilians met the Butler team as they

Source: Courtesy of Robert Brandon, Butler, PA.

Figure 4.4 Bantam #1, the very first Jeep, minutes after assembly completed on September 21, 1940. Harold Crist driving, Karl Probst leaning against the spare tire, far left

drove the BRC through the main gate at 4:30 p.m., half an hour before the deadline. About 100 individuals, including the Ford, GM and Chrysler test crews, converged on the strange little car. Accustomed to experimental vehicles of every shape and description, their initial astonishment turned to awe at seeing something uniquely different. Major Herbert Lawes, the Army procurement manager who had awarded the contract to Bantam, took the vehicle for a quick test drive.

"Upon returning," Probst recalled, "Major Lawes said he had tested Army vehicles for almost twenty years, and he said he could tell in twenty minutes whether a vehicle was good or not. He said he thought this vehicle was going to be absolutely outstanding."

In a period of three months, beginning in June 1940, this group of never-say-die individuals had designed, bid for, won the contract, and built a revolutionary new vehicle. The intrepid "band of brothers" of the American Bantam Car Company had done the impossible!

Testing

Bantam's automotive design engineer Karl Probst predicted that the BRC would undergo "the most grueling proving test imaginable". The QMC would prove his words prophetic.

Chief of the test section, of E Company, 23rd Quartermaster's Regiment, Captain Eugene Mosley, supervised the evaluation of the BRC. He assigned 35 men to conduct the trials. Sergeant Lawrence H. Ross performed as a test driver and team leader for six of the men. The intrepid Ralph Turner serviced the pilot model throughout the evaluation period. He stayed on call 24 hours a day, seven days a week.

The first "test" on September 24, 1940 was actually a demonstration. The procurement heads of the Army and Marine Corps watched as the BRC put on a display of what it could do. Captain Mosley shuttled the brass around the test track until early afternoon. Major Lawes turned the BRC over to his test section chief on September 27, when the real trials began.

A difficult path lay ahead for the audacious BRC. It begged the burning question: how long would it take for Mosley and his team to utterly destroy this upstart little truck?

The Army wasted no time putting this latest vehicle slotted for their arsenal through its paces. Among a myriad of obstacles, the Holabird proving grounds featured a mud pit called "the hell hole"—an artificial bog about 300 feet in diameter and several feet deep. Only large six-wheeled trucks and tanks had successfully traversed this treacherous quagmire.

Piloted by Captain Mosley, the BRC failed an initial attempt. After observing the effort, Probst remarked that he thought the vehicle could push through the muck if the test section chief skirted the center and went in no deeper than two feet. Following the Bantam engineer's directive, the test supervisor coaxed the car all the way across

In the weeks ahead, the BRC underwent a merciless pounding. The tests included obstacles calculated to tear the heart out of a vehicle, from being driven full-tilt over log-roads and plowed fields, through sapling forests and across sand traps.

Throughout, Ralph Turner performed his duties flawlessly, for instance when he fixed the oil pan. The testers had ripped a hole in it because it hung too low to the ground. Turner attached a skid plate beneath it to protect it from future damage. During the rugged tests, the one-piece windshield broke. Harold Crist had a new two-piece windshield shipped from Butler and installed. The chassis failed late in the testing, but Turner repaired it.

Seargeant Ross recalled, "I do not know every darn thing that broke. There were a lot of breakdowns, but I know a lot of things that broke." But Turner fixed them all. None of the breakages was catastrophic. As destiny dictated, Turner became the world's first Jeep mechanic.

Crist supported Turner by visiting the base three to four days every week. During one of his visits, on October 4, 1940, he watched a publicity demonstration for the BRC, which showcased just what Bantam's creation could do. He recalled:

> Well, the fact is the photographers, I was present at this demonstration and that particular day we had such a rough test on another car Captain Mosley drove up to me and told me, he says, "Crist, you don't have to take this treatment of your car if you do not want to, if

Source: John W. Underwood, Heritage Press, 1965.

Figure 4.5 The BRC stuck in the mud, but not for long!

you say so we will stop it," and I says, "You give her the works, we want to find out what she will do, and if she fails in these tests we will correct the condition."

And he very courteously thanked me and he said, "That is the spirit," and then he gave the fellows a very severe demonstration, his driving ability was very good, and then when he was making one of these runs through the mud and jumping out of one of the holes there, which represented a shell crater, the news photographer said, "Do it over," and he said, "Give it a little more speed," and this Sergeant Ross, he came forward, in the company of his commander, and put up a very stiff argument with the news man, and during this argument with the news reporter, the photographer said he did not believe the car was any good and it was a little more than this man Ross could stand, so he immediately exploded and said that the Jeep [as later versions would be called] could do anything.

Late in the testing, an unusual acceptance test took place. During that outing, two generals riding in the BRC became stuck in the mud hole. They stated that, if they could lift it out of that predicament, they would officially accept the car's weight. When they did so, they had found the solution to the critical issue of weight. The army eventually determined the 1,300-pound weight as unrealistic and adjusted that requirement to 2,160 pounds.

Bantam's car endured the severest tests the Army could devise. Numerous failures, corrections and comments resulted from the trials, but the BRC held up remarkably well.

The Transport Subcommittee of the Quartermaster Corp Technical Committee, the body responsible for the quarter-ton 4x4 procurement, would make the decision whether to accept or reject the new vehicle. That group did not wait for the issuance of the test reports. On October 18, 1940, in one of the greatest understatements in history, the Army approved Bantam's vehicle (emphasis added):

> The pilot model has been examined by the interested arms except for Armored Forces and is being tested at the Holabird Quartermaster Depot. The Commanding Officer of the Depot has informally reported that *the test is practically completed and the vehicle found satisfactory*, subject to modifications found necessary as a result of the test.

The incredible project that created a revolutionary new vehicle had officially succeeded.

EPILOGUE

On November 13, 1940, the Army accepted delivery of another pilot model—the Willys Quad—built by Willys-Overland Motor, Inc., at its own expense. Also, the QMC, in October 1940, had requested a prototype from the Ford Motor Company, named the Ford Pygmy. It delivered its car on November 23, 1940.

Further testing and refinement of the three prototype vehicles and their successor models (Bantam BRC-40, Willys MA and Ford GP) would occur into 1941. Despite their work to create the first Jeep American Bantam did not receive the contract to build the vehicle for the Second World War that was awarded in late July 1941. That was given to Willys Overland who eventually evolved their MA model into the vehicle for the Second World War - the Willys MB. The name Jeep would become associated with the new light trucks by early 1941, but no one knows exactly when that moniker came to exclusively identify the quarter-ton 4x4.

General George C. Marshall, the Army's Chief of Staff, who authorized the Jeep procurement, later commented that the Jeep represented "America's greatest contribution to modern warfare". Allied Supreme Commander in Europe, and future President of the United States, General Dwight Eisenhower regarded the Jeep as one of the five pieces of equipment most vital to success in Africa and Europe.

To conclude, this case study has examined the elements of prudent project management from an on-the-ground, sleeves-rolled-up perspective as applied to the creation of the first Jeep. The stakeholders achieved their objectives. The product was delivered on time and under budget. The first Jeep—a project deliverable that profoundly changed world history.

DISCUSSION QUESTIONS

1. Discuss the strategic, operational and tactical issues the first Jeep project was undertaken to address. In what ways did the project succeed or fail to address these issues? (Linking strategy to projects)
2. Examine the pros and cons of the Army using a waterfall project management model to guide the first Jeep procurement. How did Bantam's build process mirror today's agile project methodology? (Methodology)
3. How can challenging requirements, like the front-axle, weight and 49-day build time, impact projects? How should a project manager handle these difficult situations? (Requirements gathering)
4. Discuss Bantam's solutions to the three key risks. Do you agree or disagree with the company's "mitigation" efforts? (Risk management)
5. In light of Colonel Oseth's "lawyer's trick", assess the impact politics, both internal and external, can have on projects. (Power and politics and its influence on projects)

REFERENCES AND FURTHER READING

Bruno, P. R. (2014). *Project management in history: The first Jeep.* MFM Publishing.
Bruno, P. R. (2022). *The original Jeeps in pictures.* MFM Publishing.
Bruno, P. R. (2024). *The original Jeeps.* MFM Publishing.
Domer, G. E. (1976). Good things did come in small packages: The history of the American Austin and Bantam. *Automotive Quarterly, XIV*(4), 404–429.
Federal Trade Commission (1944). In the Matter of Willys-Overland Motors, Inc., Toledo, Ohio. United States National Archives, College Park, MA.
Probst, K. K., & Probst, C. O. (1976). One summer in Butler: Bantam builds the Jeep. *Automotive Quarterly, XIV*(4), 430–439.
Rifkind, H. R. (2011). *Jeep: Its development and procurement under the Quartermaster Corps, 1940–1942.* Robert V. Nortman.
Spear, W. (2016). *WARBABY: The true story of the original Jeep.* Points North Press.
Underwood, J. W. (1965). *Whatever became of the Baby Austin?* Heritage Press.
Wells, W. A. (1946). *Hail to the Jeep: A factual and pictorial history of the Jeep.* Harper & Brothers.

5 Navigating the challenges of rapid information systems implementation

Dorit Rotem

OPENING PARAGRAPHS

In a survey carried out among customers in the Israeli food industry, it was revealed that they were not satisfied with the quality of the products and services generally provided to them. Products tended to arrive late, and the percentage of defects was too high. An examination conducted by a market research consulting firm revealed that many companies in the industry were using outdated business methods.

One of the largest food companies in the country was All the Best (a pseudonym). In 2019, it owned seven factories in Israel, two in Europe, and two in the US. The company also distributed complementary products from other manufacturers, including soft drinks, disposable paper products, and more).

All the Best's food products are divided into several categories (examples from each group are provided just for clarification):

- Fresh baked goods (baguettes, bread, cakes, etc.)
- Frozen food products (frozen vegetables, falafel, etc.)
- Dry sweet baked goods (biscuits, bagels, etc.)
- Savory snacks (unique products for the local market)
- Salads (hummus, tahini, eggplants, etc.)
- Baby nutrition (formulas tailored to different age groups: newborn, two months, six months, etc.)
- Wet culinary (ketchup, mayonnaise, other sauces)
- Dry culinary (pasta, wafers, etc.)
- Ice cream.

Due to its size, All the Best was at risk of being considered by local regulators as a monopoly, subject to strict oversight laws. Therefore, the management decided to sell a portion of its manufacturing capacity and part of its distribution lines, as will be detailed later. In order not to be recognized as a monopoly, the purchasing party of the sold activities would operate entirely separately and independent from the All the Best company.

An entrepreneur named Mr Feld (pseudonym) decided, after tough negotiations, to purchase these activities and upgrade them with advanced technology. The purchase was completed in February 2019. Some All the Best employees joined the new company, named Goodies (a pseudonym), and additional new employees were recruited. Mr Feld decided to serve as the CEO of the Goodies for at least its first two years of establishment. He considered the role of CIO (chief information officer)[1] to be one of the critical roles during the startup phase and appointed Mr Hilf, who brought experience in information systems and knowledge of organizational computing infrastructure. In Feld's opinion, Hilf also possesses an innovative worldview, aligning with the fourth type of CIO according to the research by Chun & Mooney (2009).

At the beginning of November 2019, Feld had to make a decision: whether the information systems of Goodies were prepared to support the organization's commercial activities reasonably and whether it could 'go live' and approach various customers in early 2020.[2] If there were gaps, could they be bridged within the remaining time frame? Opinions among the senior management (C-level) team were divided.

The details of the case, including the nature of Goodies' activities, the functioning of the information systems department, the sequence of events, and the senior management's stance, as well as the dilemma faced by Mr Feld, are presented in detail in the following case description. In this case study, Goodies is described interchangeably as both an organization and a company, and the author occasionally replaced the titles CEO and CIO with the names of the individuals holding those roles. The notes at the end of the case description are intended to elucidate concepts for individuals who may not be acquainted with the information systems field.

BODY OF THE CASE

As mentioned, the commercial activities of Goodies were previously part of the operations of the large food corporation All the Best. When the activities were within the corporation, computing services were provided by the corporation. In February 2019, this part of the business was sold to an entrepreneur, Mr Feld.

With its establishment, Goodies intended to continue producing the same products it had previously manufactured as a subsidiary of the All the Best conglomerate. The main focus was on the snack and confectionery market, as well as frozen food products (belonging to the categories of savory snacks, dry culinary, and frozen food products, as mentioned earlier). The company planned to market both the products it produced itself and those it distributed from All the Best and other manufacturers that compete with All the Best in products such as pasta, coffee and chocolate.

The vision of the new owner was for it to become an innovative boutique company that leads in its field (frozen food and snacks) and provides attentive customer service and a comprehensive customer experience. This approach would assist in acquiring new customers and retaining existing ones, emphasizing quality, fairness, sensitivity, and integrity.

With the establishment of the company, both business and supporting departments were formed, also referred to as back-office departments. In total, there were seven departments. Each department manager reported to the CEO. Approximately two months after its establishment, Goodies employed around 600 employees in the following departments:

- Production
- Logistics (inventory, procurement, and other supply chain components)
- Marketing and sales
- Finance
- Human resources (HR)
- Operations (organizational safety, office equipment, cleaning, etc.)
- Information systems (IS).

The company's official launch date to the general public was set for January 2020. In order to support the business and support processes carried out by the organization, suitable computer systems were needed to enable these activities. Since Goodies had become a competitor to All the Best in some products, the latter refused to duplicate and sell these systems to Goodies. Therefore, Goodies had to establish its own computer systems.

Mr Feld, the CEO, had extensive business experience and had also previously served briefly as the CEO of a small advertising company. He did not, however, have experience in the field of information systems. He relied on his ability to learn and manage this area, as he had managed other areas in the past that were not within his specialization, then recruited Mr Hilf, whom he knew from the advertising agency. Hilf had worked in the field of information systems for over 20 years, and, among other roles, had previously served as the CIO of the same advertising company. Feld believed he had the appropriate competencies required for this position.

To provide the best response to the organization's needs, Hilf decided that the internal structure of the IS department would include six internal teams; with three being business-related and one treating the back-office systems, one responsible for quality assurance, and another for IT.[3] The latter two included software testers, infrastructure professionals, and information technology (IT) specialists.

The teams' organization is presented in Table 5.1 alongside their respective areas of responsibility. Each team name is prefixed with IS to indicate that it is an information systems team, handling the relevant information systems in that domain.

A team leader (also known as a team manager) was assigned to each team, and project managers were also included. The first four consisted of system analysts and developers. The IS-Infrastructure (IS-IT) team comprised experts in networks, communications, data storage, security, and so on, while the IS-Quality assurance (IS-QA) team included testers at various levels.

Table 5.1 Information systems teams and their responsibilities

Team name	Team accountabilities
IS-Production	Ensuring the ongoing stability, performance, quality, and availability of the production systems in the organization, such as bill of materials (BOM), production planning, and others.
IS-Logistics	Ensuring the ongoing stability, performance, quality, and availability of the systems that support the management of organizational inventory (raw material, finished goods, etc.), procurement, warehouses, and distribution activities of the company.
IS-Marketing	Ensuring the ongoing stability, performance, quality, and availability of the systems that support the organizational management of customer relationships and the organizational website.
IS-Back-office processes	Ensuring the continuous stability, performance, quality, and availability of the systems supporting back-office activities, namely, finance, human resource management, and other operational functions.
IS-Infrastructure (IT)	Accountable for all IT infrastructure in the organizations including servers, networks, hardware, licenses, peripheral equipment, security, and data warehouse.
IS-Quality assurance (QA)	Ensuring the quality, reliability, and performance of software applications and IT systems. This is done by several types of testing, defect management, work process evaluation, and selection.

Hilf hired 100 practitioners in the field of information systems for these departments, including 11 project managers, some of whom had extensive expertise in the field; some had less, and some had none at all. Table 5.2 shows, for each project manager (PM), the team they belong to, the number of employees in their project, and their level of experience in this role (very experienced, partially experienced, and junior).

Table 5.2 Information systems project managers and their staff

Team	Project manager	Experience	Number of projects for PM lead	Practitioners in project
IS-Production	PM1	Very experienced	1	8
IS-Production	PM2	Partially experienced	2	8
IS-Production	PM3	Junior	1	5
IS-Logistics	PM4	Very experienced	4	15
IS-Marketing	PM5	Partially experienced	1	10
IS-Marketing	PM6	Junior	1	7
IS-Back-office	PM7	Junior	3	10
IS-Infrastructure (IT)	PM8	Very experienced	1	15
IS-Infrastructure (IT)	PM9	Junior	1	8
IS-Infrastructure (IT)	PM10	Partially experienced	1	7
IS-Quality assurance (QA)	PM11	Partially experienced	1	7

On March 1, 2019, the CIO informed top management that the department planned to develop a set of IS systems. Each one would be a project in itself. Some of the commercial activities would be computerized using well-known off-the-shelf software: back-office activities would be computerized using ERP software, marketing would be managed with CRM software, production-related activities would utilize MES software.[4] The organization's remaining activities would have dedicated systems developed specifically for the organization, such as a car fleet management system, office cleaning management system, and more.[5] In total, 17 different projects were planned for the establishment of these systems, including projects for implementing off-the-shelf systems, developing systems tailored for organizational processes, and installing communication and security infrastructures.

The plan was to implement ERP, CRM, and MES systems with the assistance of integration companies specializing in these applications. Some of the dedicated systems would be developed internally and others by external suppliers. Hilf expressed confidence that all systems would be successfully deployed, believing in the professional capability of the department's team and their connections with users in various departments. These success factors go hand in hand, as documented in the literature (Tam et al., 2020).

The IT infrastructure team within IS played a critical role in the development of various system types, serving as the initial element for their creation. Establishing all types of systems requires a robust technological infrastructure, encompassing essential peripherals, reliable connectivity, network stability, equipment provisioning, licensing, security measures, and more. Some elements of this infrastructure were put in place prior to the commencement of systems development.

The overall work plan for the IS department was developed by the CIO, drawing upon his extensive years of experience in the field. He aimed to avoid consuming valuable time in meetings with the business department heads and the CEO because he wanted to dive straight into development and deploy as many systems as possible within a short time frame. He prioritized projects based on shorter time frames. In other words, systems that could be implemented more quickly were given a higher priority to allow for the concentration of resources on fewer systems at a time. He was certain that the managers of the business departments also endorsed this approach. (See Huang et al., 2013, for a review of critical success factors for successful cooperation between business and information systems.)

The CIO assigned a team of individuals, including project managers, system analysts, and programmers, to each project. Naturally, the most qualified individual, in his opinion, was assigned to projects with higher priority. (Müller & Turner, 2010 and Ahsan & Khan, 2013 address the competencies of successful project managers.)

To expedite the system development, the CIO decided, after examining several project management methodologies, that the projects would be managed using agile methodology.[6] He found agile's characteristics to be the most suitable for the situation. He also considered the use of advanced technologies such as AI in project management (Nguyen, 2015; Morris & Pinto, 2007; Aspotoni, 2006; Kashiwagi Solution Model, 2022; Richter, 2022; Abbas et al., 2023).

In accordance with the chosen methodology, the project managers planned the activities for their respective projects. The planning included sprints, each lasting up to two weeks.

Using project management software called "Monday," tasks were only scheduled for the next quarter and the one after that. Tasks for projects lasting more than two quarters were not scheduled in advance, meaning the planning was partial.

As part of managing individual projects, both internal (within the department) and external (with users), monitoring and control meetings were established to track project progress. However, portfolio review meetings covering all projects were not scheduled. Kick-off meetings with each business department separately were held on March 5, 2019.

Mr Hilf, the CIO, wanted to devote all his attention and the time available to his department to expedite the systems implementations. Beside the 100 resources hired, he felt a severe resource shortage and, as a result, made the decision to focus solely on the development and implementation of the systems. Consequently, internal monitoring and control meetings for the projects were not held on a regular schedule and took place only when there was some free time within each project. Sometimes these meetings occurred once a month, and other times once per quarter. Similarly, the oversight steering committee meetings for each project were convened in August 2019. However, after that point, due to the overwhelming workload, there was no opportunity to reconvene the oversight committee for further meetings.

Meanwhile, although there were no periodic management meetings to review the project portfolio, senior managers who felt that a particular issue was extremely urgent requested its inclusion in the portfolio and prioritized it, irrespective of the original work plan of the IS department. These ad-hoc requests were frequent and occupied approximately 50 percent of the department's total workforce. Often, changes to projects were made, sometimes urgently, and these changes affected up to 30 percent of the original overall project scope.

Two months before the company's launch date, in early November 2019, the CEO, Mr Feld, decided to assess the organization's readiness for the event. He convened the senior management team and obtained from each of them their performance status and forecast for the next two months. When it was the CIO's turn to present the project status, he presented the following:

> Most of the systems are in good condition, indicating that we have almost completed the development. It is understood that the infrastructure built was robust and supported this development. Quality and security tests will be conducted in December. The table [Table 5.3] presents the status of the systems in each business department in terms of performance percentages.
>
> To avoid overwhelming you with a lot of data, the table shows a single number (percentage) for each business department and does not detail the progress of each individual project. For your convenience, and for informational purposes only, the table also includes a general description of the projects carried out for each department. I did not find it necessary to detail projects undertaken by the infrastructure and quality assurance teams (four projects) as they are internal and, from your perspective, are transparent.

Table 5.3 The percentage of completion of the systems in each business department (CIO's perception)

Business department	Percentage complete	Project
Production	60	• Product Data Management Systems: save the drawings, specifications, and the BOM. • Change Management System: manages changes to product design, versions. • Manufacturing Execution System (MES): monitors and controls the production process on the shop floor. This team is also accountable for establishing a plant maintenance system which includes inspection, notifications, corrective and preventive maintenance, and others. • Quality System: tracks and manages quality-related processes, ensuring that products meet specified standards.
Logistics	90	• Inventory Management: handles the movement of raw materials and goods (within the ERP system). • Procurement: manages orders from suppliers and subcontractors of raw materials, other products, and services (within the ERP system). • Warehouse Management System: manages the movement and storage of raw materials and finished goods. • Distribution System: manages the distribution of the company's products to various customers.
Marketing	70	• CRM: manages the customer relationships, streamline processes, and increase profitability. • Organizational Website: provides an easily accessible representation of the brand, values, and offerings. This project is 50% complete.
Finance	60	• Financial Accounting: handles the general ledger of the organization, the incoming and outgoing payments, organizational assets, and other financial issues (within the ERP system).
HR	90	• HCM (human capital resources): manages employees' details, their assignments, attendance, and training. It also supports payroll processes and recruitment processes (within the ERP system). Incentive system has been developed.
Other back-office activities	90	• Other support systems: handle other ongoing processes, such as vehicle fleet management, office equipment management, various services (cleaning and others), and service call management safety).

The CEO requested feedback from the other members of management regarding the status that was presented. The following dialogue reveals some of the responses.

HR Manager: I have an almost fully operational system; employees' personal records and training records are ready as well. They even developed an application that was not in the original plan, which is a system for employee benefits and incentives. Good job!

Operations Manager: Everything is working reasonably well on my end too. We need some further completion, but it's doable. From my perspective, we can move forward.

CIO: Thank you both very much. We worked hard to get to this point.

Production manager: The system is not functioning. There are no alerts for production malfunctions, which is critical, and the equipment maintenance issue has not been resolved yet. I need it urgently.

CIO: I am aware of the issue with fault detection, which stems from problems in the operation of the machine learning system we acquired. It will be resolved before long. Regarding the equipment maintenance system, my assumption was that, since it involves new equipment, there wouldn't be any issues in the near future. Given the severe shortage of manpower, I put it aside. If you say it's mission-critical to get it up and running, we'll prioritize it.

CFO (Chief Financial Officer: *I've submitted my requirements for the finance module* in the chosen ERP system. These requirements are quite basic and generic, and I'm not sure what has been done with them. I've seen a presentation explaining how profit and loss reports will look, which seemed trivial, but I haven't seen any invoice records yet. It's still unclear to me how they relate to customer supplies, and I don't know when acceptance testing for the system will take place. I tried to inquire with the implementing vendor, but they haven't been responsive.

CIO: Don't worry, the vendor is in close contact with my project manager, and the matter of invoice records, and profit and loss reports is indeed quite generic across all organizations, so there was no need to involve you. My team is handling the acceptance testing. Trust me; the financial module is functioning as expected.

Marketing manager: My response is mixed. From the checks my team has conducted, it appears that, on one hand, the system monitoring our sales performance is working well and also displays some customer data, although not all of it. By the way, when will we see all the customer data, and who is responsible for inputting this data into the system? On the other hand, we've developed the organization's marketing website, but the system does not showcase all our products, and customers cannot make purchases through the website, which is quite basic. What good is a site that only displays information without allowing orders? Sales will have to be conducted physically through sales representatives, just like a century ago. I could start working this way, but it's not efficient at all and requires more field salespeople.

CEO: I haven't seen that the website reflects our company's values and what sets us apart from others. It doesn't showcase our business innovation and desired reputation.

CIO: I'm pleased with the part that's working well. Regarding customer data, it's clear that your department is responsible for it. The responsibility for data always lies with the user. As for the website, we developed what we considered most urgent. The entire website wasn't part of the original plan; your representatives added this requirement only in June. I'm satisfied with what we've achieved so far. You also mentioned that it's possible to work this way. We seem to share the same opinion on this matter. Adding a page that describes our desired reputation for the system is not a problem.

Head of logistics: While inventory and procurement are working smoothly, we can make local and international purchases. However, the system cannot generate shipping certificates and approval certificates from the Ministry of Health's veterinarian for goods that need to be distributed. Without these certificates, we are not allowed to release the merchandise.

CIO: You [head of logistics] kept changing your requirements regarding the application all the time. We started developing those certificates, and you changed the requirements three times during development. Therefore, we put those certificates aside and focused on what was clear. When it's decided how the shipping certificate should look and what details you want to display on the veterinarian certificate, we will start developing them.

Following the statements made by the heads of the departments, the CEO said: At this point, I expected a much higher readiness of the organizational information systems. When do you, Mr Hilf, think all the work will be completed?

CIO: We worked on many systems in parallel despite the severe shortage of employees in the IS department and despite the numerous changes requested by various departments. The changes were not only at the level of individual project changes but also included requests to introduce entirely new systems. Despite this, I think I can present the completion in the first third of December.

CEO: The performance percentage you presented does not match what the department heads claimed. Now, with your assistance, we will prepare a table summarizing the number of months of work required to complete each system.

Table 5.4 presents what was prepared in the collaborative work.

CEO Mr Feld summarized, "Significant gaps have been identified here between what is desired and what is currently in place. The question is, can these gaps be bridged within the remaining time until the end of December 2019? What does the organization need to do to meet this deadline, and how can we be sure in December that the systems are truly ready?" At

Table 5.4 Estimate manpower months to completion (CEO's and C-level members' perception)

Business department	Problematic elements of the systems	Estimate months to completion
Production	MES: fault alert. Maintenance: no support for maintenance processes.	70
Logistics	Impossible to deliver goods to customers (within the ERP).	12
Marketing	CRM: customer records are missing. Website: company's products only partially displayed; it is not possible to place customer orders on the website; company's values are not reflected on the website.	5
Finance	It is not clear what the system is doing. The system was not presented to the users (within ERP).	50
HR	Minor changes are required in the incentive system.	5
Operation	Vehicle fleet system and safety system require several compliances.	5

this point, he had to make a decision on whether to open the company's doors to the public. Since he wasn't a computer expert, he decided to hire consulting services from experts in the field of information systems.

The consultants interviewed all the top managers and the heads of teams in the IS department. They also examined the overall plan and the work plans of each department and the work plans of three randomly selected projects. Additionally, they requested to review the minutes of meetings attended by members of the IS department and future users of these systems.

CONCLUSION

The company, Goodies, founded in February 2019, was a startup that aimed to open its doors in January 2020. To achieve this goal, it had to, among other things, establish all of the organization's computer systems/applications in a short period of time. This case relates to the management of the organization's information systems department from the perspective of planning and executing the portfolio and its programs, as well as the management of the individual projects that make up this portfolio.

The results produced by this management approach placed the CEO in a dilemma where every decision he made carried a certain level of risk. On one hand, opening on the planned date exposed the company to the possibility of operational failures; on the other hand, delaying the opening could lead to cost overruns, missed opportunities, and damage to the company's reputation.

DISCUSSION QUESTIONS

1. What do you believe are the primary challenges in project management and portfolio management today?
2. What work methods (or procedures) should this company consider adopting before the official launch to customers, and what strategies can be implemented after the launch for a successful post-launch phase?
3. How much do you assess the CIO's comprehension of the organization's business processes, and, in your view, how significant is this understanding?
4. Have the CIO and the project managers identified all the stakeholders in this case study? Is there an unknown or unidentified stakeholder?
5. Was the allocation of personnel to the different projects reasonable (referring to the rank-and-file level)?
6. What can you say about the communication channels activated during this stressful period, as well as the way the ongoing projects were monitored?
7. What, in your view, accounts for the difference in perspectives between the CIO's assessment of project statuses and the CEO's perception of the situation?
8. When it comes to assessing the status of projects in November 2019, what is the most effective way for the CEO and the CIO to reach a mutually agreed-upon, fact-based evaluation of the project status?

NOTES

1. The CIO is a senior executive in an organization responsible for managing the IT and digital systems that support the organization's operations and strategic objectives. The key aspects of the CIO role in the context of this case are: a) overseeing the design, implementation, and management of the organization's technology infrastructure; b) digitalization of business processes and customer experiences through the adoption of emerging technologies; c) establishing and enforcing governance frameworks for project planning, execution, and control; d) ensuring projects are delivered on time, within budget, and aligned with organizational goals; and e) fostering and leading innovation and continuous learning among information system staff.
2. Going live refers to the point in a project or implementation process when a new system, software, application, or website is officially launched and becomes fully operational for its intended users or customers.
3. The role of an IT team within Goodies is to manage and support all types of technology infrastructure, systems, and services that enable the efficient and secure operation of the business. This includes managing servers, storage systems, and data centers to ensure application systems are running efficiently.
4. Off-the-shelf software refers to pre-packaged software applications and solutions, in a certain domain, available for purchase and use by organizations usually with minimal adjustments of customization (or configuration). This software is usually designed to meet common or generic needs and is produced by software providers for a wide variety of users. ERP (enterprise resource planning) systems deal with financial management, logistics (inventory, procurement), human resources, and more. CRM (customer

relationship management) is used to manage and analyze interactions and relationships with customers and potential customers. MES (manufacturing execution systems) are used in manufacturing and production processes to track, monitor, and manage various aspects of production in real-time.

5. A dedicated system is a specialized computer system or hardware configuration designed for a specific purpose or function. These systems are tailored to excel in their intended tasks, offering reliability and performance advantages in their dedicated domains.
6. Agile is derived from the scrum methodology and is a project management approach that seeks to perform work as a team in small pieces at a time (in information systems, it is customary to call them sprints), with continuous experiments and feedback loops along the way for learning and improvement. Scrum helps people and teams deliver value incrementally in a collaborative way. As an agile framework, scrum provides enough structure for people and teams to fit into how they work, while adding the right practices to optimize their specific needs. This methodology has supporters and opponents.

REFERENCES AND FURTHER READING

Abbas, Q., Younus, W., Malik, S., & Hassan, M. H. (2023). Incorporating ChatGPT in software project management. *IEEE-SEM*, *11*(9), 1–9.

Ahsan, K., Ho, M., & Khan, S. (2013). Recruiting project managers: A comparative analysis of competencies and recruitment signals from job advertisements. *Project Management Journal*, *44*(5), 36–54.

Aspotoni, G. (2006). An introduction to Scrum. *Developer's Journal*, *6*, 1–10. Retrieved October 2023 from http://giovanniasproni.com/articles/AnIntroductionToScrum_SDJ_06-2006_EN.pdf

Chun, M., & Mooney, J. (2009). CIO roles and responsibilities: Twenty-five years of evolution and change. *Information & Management*, *46*(6), 323–334.

Huang, S.-J., Wu, M.-S., & Chen, L.-W. (2013). Critical success factors in aligning IT and business objectives: A Delphi study. *Total Quality Management & Business Excellence*, *24*(9–10), 1219–1240.

Kashiwagi Solution Model (2022, March 23). *Dr. Dean's experience with agile project management* [video]. YouTube. www.youtube.com/watch?v=skshYYyUmbk

Morris, P. W. G., & Pinto, J. K. (2007). *The Wiley guide to project, program, and portfolio management*. John Wiley & Sons.

Müller, R., & Turner, R. (2010). Leadership competency profiles of successful project managers. *International Journal of Project Management*, *28*(5), 437–448.

Nguyen, A. P. (2015). *Relationship between IT project managers' emotional intelligence and project success*. [Doctoral dissertation]. Retrieved on October 2023 from https://scholar.google.co.il/scholar?hl=en&as_sdt=0%2C5&q=+Nguyen%2C+A.+P.+%282015%29.+Relationship+between+IT+Project+Managers%27+Emotional+Intelligence+and+Project+Success&btnG=

Rao, K. N., Naidu, G. K., & Chakka, P. (2011). A study of the agile software development methods, applicability and implications in industry. *International Journal of Software Engineering and Its Applications*, *5*(2), 35–46.

Richter, L. (2022). *How to choose the right project management methodology* [video]. YouTube. www.youtube.com/watch?v=6xQ6JB2PDio

Tam, C., Moura, E. J. da C., Oliveira, T., & Varajão, J. (2020). The factors influencing the success of on-going agile software development projects. *International Journal of Project Management*, *38*(3), 165–176.

6
Avenue to project success: a decision scenario based on the success management approach

Nilton Hideki Takagi and Thiago Meirelles Ventura

OPENING PARAGRAPHS

The cases examined in this chapter involved two information systems projects, with the executor being a center of a public university in Brazil with a background in information systems and technologies (IST). The public university has almost 100 courses, more than 15,000 active students and more than 3,000 employees, the majority of whom are professors. The human resources capacity of the IST Center changes according to the projects being carried out, but it has a permanent staff of around 30 professors.

One focus of the Center is to offer IS services to other public institutions, known as government-to-government (G2G) projects. G2G projects have particular characteristics: on the one hand, they make it easier for the client (another public institution) to trust them because, for example, they have another public institution as the executor, which will not "go out of business" during the project. On the other hand, there is the challenge and need to fulfill the bureaucracies of public institutions on both sides.

The first project explored here took place between 2016 and 2020, and the second between 2020 and 2021. The total budget for both projects was more than $1 million. Both projects are important to the IST Center and citizens; thus, success needs to be achieved. In this way, the project manager in round one needs to define project management methodology and look for integrated success management activities, focusing on planning and controlling success factors (what can impact success) and success criteria (how success will be measured). In the second round, after identifying the success criteria and factors, the project manager can understand which of the usual areas of project management (schedule, cost, risk, quality, resources, communication, and so on) need to be managed more closely with the project team. Besides the importance of the success factor in managing the project, in this work, the main focus is to achieve success, with attention to success criteria.

BODY OF THE CASE

The clients were the State Health Secretariat and the State Public Security Secretary. The Brazilian state in which the client public institutions are located has a geographical size that is close to the size of Germany and France combined and a population of more than 3 million. There are more than 140 municipalities, some of which can only be reached by unpaved roads. From a management point of view, it is not easy to access the citizens to provide health and public care, the two areas in which the projects took place. The systems envisioned within the scope of the project aim to improve the efficiency of the public services provided, thereby reducing the discrepancy in access to information in the municipalities.

In 2015, the IST Center was invited to evaluate a project opportunity with the State Health Secretariat, which we will call Case Study 1 (CS1). It was the first contact; the first opportunity for the two parties to work together, and the IST Center was duly invited to carry out the project. This first project took place between 2016 and 2020. Because of the results of the first project, in 2019 the project manager of CS1 was contacted for another project at the State Secretariat for Public Security. This second project took place between 2020 and 2021, Case Study 2 (CS2).

CS1 was the development of two systems. One was related to health control and would be used by the state's more than 140 municipalities. The other was the development of a platform for state health indicators, which would be used to consolidate data from a wide variety of sources and support decision-making. A pressing issue was the Covid-19 pandemic. The State Health Secretariat needed to collect data and provide transparency on infection cases and deaths, for example. Among other functionalities, the system under development for health indicators was adapted to be the integrated channel between the state's health institutions, providing consolidated information on Covid-19 cases. In this case, the Center adopted a hybrid approach to project management. CS2 was the development of an integrated system, which aimed to replace three legacy systems. The initial team was based on the project team with the State Health Secretariat. In this case, the Center adopted an agile approach to project management.

These two projects were the first with a very high budget. One of the concerns was to understand the profile of who could take part in the project and what challenges might lie ahead. The results of these projects would be the cover letter for the IST Center, meaning that the results of the projects could open up or close down opportunities. It was crucial to achieve success in both.

Success Factors and Success Criteria

Strengths and weaknesses are elements that can have an impact on the success of a project, and we can call these elements *success factors*. Another important facet of success management is how we can evaluate the project's success; what we can identify as *success criteria*. Both are important in managing the project, and a project manager needs to understand the difference.

Strengths

The team formed to lead the projects was focused on technical learning capacity, management capacity and the relationship of trust with the manager assigned to the project. Many of the strengths at the start of the project were related to hard skills.

Project manager competences

The project manager had already worked in systems development team management and had taken a specialization course in project management as part of his academic background. The project manager had no experience of the technology chosen by the client, nor did he know the client's business rules, a common situation in project management. However, he had the freedom to develop a technical team to cover the specific technical part of the projects.

Technical competences of the project team

The technical team was made up of technical coordinators, senior systems analysts, junior systems analysts and trainees from the university. Some had experience in the chosen technology; others had experience in the rules of this business as they had already worked for the client. The technical coordinators were professors from the IST Center. In order to hire and maintain an effective technical team, senior and junior analysts were hired at a salary above the market rate.

Project management competences of the project team

For CS1, a small group was set up to help manage the project. One of the people involved in this sub-team was certified in project management and had extensive experience of managing projects both inside and outside the IST area. Together with the project manager, this sub-team defined the management methodology and helped monitor the project.

Project management method

The project manager and the team responsible for the project management had more experience in certain aspects of project management. They defined an approach that suited the type of the project, the project team's experience, and the requirements of communication and engagement with the client.

Relationship between project team members

When selecting the project team, the project manager considered behavioral competences to be a strong component. Good relationships were one of the important points that the project manager wanted for the project, and which could be crucial to achieving the project's results. The team also needed to be committed to the deliverables defined with the client right from the start of the project.

Weaknesses and challenges

Many doubts arose at the start of the project, whether these were seen as weaknesses or challenges, as it was the IST Center's first project on this scale.

Lack of knowledge of the client profile

Being new to each other is often one of the weaknesses at the start of a project. In these case studies, it was no different: the Center did not know how the client might behave or what the commitment would be like during the project. Lack of commitment could delay everything from collecting requirements to validating the artifacts.

Performance of the project team

Although some were known to the project manager, the project participants had not worked together before. In an IST project, it is not easy to get quick wins; you need time to assess the requirements, to implement and deliver something that can be used by the client. In a team that does not yet know how each other will perform in practice, results can take even longer.

Clarity, or not, of the final product

In IST projects, it is often unclear what the end product will be. When developing systems, this is one of the challenges. The project team may have a different view of the client's expectations, especially at the beginning of the project.

Sufficient budget

With a lack of clarity at the start of a project, there is always doubt. Will the budget be enough to deliver everything the client expects? Alignment between the available budget and the client's expectations of results is fundamental to the success of the project.

Evaluating Project Success

It is necessary to know, from the stakeholders' perspectives, what will actually be evaluated in order to say whether the project has been conducted and completed successfully. For these evaluations, the following are some of the criteria found in the literature.

- The client is using the product. Projects can end up with the product already out of date or not meeting all the requirements to make it operational. There have also been reports in the public sector that some systems have not been put into operation due to resistance from civil servants. This is a post-delivery criterion to be aware of.
- The product or result is user-friendly. In the IST area, a system that is difficult to use will consequently, in the short and medium term, lose performance or even no longer be used at all.
- Increased control of business processes. One of the objectives of IST projects is usually to increase project monitoring and control. In these case studies, all the systems developed had this criterion included, whether it was the integration of health indicators or the replacement of legacy systems in public security.
- Regulations and legislations compliance. With public institutions as clients, standards, and legislation that define business processes must be followed to the letter. Of course, when developing products for private institutions, it is also necessary to follow

guidelines or definitions in legislation relating to the sector in which they operate. However, in private organizations, changes to standards that define processes often only depend on them. In the case of public institutions, they usually need to be evaluated by other state institutions and this may even occur at national level.

- Scope compliance. Meeting all of the client's defined requirements is usually an important criterion and one that impacts on a number of other criteria, such as time and budget. In the case of developing and implementing new systems, the scope at the start of the project may not even be clear to the client. The experience of the execution team can be a decisive factor in guiding the client to pin down what they really need.
- Budget compliance. On the client's side, if it is a public institution, the project budget is likely to be defined at the start, without much flexibility once the project has been accepted. On the side of the contractor, as the team is formed for the project, if the budget is not well managed, it may be necessary to demobilize the team regardless of whether the project is finished or not. There is no possibility of taking the "loss" by keeping the team until the end. Staying within budget is a criterion that needs to be taken into account, as it can have a direct impact on other success criteria.
- Schedule compliance. Along with the budget, time compliance is one of the criteria most valued by clients and project managers. There are a few reasons for this. These are commitments that, if not met, can cause wear and tear on both sides. Another reason is that time is "easy" to measure; the schedule is a tool for which you do not need to be an expert to understand the minimum of what it contains.
- Client and end user satisfaction. As it is the first project, a good impression from the contractor is crucial to attracting new projects. Good client satisfaction is also related to good satisfaction among the end users of the product developed in the project.
- Team project satisfaction. The selection of the project team should take into account, as in these case studies, behavioral aspects as well as technical aspects. The satisfaction of the project team goes beyond the question of keeping them motivated; it goes to the need to be able to count on them in future projects.
- Low cost of maintenance in the operation phase (post project). Once the products have been delivered, the cost of maintenance is something that needs to be weighed up. Technology and development standards can directly impact on the need for more or less maintenance by the client once the product is in operation.
- Impact of the result on the internal environment and the external community (including the public). For a project in the public sector, the impact on communities, other public institutions, and citizens directly influences the perception of the project's success from the point of view of the client and the execution team. The greater the positive impact, the greater the perception of success is likely to be.

Project Management

In project management, there are several areas that need attention from the project manager and their management team, including budget, schedule, risk, procurement, communication, resources, stakeholders, quality, and scope These areas are presented, with some minor differences in concept, by most project management references, such as the Project Management Body of Knowledge (PMBOK),[1] ISO 21500 (and ISO 21502), PRojects IN Controlled Environments (PRINCE2), Project Management Methodology (PM²) and scrum, among others. Particular tools and techniques tend to be applied to these management areas. Project management processes are also carried out within a project life cycle. An overview of how project management works based on these management references is shown in Figure 6.1.

When we evaluate management processes in process groups, the references generally identify four sequential groups (initiating, planning, executing, and closing) and one transversal group (monitoring and controlling). Throughout the project, these process groups require different efforts from the project team. Figure 6.2 represents the level of effort in the project life cycle, with a transition between the sequential process groups.

The process groups in which the most processes are concentrated are planning and monitoring and control. Figure 6.3 and Figure 6.4 show the processes set out in different project management references for the planning and monitoring and control process groups.

Many of the evaluation criteria for assessing the success of a project only become apparent once the phases or project have been closed. These closure processes direct deliveries to clients, who can start to operationalize them and enable the evaluation of the criteria in practice. The closure processes in the various project management references are shown in Figure 6.5.

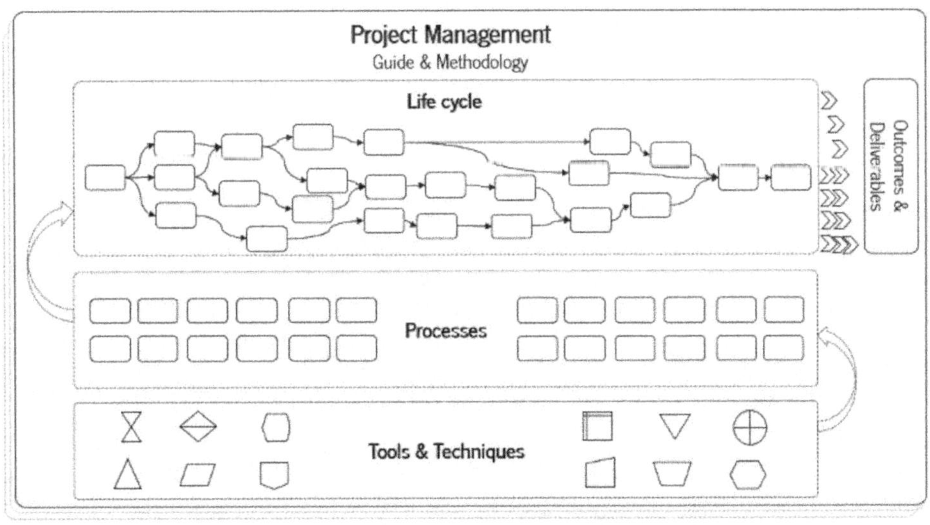

Source: Authors.

Figure 6.1 General visualization of project management

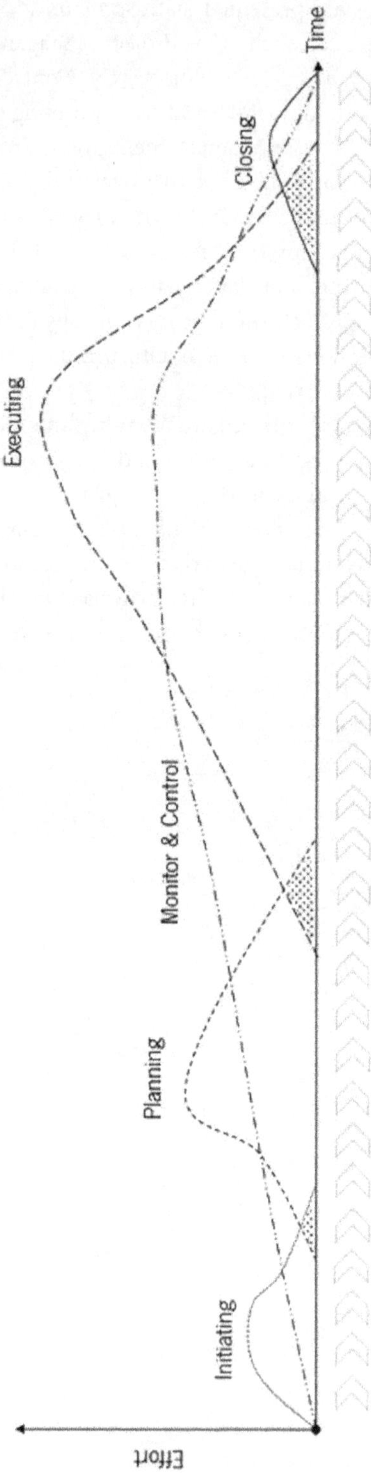

Source: Authors.

Figure 6.2 Effort level in the life cycle of the project

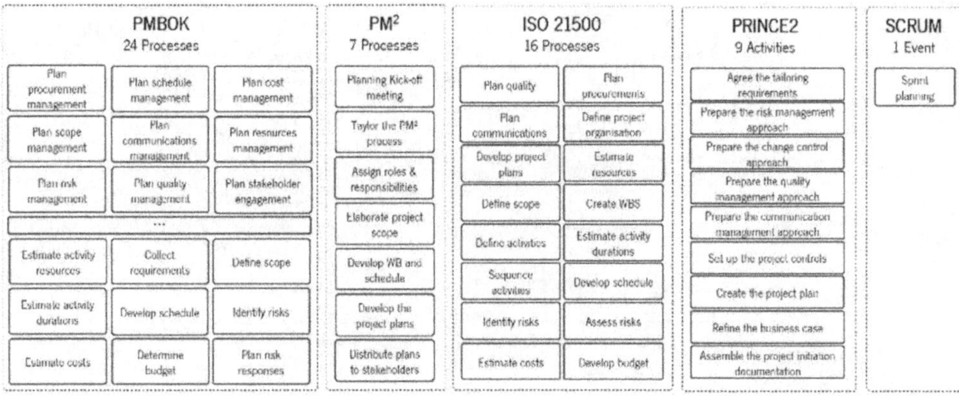

Source: Authors.

Figure 6.3 Processes in the planning group

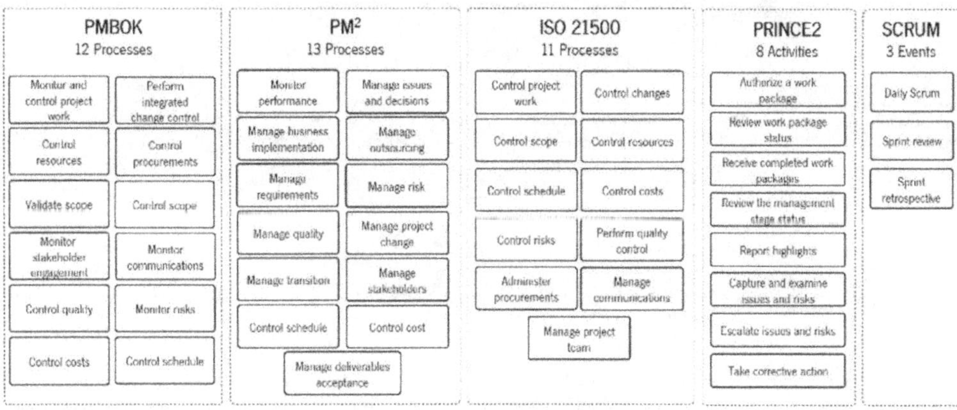

Source: Authors.

Figure 6.4 Processes in the monitoring and controlling group

Success Management

Success in projects is the goal of project managers and organizations; however, many do not achieve the success expected. Success should notcan rarely be measured simply by compliance with budget, deadlines, and/or quality, as might typically be expected in the project management field. Conducting a project to success is complex and has many variables, which project managers need to be prepared to deal with.

Success management (SM) is a way to manage the elements of success in a project. SM is proposed in the literature as a new knowledge area of project management. Some works have detailed the activities of SM, such as planning how SM will be conducted in the project,

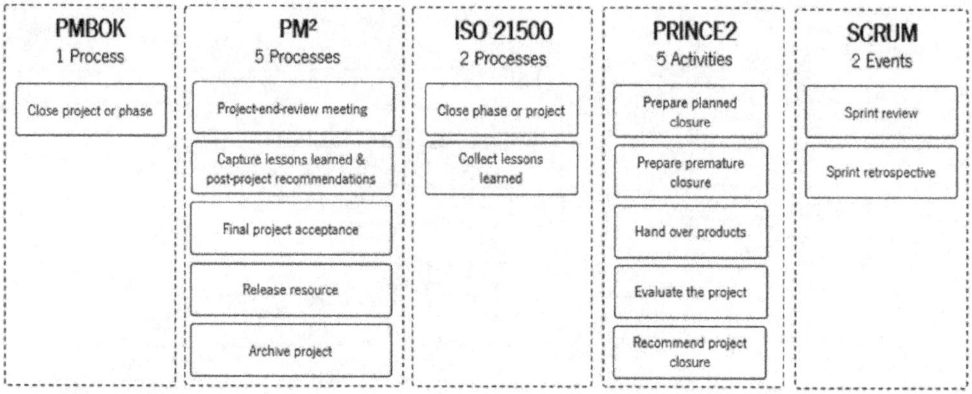

Source: Authors.

Figure 6.5 Processes in the closing group

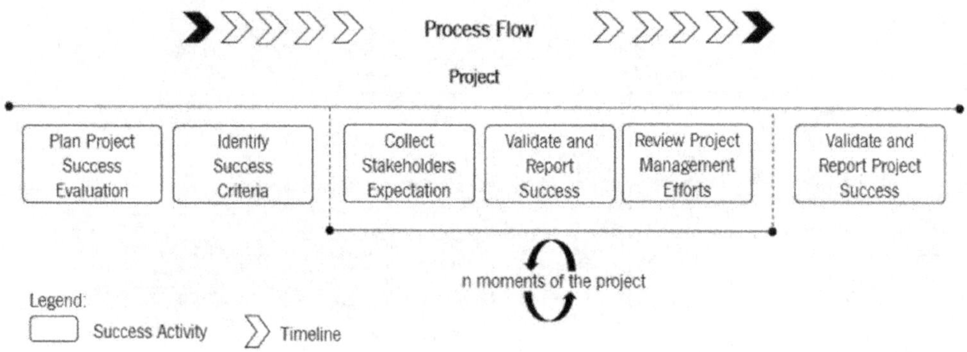

Source: Authors.

Figure 6.6 Management of success criteria

identifying success factors and success criteria, monitoring and controlling the success, among other suggested activities. Other works have integrated SM into project management methodologies such as PMBOK, PRINCE2, PM^2, ISO 21500, ISO 21502 and scrum.

To evaluate success following the SM process, the main element is success criteria. The success criteria can be related to different areas of project management, such as compliance with the schedule (schedule area), compliance with the budget (cost area), compliance with the laws and regulations defined (scope area), client satisfaction (stakeholder area), satisfaction of the execution team (stakeholder area), among other criteria (project management area).

The SM process has defined activities for the various stages of the project, from planning, through monitoring and control, to closure. For the case studies in this chapter, the evaluation activities were focused on the success criteria. Figure 6.6 shows these success evaluation stages based on the literature.

Purpose and Objectives

This scenario presents the opportunity to help define the management method that can bring the project closer to success. The main purpose of the project manager is to achieve project success and open up future opportunities for new projects. In this scenario, we have several different avenues that could be followed when defining project management methods:

- Adopt a well-established project management methodology. (The different methodologies all detail how the project manager should carry out the management processes, and some even provide templates for the management artifacts to be developed.)
- Adopt an agile, iterative, and incremental framework, as this is an IST project. (Agile approaches gained momentum following a manifesto from the information technology community. Although these agile approaches can be used in any area, in the field of IST they are very frequently used.)
- Adopt a hybrid approach, combining waterfall references and agile project management approaches.
- Rely on the experience of the team assigned to help manage the project. At least one of the members has a lot of experience and will certainly bring good solutions.
- Focus on success management activities and direct the management effort based on the success criteria identified.
- A combination of previous options.

There are many variables to consider when defining project management processes. Some elements include strengths, weaknesses, challenges, types of management approach, activities to manage success criteria, risks associated with changes in legislation, changes in external scenarios that could impact the project (such as another pandemic), and so on. The very definition of the management methodology can be complex, as can the management of the criteria that will impact the success of the project. In this context, we have the following learning objectives:

- Know how to identify which variables can impact the definition of the project management method.
- Realize that there are various project management references that can help define the management method for each project.
- Understand how to integrate activities to manage and evaluate project success into the project management method.
- Understand how the success criteria can impact the management effort of the project management areas.
- Understand who would be the main stakeholders to consider when evaluating success.
- Realize that the success criteria are not static; they can change in importance over the course of the project.
- Reflect on how to manage the different stakeholder perspectives in relation to project success.
- Assess how to manage the risks associated with the success criteria.

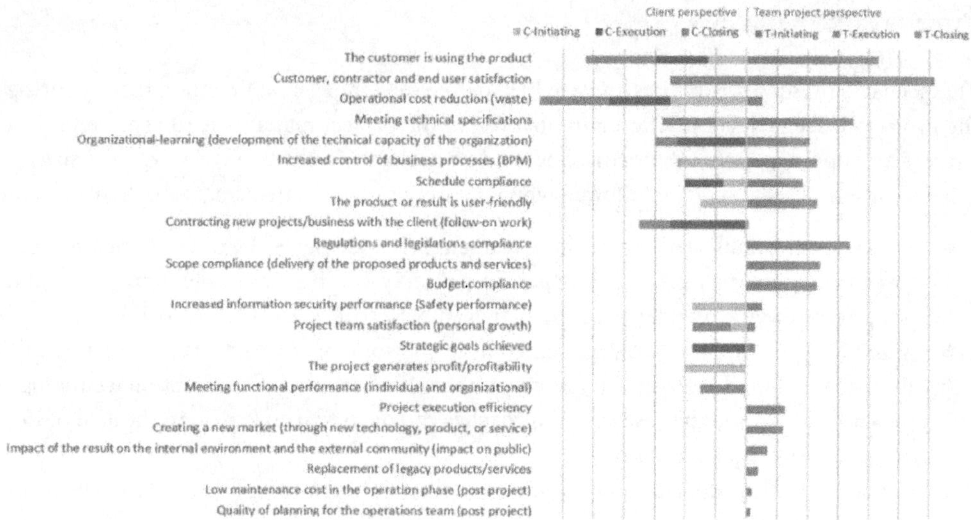

Source: Authors.

Figure 6.7 Success criteria rankings, results for case studies 1 and 2

We have been looking at scenarios of IST projects in the public sector. In this context, identifying and managing success criteria is the main target of the methodology. Note that the success criteria are related to the various areas of project management, which can direct management efforts towards the process or activity that can most impact the success of the project. As the success criteria may change over the course of the project, it is important to evaluate such evolution over the course of the project. Figure 6.7 presents the consolidated results of the collection and prioritization of success criteria in CS1 and CS2. The result shows the level of importance at the *beginning*, *during*, and *at the end* of the project for each success criterion. The results are sorted by the success criteria that, when added together (project team and client perspective), were most representative. It can be seen that some criteria were important only for the project team, while others were only for the client. Take the learning from this evaluation, and from the changes over the course of the project, and expand the vision of evaluating success to the following questions.

DISCUSSION QUESTIONS

1. In a project there are different types of stakeholders, such as managers, employees, shareholders, suppliers, competitors, clients, and so on. In your opinion, what types of stakeholders should be questioned to help define the success criteria of a project?
2. Think of a methodology to define the success criteria for a project. Who would provide information? How would this information be collected? How should you prioritize the reported success criteria? In the end, how many success criteria would be selected? How often and at what phase of the project would these criteria be reviewed?

3. Imagine that, as someone responsible for identifying the success criteria in a specific project, you noticed that the main success criteria changed during the execution of the project. In your opinion, what would be the best approach to handle this change?
4. When conducting interviews with two people involved in the project, you noticed a big difference between the opinions of what should be considered to determine the success of the project. Each interviewee listed three different success criteria. What would be your decision in a scenario like this?

NOTE

1. In this chapter, we mention the processes of the sixth version of the PMBOK. These processes are also presented in the first version of *Process Groups: A Practical Guide* from the PMI, 2022.

REFERENCES AND FURTHER READING

Atkinson, R. (1999). Project management: Cost, time and quality, two best guesses and a phenomenon, its time to accept other success criteria. *International Journal of Project Management, 17*(6), 337–342.

Cserháti, G., & Szabó, L. (2014). The relationship between success criteria and success factors in organisational event projects. *International Journal of Project Management, 32*(4), 613–624.

Pankratz, O., & Basten, D. (2014). Ladder to success: Eliciting project managers' perceptions of IS project success criteria. *International Journal of Information Systems and Project Management, 2*(2), 5–24.

Pereira, J., Varajão, J., & Takagi, N. (2022). Evaluation of information systems project success: Insights from practitioners. *Information Systems Management, 39*(2), 138–155.

Takagi, N., & Varajão, J. (2019). Integration of success management into project management guides and methodologies [Position paper]. *Procedia Computer Science, 164*, 366–372.

Takagi, N., Varajão, J., & Ventura, T. (2024). Implementing success management on Government-to-Government projects: An integrated perspective with the PMBOK guide. *International Journal of Managing Projects in Business*, 17(1), 153-171.

Takagi, N., & Varajão, J. (2021). *Success management and scrum for IS projects: An integrated approach.* Pacific Asia Conference on Information Systems: Association for Information Systems (pp. 1–8).

Takagi, N., & Varajão, J. (2022). ISO 21500 and success management: An integrated model for project management. *International Journal of Quality & Reliability Management, 39*(2), 408–427.

Takagi, N., & Varajão, J. (2025). ISO 21502 and success management: A required marriage in project management. *SAGE Open*, 15(3), 1-11.

Takagi, N., Varajão, J., Ventura, T., Ubialli, D., & Silva, T. (2024). Managing success criteria and success factors in a BPM project: An approach using PRINCE2 and success management on the public sector. *Cogent Business & Management*, 11(1), 1-20.

Varajão, J. (2018). A new process for success management bringing order to a typically ad-hoc area. *Journal of Modern Project Management, 5*(3), 92–99.

Varajão, J., Magalhães, L., Freitas, L., & Rocha, P. (2022). Success management: From theory to practice. *International Journal of Project Management, 40*(5), 481–498.

PART II
POWER SKILLS

7
Navigating complexity: integrating collaboration in public infrastructure projects

Caroline Coulombe and Jonathan Harvey

OPENING PARAGRAPHS

In the bustling heart of Quebec's vibrant urban landscape, in the early months of 2025, Dr Sandra Williams, managing strategy director of the Governmental Public Infrastructure Society (GPIS), found herself at a pivotal crossroads. GPIS, a cornerstone in Quebec's public infrastructure landscape since its inception, was facing a period of unprecedented challenges. The organization, responsible for overseeing a vast array of public infrastructure projects, including the management of over 1,200 buildings and an extensive portfolio of projects valued at billions, was in a state of disarray.

The crux of GPIS's dilemma revolved around the necessity to fundamentally overhaul its construction process. This need was made evident through a series of intense discussions and meetings that Dr Williams had with the CEO and various directors of GPIS, unfolding over the previous months. Each conversation, while unique in its specifics, invariably circled back to the same core issues: a severe shortage of resources, escalating conflicts with contractors, and the pressing constraints of time and funding.

Dr Williams, known for her sharp analytical skills and strategic thinking, was at the helm of making crucial decisions to navigate these turbulent waters. Her decisions would not only impact the immediate future of GPIS but also set a precedent for how public infrastructure projects would be managed in the region. The complexity of the problem was compounded by the current market conditions – a labor crisis in the construction industry marked by dwindling productivity and quality.

As she sat in her office in early 2024, Dr Williams knew that the path ahead would require not just strategic changes but a paradigm shift in how GPIS approached its projects. She contemplated the implementation of the integrated design process (IDP), a methodology celebrated for its collaborative and interdisciplinary nature, as a potential solution. This approach, if successful, could transform the very fabric of GPIS's operational and management practices, ushering in an era of efficiency, sustainability, and enhanced collaboration. The stakes were high, and the eyes of the entire organization – and indeed, the industry at large – were on Dr Williams, waiting to see how she would steer GPIS into the future.

BODY OF THE CASE

Dr Williams, the managing strategy director, settles into her chair, a contemplative frown creasing her forehead. The echoes of her recent phone conversation with the CEO and various directors of the Governmental Public Infrastructure Society (GPIS) still linger in the air. These discussions have become a familiar routine, with similar calls peppering the past few months, each marked by a progressively tense atmosphere. It is clear that GPIS is grappling with a significant challenge in its construction projects.

Each phone call, though varied in specifics, circles around a central issue: the need for a fundamental overhaul of the construction process. The directors' concerns are as diverse as their backgrounds – some plead for additional resources, others report ongoing conflicts with contractors, and a few grapple with the twin demons of insufficient funding and time constraints. After a series of such deliberations, Dr Williams steps up, shouldering the responsibility to devise a strategy that would steer the organization out of troubled waters. One aspect is glaringly apparent to her: the current process suffers from a severe lack of collaboration – a deficiency she is determined to address.

Addressing the issues at GPIS is no small feat, considering the magnitude and scope of its mission. The organization plays a pivotal role in aiding public entities with managing their public infrastructure projects alongside developing, maintaining, and managing an extensive real estate portfolio tailored to these entities' needs. The scale of operations is vast: GPIS oversees the management of more than 1,200 buildings, including over 450 properties under its own ownership. Additionally, the organization is at the helm of managing over 160 projects, collectively valued at approximately $45 billion, while being involved in nearly 27 projects together worth around $30 billion. The sheer volume and complexity of these megaprojects underscore the potential for significant tensions to arise from the intricate web of stakeholders engaged across various stages of these projects.

Dr Williams is acutely aware of the prevailing market challenges impacting the construction industry. The sector is navigating a crisis marked by a burgeoning labor shortage and a general decline in productivity and quality. Contractors are struggling to recruit sufficiently skilled workers, often failing to meet project timelines as a consequence. Compounding these issues, GPIS's methodologies remain inflexible and deeply entrenched in stringent contractual frameworks. This rigidity is proving to be a significant hurdle, especially when there is a pressing need for projects to adopt more adaptable approaches and implement cost-saving measures.

Solution: IDP and Collaboration

Confronted with these multifaceted challenges, Dr Williams, in concordance with her fellow directors and the CEO, spearheaded the implementation of the integrated design process (IDP) at GPIS. This methodology, celebrated for its collaborative and interdisciplinary essence, is applied from the very inception of a project. The central aim of IDP is to nurture the development of solutions that are not just efficient and well-integrated but also optimal, forward-thinking, and sustainable. Guided by clearly articulated objectives that span functional, economic, social, and environmental dimensions, the IDP provides a holistic framework that encapsulates the full life cycle of an infrastructure endeavor.

At GPIS, the operationalization of IDP involves the formal and systematic execution of integrated design workshops enhanced by professional facilitation. Central to this approach are iterative feedback loops, incorporating regular thematic meetings and workshops, which serve as pivotal forums for ongoing evaluation and decision-making throughout the project's evolution. Dr Williams recognizes that the key to success lies in ensuring active participation and collaboration from all stakeholders at every stage of the project. This requirement presents its own set of complex challenges, necessitating skillful navigation and management. It is this realization that propels Dr Williams to explore mechanisms for effectively measuring and enhancing collaboration within these project environments.

In her exploration, Dr Williams discovered that, within the context of a construction project's ideation and planning phase under the IDP framework, collaboration is multifaceted, encompassing eight distinct dimensions. Each dimension, with its unique characteristics, contributes to the collaborative process (Table 7.1).

Each of these dimensions plays a crucial role in enhancing and measuring the effectiveness of collaboration within the IDP framework, guiding Dr Williams in her efforts to improve project outcomes at GPIS. Recognizing the need to quantify these aspects of collaboration, Dr Williams discovered the collaboration indicator created in Canada by the Observatory of research on collaboration in Quebec (OQRC), a tool designed to measure and improve the effectiveness of collaborative efforts in a structured and objective manner. The collaboration indicator serves several vital objectives that align with Dr Williams' goals. It provides a reliable and structured method to gauge the level of collaboration in projects. It also assesses the collaborative maturity of project teams, from their formation and through the entire project duration, on a multilevel governance perspective. This tool is pivotal in enabling proactive measures and offering solutions to reduce the risks linked with collaboration difficulties. Importantly, it also supplies project managers with a continuous and reliable indicator that is instrumental in guiding projects towards successful outcomes.

As Dr Williams gears up to implement the IDP and the newly discovered collaboration indicator at GPIS, she realizes the necessity of applying these tools in a real-world scenario. The construction of a new school has been selected as the ideal project to initiate this endeavor. The school construction project, with its diverse stakeholder group (Table A7.1) and complex requirements, provides a dynamic practical environment to assess the effectiveness and refine the collaboration indicator and the multidimensional approach of the IDP methodology. This

Table 7.1 Collaboration dimensions with descriptions

-	Dimension	Description
1	Communication – preparation	Emphasizes the importance of adequate preparation before meetings.
2	Communication – structure	Concerned with the relevance and effectiveness of workshop activities.
3	Trust	Fundamental to team dynamics, focusing on the trust among team members and in the process itself. It involves openly expressing the expectations of all stakeholders.
4	Facilitation process	A critical element for structuring collaboration, involves the facilitator's role in building stakeholder confidence.
5	Interdisciplinarity	Highlights the variety of professions, expertise, and perspectives involved. Stresses the added value brought by the presence of experts.
6	Governance	Pertains to the mechanisms and structure of the steering committee and the dynamics within this committee.
7	Collaborative leadership	Addresses the functioning and respect between the project manager and the facilitator, along with the facilitator's role in fostering stakeholder confidence.
8	Decision process	Deals with the ambiguity and balanced maintenance of tensions. Emphasizes the clarity of options and steps in the decision-making process.
9	Stakeholders	Focuses on including the expectations of a broad spectrum of stakeholders and the added value of client participation.

initiative marks a significant step forward in Dr Williams' journey to transform project management practices at GPIS, aiming to foster a more collaborative, efficient, and sustainable approach to public infrastructure development.

School Construction Project and its Stakeholders

The school construction project embarked upon by GPIS is not just another building; it represents a bold step into the future of educational architecture. Envisioned as a beacon of sustainable development, the school's design is a pioneering model featuring innovative architectural concepts with open, multifunctional areas and diverse activity zones catering to various educational needs. Central to the design philosophy is the emphasis on inclusivity, with spaces crafted to welcome and nurture a wide array of student experiences and learning styles. This progressive approach necessitates a rich tapestry of perspectives and ideas, making the project an ideal candidate for Dr Williams' collaborative methodologies. By ensuring the highest level of collaboration, GPIS aims to bring together varied insights and expertise, ensuring that the school not only stands as a testament to advanced architectural design but also as a nurturing ground for the inclusive, holistic development of its students. This project, therefore, is more than just a construction endeavor; it is a commitment to shaping a future where educational spaces are inclusive, sustainable, and thoughtfully designed.

In orchestrating the school construction project under the IDP, Dr Williams carefully curated a team of stakeholders, each chosen for a specific purpose. She appointed Alistair

Sterling as the project director to steer the project with his strategic insights and broad vision. Recognizing the need for meticulous day-to-day oversight, she entrusted Elara Moreau with the role of project manager to ensure seamless collaboration and effective dialogue among the team.

Dr Williams, alongside Alistair Sterling and Elara Moreau, formed a strategic team to select the remaining key stakeholders. Together, they recognized the need for a facilitator who could ensure seamless collaboration and effective communication within the team, leading to the inclusion of Jasper Tremblay. They also understood the importance of incorporating the users' perspectives into the project, so needed representatives from the school. This insight led them to bring in Evelyn Rosario, who would provide valuable insights into the school's functional needs and expectations. To align the project with the client's broader objectives, they involved Mario Bouchard, ensuring the project remained anchored to its foundational goals.

The team was further strengthened by the addition of specialized technical expertise. Zara Alvarado, an innovative architect, was chosen for her creative and sustainable design approaches. Hiroto Nakamura, an electromechanical engineer, was selected to integrate efficient and modern systems into the building's design. Finally, recognizing the importance of cutting-edge planning tools, the team brought in Sienna Gérard as the BIM Building Information Modeling) consultant, adding a layer of advanced digital modeling to the project's planning and execution.

Meetings and Collaboration Evaluation

On the eve of the school's construction journey, a steering committee meeting was convened on April 15, 2022, laying the groundwork for the first integrated design workshop set for the following week. This meeting was crucial in establishing the project's core – its mission, vision, and values – and marked a series of firsts for the key participants. The project manager, Elara Moreau, though seasoned in managing school infrastructure projects, was navigating uncharted waters, as this was her inaugural venture into a workshop involving a broad spectrum of stakeholders. Her expertise in traditional project management was about to be challenged, and augmented, by this new collaborative and interdisciplinary approach of the IDP. In the case of Jasper Tremblay, the facilitator, who also has experience in guiding construction infrastructure project design workshops, this was his first involvement with GPIS, which brings fresh perspectives and seasoned facilitation skills to the table. The representatives of the school, pivotal in providing client insights, were also stepping into new territory. Not only was it their first experience in a school construction project of this magnitude; it was also their first experience of participating in facilitated design workshops. In summary, all participants, though experienced in their respective fields, were embarking on a novel approach with this particular project, bringing together their diverse skills and experiences to create a collaborative, innovative, and well-formed approach to the school's construction.

As Dr Sandra Williams sat in her office, the reports from the various stakeholders about the preparations for the upcoming integrated design workshop for the school project began to trickle in. Each piece of information painted a picture of the preparatory phase, highlighting the challenges and nuances of communication and coordination among the diverse team.

Evelyn Rosario's email expressed her enthusiasm for the upcoming workshop, but her excitement was tinged with uncertainty. She had been inquiring about the workshop details, only to find that no one seemed able to address her queries – the presentations, it appeared, had not yet been circulated. Evelyn pondered whether this was a deliberate aspect of the creative process or a lapse in the IDP.

Meanwhile, Dr Williams was mulling over the implications of Hiroto Nakamura's absence from the initial IDP briefing. She questioned whether this was a sign of a flaw in the process structure or preparation, or if it simply indicated a lack of engagement on Hiroto's part.

As Dr Williams reflected on all this input, she recognized the intricacies and challenges inherent in launching a new collaborative process, especially one that necessitated such active stakeholder involvement from the outset. She acknowledged that these initial observations might point to more profound issues in collaboration, practices, or processes that could impact the alignment necessary for the successful completion of the school project. However, rather than rushing to conclusions, Dr Williams opted for a more observant approach. She decided to reserve judgment until after the first few meetings, intending to use them as a learning opportunity and assess the overall collaboration performance scores. This approach would enable her to make more informed decisions moving forward.

After couple of meetings, Dr Williams reflected on the latest school project meeting. She recalled the details with vivid clarity. The hybrid meeting space was bustling with the energy of 24 key stakeholders, a microcosm of the project's diverse team. Most were physically present, clustered around the conference table or leaning against the walls, while others' faces flickered on the computer screens.

The atmosphere had shifted when Alistair Sterling, the project director, walked in. Dr Williams remembered noticing the ripple of surprise that went through the room. Although the project manager knew of Alistair's attendance, many others were caught off guard. Alistair's early intervention was decisive. He didn't waste any time in setting the meeting's tone, emphasizing that the focus should be on identifying issues and brainstorming viable solutions rather than just reaching a consensus. Dr Williams admired the clarity and direction Alistair brought to the table.

Then there was Hiroto Nakamura, the electromechanical engineer. Dr Williams could almost see him again, standing awkwardly at the front, papers in hand, his face a mixture of confusion and apprehension. His presentation, dense with technical terms, failed to resonate with the non-technical members. Hiroto's efforts to keep it concise were thwarted by the barrage of questions from the audience, leading him to overrun his time. Dr Williams could sense his disengagement, a likely result of his limited role in the workshop.

Zara Alvarado's assertiveness stood out in Dr Williams' memory. The architect unexpectedly added a new item to the agenda, catching many off guard. Later, her impromptu facilitation to clarify Hiroto's technical content was a welcome surprise, albeit slightly disorienting for Jasper Tremblay, the official facilitator. Dr Williams pondered whether Zara's spontaneous contribution could have been better integrated with a more structured approach.

The tension between Elara Moreau and Jasper was palpable. Their lack of alignment and the resulting contradictions created confusion among the stakeholders, particularly evident in Evelyn Rosario's reactions. As the client representative, Evelyn seemed to struggle with any unclear leadership, often looking perplexed about the next steps in the workshop process.

Dr Williams thought about Jasper's role. His introduction, intended to establish the IDP's objectives and foster a collaborative environment, was overshadowed by his struggles with time management and guiding the discussion. Jasper's evident surprise at Alistair's attendance and his oversight in not setting clear workshop success rules from the start seemed to have led to disengagement among some participants. Evelyn's disappointment at not being more involved in presenting the school's issues and the many cameras remaining off during the virtual part of the meeting were telling signs.

Mario Bouchard's concern raised about the absence of a ministry representative highlighted a significant gap, considering the project's scale and importance. Zara Alvarado's agreement with Mario's observation, coupled with her mention of her routine involvement in such workshops, underscored the varied experience levels within the team regarding the IDP process.

Towards the end of the meeting, Dr Williams recalled Zara and Jasper having a brief discussion. They talked about how Zara's contributions could be better integrated into future workshops, perhaps by adding her insights to the agenda beforehand and tailoring the meeting structure to incorporate her input more effectively. It was a constructive conclusion to a meeting with its fair share of challenges.

Dr Williams reclined in her chair, lost in thought as she digested the intricate details of the meeting. The nuances of each interaction, the subtle tensions, and the unexpected turns were not mere happenings in isolation. To her, they were clear indicators of deeper issues around collaboration, communication, and leadership that permeated the project. These areas needed her attention and skillful navigation to steer the project towards success.

Mid-contemplation, the soft ping of a notification from her computer broke her train of thought. She turned her attention to the screen, focusing on the email that had just popped up. It was the latest survey score, a crucial piece of data that would offer additional insights into the team's dynamics and the project's progress so far. Dr Williams clicked on the email, ready to analyze this new information and incorporate it into her strategy for guiding the school project forward (Table 7.2).

Dr Williams perused the survey results, thinking over each score that told an unfinished story of the project's journey. The communication aspects clearly required attention. Workshop preparation, marked at 3.91, in the yellow zone, indicated a moderate level of readiness among the team, a point she noted for further exploration. The score of 2.84 for workshop structure, however, was a more pressing concern, highlighting the need for significant improvements in how the meetings were organized and conducted.

She did feel some cautious satisfaction at the trust score of a near-green 4.21. In the midst of adapting to a new process, maintaining such a level of trust among the participants was an encouraging sign. But the very low score of 1.98 for the facilitation process, firmly in the red zone, was troubling. Dr Williams recalled the meeting's immediate feedback, pondering whether the issue lay with the facilitator or the facilitation approach itself.

Table 7.2 Survey results latest meeting

Dimension/measure	Survey score (Maximum: 5)
Workshop preparation	3.91
Workshop structure	2.84
Trust	4.21
Facilitation process	1.98
Interdisciplinarity	3.73
Governance	4.3
Collaborative leadership	2.49
Decision process	4.12
Stakeholders	4.7

Note: The scale is divided into three colour bands that match the visual gauge in Figure A7.1 within a range of 0 to 5; 0 being very weak and 5 very strong. Red (left portion, 1.00 – 2.00) signals a zone that calls for swift corrective action. Yellow (central portion, 2.01 – 4.19) indicates moderate performance and scope for improvement. Green (right portion, 4.20 – 5.00) reflects a healthy dimension.

The score for interdisciplinarity stood at 3.73, reflecting a promising start and suggesting there were areas for growth. The governance score, at 4.3, comfortably in the green zone, was reassuring. Dr Williams felt validated in the efforts she and her fellow directors had put into providing the necessary resources and time to establish this new process.

However, the collaborative leadership score of 2.49 presented a conundrum. It was perhaps to be expected, given the dynamic between the project manager and the facilitator, but it was an area that clearly needed addressing.

The decision process, scoring a robust 4.12, was a brighter spot in the survey. Dr Williams was curious about the elements that made this aspect particularly effective. Similarly, the stakeholder score, at 4.7, was another high point. The level of satisfaction here was a key indicator, prompting her to consider how these positive aspects could be replicated across other project dimensions.

Dr Williams sat back in her chair, her mind a bustling hub of thoughts and strategic considerations. The survey results laid before her painted a complex project landscape, mingling achievements with intricate challenges. She understood that, to navigate this terrain, she needed to dig deeper into the scores to unravel the stories they were silently narrating. Several critical questions arose from her analysis, each demanding attention and resolution.

First, she contemplated the team's readiness score. Was this an indication of people's level of comfort with the current process, or were there unexplored gaps in their preparation that needed to be addressed? This uncertainty prompted Dr Williams to consider what improvements could be made to elevate the team's preparedness. Then, she pondered the trust factor. What were the finer aspects that had cultivated such trust among the team members, and how could these elements be further strengthened to fortify that trust? The question of interdisciplinarity also loomed large. While the current level of cross-disciplinary collaboration was promising, Dr Williams wondered what more could be done to fully leverage the diverse expertise and perspectives within the team. She also reflected on the governance aspect. What specific elements of the governance structure resonated positively with the team, and how could these successful components be applied to other areas needing improvement? The dynamics of collaborative leadership particularly intrigued her. What was the root cause of the apparent disconnect between the project manager and the facilitator, and how could this relationship be realigned for more effective collaboration? Last, she considered the high satisfaction levels in stakeholder engagement. What factors had contributed to this success, and could these be replicated across other project dimensions?

Each of these questions formed a piece of the larger puzzle that Dr Williams was determined to solve. She knew that the answers to these questions would be instrumental in charting the course for the successful completion of the school project. Her insights, drawn from the surveys and her strategic analysis, would serve as the guiding light for the next phase of the project, aiming to enhance collaboration, streamline processes, and ultimately achieve the project's ambitious goals.

Concluding Remarks

In this case study, Dr Sandra Williams, managing strategy director of the Governmental Public Infrastructure Society (GPIS), is confronted with a significant challenge: overhauling the organization's construction process amid diverse concerns from directors and a tense atmosphere. The vast scale of GPIS's operations, managing over 1,200 buildings and projects valued in billions of dollars, combined with industry-wide issues such as labor shortages and declining productivity, exacerbates these challenges.

Dr Williams identifies a critical deficiency in the current process: a lack of collaboration. To address this, she advocates for implementing the integrated design process (IDP), known for its collaborative and interdisciplinary approach. The IDP aims to nurture efficient, sustainable solutions from inception on through the fully life cycle and completion of infrastructure projects. Emphasizing the importance of stakeholder participation at all stages, Dr Williams navigates through complex challenges to enhance collaboration within the project environments.

During the critical phase of a school construction project, Dr Williams carefully selects a team of stakeholders, each with a specific role to ensure the success of this innovative educational facility. The project, envisioned as a model of sustainable and equitable development, demands diverse perspectives and inclusive strategies, aligning with Dr Williams' approach.

However, initial meetings reveal underlying issues in communication, leadership, and facilitation. Survey results from these meetings indicate mixed feelings among team members regarding various aspects of the project. While some dimensions, like trust and governance, score well, others, like facilitation process and collaborative leadership, fall short, necessitating immediate attention. The highest satisfaction in stakeholder engagement is a positive indicator, yet the varied levels of satisfaction across the dimensions point to the need for a more in-depth understanding and strategic improvements.

Dr Williams, equipped with these insights, realizes the complexity of the task ahead. She contemplates the survey results, recognizing the necessity to delve deeper into the scores to fully interpret the team's feedback. Her commitment to transforming the project management practices at GPIS remains steadfast, as she aims to guide the school project towards a successful and collaborative completion, while considering the nuances revealed by the recent survey and the challenges observed in the meetings.

DISCUSSION QUESTIONS

1. Identify and discuss the primary challenges GPIS is facing during the transition to the IDP. How are these challenges reflected in the collaboration between the stakeholders?
2. Discuss the importance of stakeholder management in the context of GPIS's school construction project. Evaluate the role of the dimensions of collaboration in the current context, using the indicator as a base for discussion.
3. The case study outlines eight dimensions of collaboration identified by Dr Williams. Evaluate how these dimensions were addressed or manifested during the initial IDP meetings and workshops for the school construction project. Which dimensions appeared to be strengths, and which presented challenges?
4. Reflect on the leadership dynamics between Dr Williams, the project director, the project manager, and the facilitator within the context of the school construction project. How did their interactions and leadership styles impact the collaborative environment and project progress?
5. Dr Williams implemented the collaboration indicator tool to measure and improve the effectiveness of collaborative efforts at GPIS. Based on the survey results shared in the case study, critically assess the tool's effectiveness. What insights do the survey results provide about the team's collaboration, and how might Dr Williams use this information to guide future projects?

REFERENCES

Coulombe, C., & Harvey, J. (2022). La mutation organisationnelle orchestrée dans une pratique collaborative des équipes en contexte pandémique: L'effet véloce des tensions. *AdMachina*, *6*(1), 13–25.

Coulombe, C., & Harvey, J. (2023). Variation de la collaboration selon la temporalité, les phases et le secteur: Analyse des courbes collaborative. *Revue Interdisciplinaire Droit et Organisations (RIDO).* www.revue-rido.com/articles/variation-de-la-collaboration-selon-la-temporalite-les-phases-et-le-secteur-analyse-des-courbes-collaboratives-dans-les-equipes-projets

Coulombe, C., Harvey, J., Haineault, C., Monette, J., & Leroux, M. (2023). A new project performance indicator: Research action for measurement of stakeholder collaboration in major public infrastructure projects, European Academy of Management (EURAM), Dublin - June 2023, ISSN: 2466-7498, ISBN 978-2-9602195-5-5

Coulombe, C., Leroux, M. P., Harvey, J., & Monette, J. (2023). La recherche intervention comme catalyseur de compétences collaboratives: Un changement organisationnel qui influence la gestion des grands projets d'infrastructures publiques, *AdMachina*, *7*(1), 2–30.

Coulombe, C., et al. (2023a). *Major public infrastructure project adopting front-end collaboration.* British Academy of Management.
Coulombe, C., et al. (2023b). *Performance measure of collaborative governance.* British Academy of Management (BAM).

APPENDIX

Table A7.1 School project stakeholders

Name	**Position**
Alistair Sterling	Project director
Elara Moreau	Project manager
Jasper Tremblay	Facilitator
Evelyn Rosario	Client user (school)
Mario Bouchard	Client owner
Zara Alvarado	Architect
Hiroto Nakamura	Electromechanical engineer
Sienna Gérard	BIM consultant

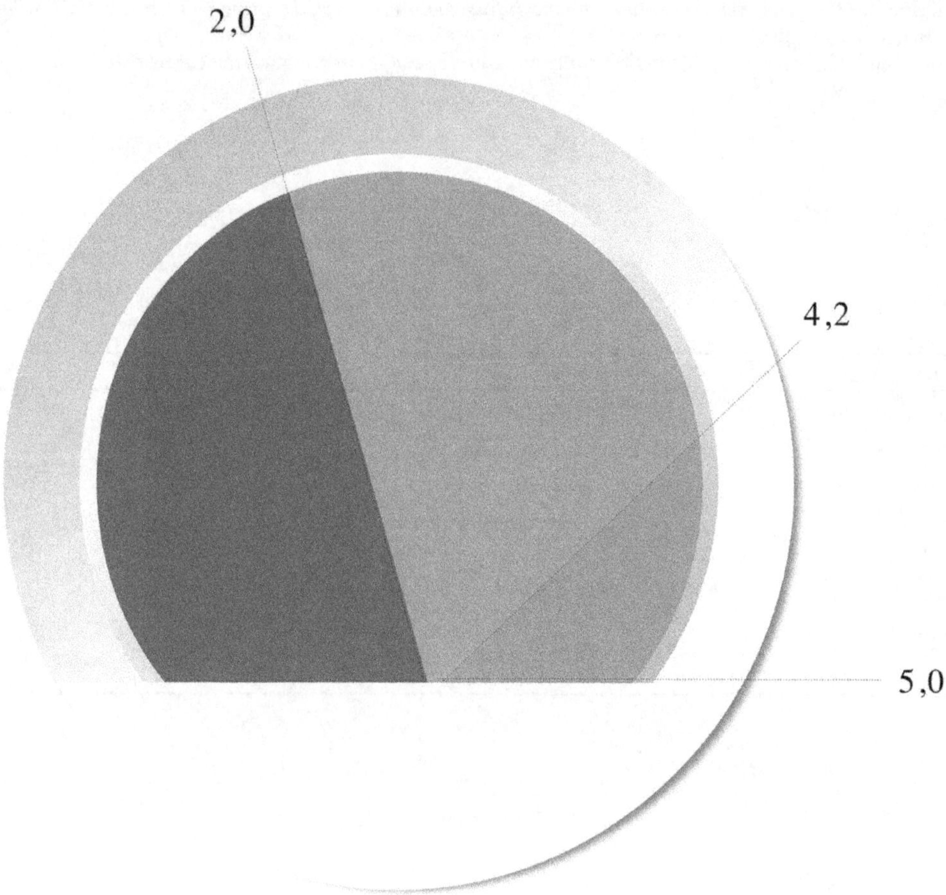

Source: Authors.

Figure A7.1 Representation of collaboration indicator tool

8
Scrum team tales: conquering challenges with scrum masters and product owners

Simona Bonghez

OPENING PARAGRAPHS

InnovaTech Solutions, founded by Elona Task five years ago, has swiftly ascended to become a beacon of innovation in software development within the healthcare sector. With a mission rooted in continuous learning, and an agile-centric culture, the organization has made significant strides. However, the introduction of agile methodologies across diverse teams with varying levels of agile familiarity has brought up numerous challenges. This case study delves into these situations across multiple teams within InnovaTech to explore the effectiveness of different roles and strategies in fostering agile adoption and overcoming operational hurdles.

In Scenario 1, Team Phoenix, a newly formed group with diverse agile experiences, faces challenges in collaboration and understanding due to an inexperienced product owner and the complex dynamics of adopting agile practices. Scenarios 2 and 3 introduce the MediCore team, which initially benefits from stakeholder engagement but later struggles with changing requirements and dwindling stakeholder involvement, highlighting the pressures of agile environments in maintaining product vision and team morale.

Further complicating these dynamics, Scenario 4 discusses conflicting priorities within Team Phoenix, showcasing the complexities of stakeholder management and the necessity of clear communication and effective prioritization strategies. Lastly, Scenario 5 captures the challenges of scaling agile teams and integrating new members into established teams, emphasizing the importance of maintaining quality and cohesion.

Through the detailed analysis of each scenario, the case study enables the identification of key role performances and strategic recommendations aimed at improving agile practices, enhancing team collaboration, and optimizing project outcomes at InnovaTech Solutions.

BODY OF THE CASE

Context Information: Company Profile

Elona Task (ET to friends and colleagues) founded InnovaTech Solutions five years ago, aiming to create a dynamic and innovative software development organization. In just a few years, the company has flourished, earning a reputation for groundbreaking solutions and consistent growth. Its blend of cutting-edge technology and a customer-centric approach has distinguished it as a rising star in the tech sector, attracting diverse clients and a talented team of professionals dedicated to pushing the boundaries of what is possible in software development for the healthcare sector. ET has always been deeply committed to a culture of continuous learning and improvement, strongly advocating for the agile mindset. "This approach is crucial for driving innovation and success in the fast-paced tech industry," she often says, emphasizing agile's role in InnovaTech's success.

Scenario 1: Newly Formed Team

Team Phoenix, established early this year at InnovaTech Solutions, was tasked with a vital project: developing a software tool for healthcare professionals to streamline complex data analysis. The application aims to be intuitive, aiding specialists in making prompt, precise data-driven decisions. The project combines skills in software development, data analysis, and user experience design. To achieve the objectives, InnovaTech chose the scrum framework for this team, aiming to enhance collaboration, enable swift development cycles, and gather continual feedback to align the product closely with the evolving needs of healthcare users.

All the Phoenix team members are new to InnovaTech Solutions (having been hired less than six months ago), each bringing strong technical skills but with varied experience in agile methodologies. Their backgrounds range from comfortable familiarity with various agile frameworks to complete newness in agile practices. The team includes four senior developers, a data analyst, a UX/UI (user experience, user interface) designer, and two QA (quality assurance) testers. The most experienced developer was also asked to take on the role of scrum master.

Their first challenge proved to be the product owner, a role undertaken by a representative from the client healthcare company. He was new to this role, and his lack of agile experience filled the ceremonies with hesitancy and confusion. Misunderstandings were common, and there was palpable tension in meetings. The lack of a shared language and understanding around agile principles led to frustration, and the team's morale began to dip. Collaboration, a cornerstone of agile, was also proving to be a challenge. The team members, each accomplished in their own right, struggled to sync their efforts. The scrum master found himself uncomfortable and overwhelmed with his additional responsibilities and preferred to focus on developing the application. This situation amplified the team's issues with communication gaps, mounting friction during meetings, and obstacles in their collaborative efforts. Their differences and unfamiliarity with one another were highlighted, rather than mitigated, and some of them began to question the benefits of using agile, blaming the scrum framework for their growing frustrations and perceived lack of progress in the project.

Discussion questions for Scenario 1

1. Role analysis: Review the Team Phoenix case at InnovaTech Solutions. Determine which roles among the scrum master, product owner, and agile coach, individually or in combination, are most effective in guiding the team towards successful agile adoption. Base your decision on the specific challenges the team is facing.
2. Strategic recommendations: Provide targeted recommendations for the chosen role(s) to address the team's struggles, focusing on strategies that encourage open communication, foster an understanding of scrum principles and scrum accountabilities, and create a supportive environment where team members feel comfortable asking questions and seeking guidance. The aim is to help the team embrace the benefits of agile and start experiencing its positive impact on project delivery and team collaboration.
3. Action plan for agile principles implementation: Create an action plan for Team Phoenix to improve the understanding and implementation of agile principles. This plan should include specific steps for training, team-building activities, and regular check-ins to assess progress. Address how the team can integrate Agile practices into daily work to enhance efficiency and productivity.

Scenario 2: Changing Requirements

The MediCore team at InnovaTech is working on a comprehensive software application designed for medical records. This application is tailored to support over 50 different medical specialties. It aims to provide specific functionalities and content relevant to each specialty, ensuring that healthcare professionals can access and manage patient records efficiently and effectively. This project is complex due to the diverse requirements of different medical fields, requiring a nuanced understanding of each specialty's needs and workflows.

The team, consisting of two senior developers, two mid-level developers, one junior devel oper, and two QA testers, is skilled in scrum and has a good understanding of agile principles. While they started the project with a high level of enthusiasm and energy, now, after three months from the project initiation, the team is struggling with frequent changes in project requirements. These constant shifts have taken a toll on the team's morale, leading to frustration and a sense of uncertainty. The once smooth and efficient workflow is now disrupted, causing delays and confusion. As the team navigates these changes, the initial excitement has given way to a feeling of being overwhelmed, impacting not just productivity but also overall job satisfaction.

The minimum viable product (MVP) was defined and agreed upon before starting the development, but is now at risk due to constant requirement alterations. The scrum master's efforts to seek support from the product owner have been in vain. The product owner, focused on pleasing the client who is funding the project, has been agreeing to all client requests, even imposing changes on tasks already in progress (the team is operating in two-week sprints).

This has exacerbated the team's challenges, further complicating the path to meeting the MVP delivery deadline.

Discussion questions for Scenario 2

1. Role analysis: Examine the roles of the scrum master, product owner, and team members in the MediCore project. Discuss how each role can contribute to managing the frequent changes in project requirements and improving team morale.
2. Client–team dynamics: Analyze the role of the product owner in balancing client demands with the team's capacity. Suggest ways the product owner could negotiate with the client to prioritize essential features while maintaining realistic project goals.
3. Strategy development: Propose strategies that the scrum master could implement to support the team in adapting to changing requirements while maintaining focus on the MVP. Consider approaches to enhance communication, team cohesion, and stress management. Reflect on the impact of frequent requirement changes on an agile project. Discuss how these challenges could be addressed in future projects to prevent similar issues.

Scenario 3: Lack of Stakeholder Engagement

The MediCore team at InnovaTech is working on a comprehensive software application designed for medical records. This application is tailored to support over 50 different medical specialties. It aims to provide specific functionalities and content relevant to each specialty, ensuring that healthcare professionals can access and manage patient records efficiently and effectively. This project is complex due to the diverse requirements of different medical fields, requiring a nuanced understanding of each specialty's needs and workflows.

Initially, the team enjoyed productive collaboration with stakeholders in developing their medical records software. Stakeholders, including healthcare professionals, provided valuable input, ensuring the product aligned with user needs. However, over the last three sprints, stakeholder engagement has drastically declined. The team now finds itself without critical feedback, leading to uncertainty in task prioritization and potential misalignment with user requirements. This sudden drop in engagement is affecting the project's progress and risks compromising the value delivered to the end users.

Upon investigating this sudden decline in stakeholder engagement, the product owner discovered two primary reasons. First, the healthcare professionals, crucial stakeholders, had to shift their focus to an unexpected surge in patient care, reducing their availability for the project. Second, several key project advocates among the stakeholders were reassigned to other pressing duties, leading to a significant decrease in communication and support.

Discussion questions for Scenario 3

1. Role analysis: Discuss the effects of reduced stakeholder engagement on the MediCore team's ability to deliver a product that effectively meets the diverse needs of the healthcare specialties. Assess the roles of the scrum master, product owner, and team, focusing on their potential contributions to resolving the stakeholder engagement issue.

2. Strategic recommendations: Develop strategies for these key roles to re-engage stakeholders, adapt to their limited availability, and maintain effective communication and feedback channels.
3. Long-term engagement planning: Propose long-term engagement strategies to prevent similar challenges in future projects, ensuring consistent stakeholder involvement throughout the development process.

Scenario 4: Conflicting Priorities

Team Phoenix, established early this year at InnovaTech Solutions, was tasked with a vital project: developing a software tool for healthcare professionals to streamline complex data analysis. The application aims to be intuitive, aiding specialists in making prompt, precise, data-driven decisions. The project combines skills in software development, data analysis, and user experience design. To achieve the objectives, InnovaTech chose the scrum framework for the team, aiming to enhance collaboration, enable swift development cycles, and gather continual feedback to align the product closely with the evolving needs of healthcare users.

The team includes four senior developers, a data analyst, a UX/UI designer, and two QA testers. After an experienced scrum master joined the team to overcome some initial challenges (see Scenario 1), Team Phoenix made significant progress. Now, six months into the project, they encounter a new set of issues. As the healthcare professionals began to experience the benefits of the developing tool, they started to provide a multitude of feedback points and requests. This influx of input led to an array of parallel and sometimes conflicting demands for additional features and improvements.

As the product owner of Team Phoenix sought to address the issue of conflicting priorities, they decided to bring all involved stakeholders together for a planning meeting. The turnout was remarkable, with 23 participants attending, representing a mix of several specialties within the healthcare field. The intent of the meeting was to bring forth clarity and consensus; however, as discussions unfolded, it became evident that each represented specialty had its own set of specific requests. Every group expressed a strong desire for its particular needs to be included in the upcoming sprint.

The meeting, initially aimed at fostering understanding and alignment, quickly transformed into a platform for competing demands. Stakeholders, driven by their commitment to their respective specialties, passionately presented their requirements. Unfortunately, these varied and often conflicting opinions did not align with one another, nor did they consistently reflect the project's original scope and objectives. This divergence presented the product owner with a substantial challenge: stakeholders were not only reluctant to have their requests sidelined, they were also advocating for an increase in team capacity as a means to incorporate all their needs within the project's tight timelines.

This suggestion, while well-meaning in its attempt to address workload challenges, introduced an additional layer of complexity. It raised questions about the feasibility of scaling the team effectively under the current constraints and the potential impact on the project's cohesion and direction. For the product owner and the team, the situation was becoming increasingly intricate, entangling them in a web of stakeholder expectations and project realities.

Discussion questions for Scenario 4

1. Role analysis: Identify which role among scrum master, product owner, developers, or agile coach, individually or in combination, is best equipped to address the challenge of conflicting priorities in the Team Phoenix scenario. Justify your choice based on the specific responsibilities and influence of the selected role(s).
2. Role-specific recommendations: For the chosen role(s), provide specific recommendations to manage and resolve the conflicting stakeholder demands. Focus on strategies related to prioritization, stakeholder communication, and negotiation techniques.
3. Team dynamics and support: Discuss the impact of the conflicting priorities on Team Phoenix. Propose methods the scrum master could use to support the team, ensuring focus and morale are maintained.
4. Scalability and resource management: Analyze the suggestion to increase the team's capacity. Discuss its potential benefits and drawbacks, and suggest alternative strategies for managing increased workload and stakeholder expectations.

Scenario 5: Collaboration Clash

Team Phoenix at InnovaTech Solutions, established seven months ago, has been working diligently on a crucial project using the scrum framework. The task is to develop an intuitive software tool for healthcare professionals, designed to simplify complex data analysis and assist in making swift, accurate, data-driven decisions. The project demands a diverse set of skills, combining software development, data analysis, and user experience design. The original team composition included four senior developers, a data analyst, a UX/UI designer, and two QA testers, all experienced in agile methodologies and committed to the scrum principles of collaboration, iterative development, and continuous feedback.

Three sprints ago, in response to increasing demands from stakeholders and the complex nature of the healthcare project, Team Phoenix expanded its capacity. It welcomed a new data analyst and two junior developers, aiming to enhance the ability to address the evolving needs of the project. However, this expansion brought unexpected challenges, especially highlighted in the last two sprint reviews. It was observed that several user stories, primarily handled by the two new junior developers, failed to meet the team's Definition of Done, a cornerstone of maintaining quality and consistency in scrum projects. This raised serious concerns about the onboarding process for new team members and their integration into the existing agile framework and team culture.

The situation took a turn just before the upcoming retrospective meeting. The four senior developers, who had been with Team Phoenix since the project's inception, formed an informal coalition. This action, while perhaps unintentional, signified a growing rift between the original team members and the newcomers. The junior developers, still acclimating to the project and the agile framework, found themselves somewhat isolated and without adequate guidance.

As the scrum master prepares to lead the retrospective, they are confronted with these pressing issues: integrating new team members effectively, ensuring adherence to the project's quality standards, and addressing the emerging divide within the team.

Discussion questions for Scenario 5

1. Role analysis and intervention strategies: Determine which roles among the scrum master, product owner, and agile coach are best suited to address the collaboration challenges faced by Team Phoenix. Develop specific intervention strategies for the chosen role(s) to resolve the divide between the original team members and the new joiners and to facilitate effective integration of the new members into the team.
2. Defining and maintaining the Definition of Done: Discuss the importance of the Definition of Done in scrum projects. Propose methods for ensuring that all team members, including new joiners, understand and adhere to these criteria. Consider how the team can maintain quality standards while accommodating the learning curve of new members.
3. Retrospective planning: As the scrum master, plan how to conduct the retrospective meeting to address these issues effectively. Outline the key topics to be discussed, how to facilitate open and constructive communication, and how to ensure that action items are identified and followed up on.
4. Long-term strategies for team growth and adaptation: Propose long-term strategies for Team Phoenix to adapt to changes in team composition and to manage growth effectively while maintaining high standards of work and a positive team dynamic. Consider how the team can prepare for and manage future expansions or changes in team composition.

REFERENCES AND FURTHER READING

Adkins, L. (2010). *Coaching agile teams: A companion for scrum masters, agile coaches, and project managers in transition*. Addison-Wesley Professional.

Beck, K., Beedle, M., van Bennekum, A., et al. (n.d.). *Manifesto for agile software development*. Accessed 30 November 2023 from https://agilemanifesto.org

Cohn, M. (2010). *Succeeding with agile: Software development using scrum*. Addison-Wesley Professional.

Derby, E., Larsen, D., & Schwaber, K. (2006). *Agile retrospectives: Making good teams great*. O'Reilly Media.

Perri, M. (2018). *Escaping the build trap: How effective product management creates real value*. O'Reilly Media.

Project Management Institute (2021). *A guide to the project management body of knowledge (PMBOK guide)* (7th ed.). Project Management Institute.

Schwaber, K., & Sutherland, J. (2020). *The scrum guide: The definitive guide to scrum: The rules of the game*. Scrum.org.

Scrum Alliance (n.d.). *Scrum roles demystified*. Accessed 30 November 2023 from https://resources.scrumalliance.org/Article/scrum-roles-demystified

Sutherland, J., & Altman, I. (2017). *The art of doing twice the work in half the time: How to use scrum to make your agile more agile*. Random House Business.

9
Unraveling the ethical knot: a case study on deteriorating team dynamics

Simona Bonghez

OPENING PARAGRAPHS

Ethics and professional behavior play a critical role in project management, shaping the behavior, decision-making, and overall culture within a project team. They significantly influence stakeholder trust, risk mitigation, team morale, and decision-making processes. Today's landscape increasingly shows a concerning trend where ethical boundaries are crossed in various fields including business, government, education, and sports. There appears to be a growing belief that success justifies the bending or breaking of ethical norms (Blanchard & Peale, 1988). This shift in attitude not only questions the core values of society, it also signals a critical need for individuals and organizations to re-evaluate and strengthen their commitment to ethical principles in their pursuits and interactions. Yet, this topic is not equally covered in discussions and specialized literature; books on project management barely dedicate a few paragraphs to this subject (Müller, 2014).

This case study is designed to offer a comprehensive exploration of ethical considerations in project management and their practical application. The study is divided into two distinct parts, each contributing to valuable experiential learning. The first part (discussion questions) prompts readers to understand and analyze the root cause of the team's ethical challenges and their consequences on trust, collaboration, and overall project performance. The second part presents readers with an engaging activity with the opportunity to study an Ethics Toolkit, select the most suitable tool, and articulate their reasons for the selection.

This exercise encourages readers to critically analyze the ethical challenges faced by the project team and identify effective tools to address those challenges. By justifying their tool selection, students and participants demonstrate their understanding of the toolkit and its real-life application. In providing arguments for their tool selection, readers engage in thoughtful decision-making and problem-solving based on an evaluation of the pros and cons of each tool's potential application in the given scenario. This type of activity falls in line with the characteristics of a "decision scenario" case study, where readers are prompted to make informed decisions or take specific actions based on their understanding of the project and available tools.

BODY OF THE CASE

The Company

In the heart of the tech world stands Innovatech Solutions, a colossus born from humble beginnings. Its shimmering facade in the tech district is a far cry from its early days in a modest apartment building. As a beacon of innovation, Innovatech's journey from a fledgling startup to a global powerhouse is a story of ambition, vision, and the relentless pursuit of progress.

Once, Innovatech Solutions was the embodiment of the startup spirit. Agility and adaptability were not just concepts; they were the very essence of its existence. Teams operated in tightly knit groups, ideas flowed freely, and decisions were made swiftly. This environment was fertile ground for pioneering technologies, nurturing products and solutions that redefined the industry. But, as Innovatech grew, its success began to reshape it. The company expanded, spreading its wings across the globe, attracting top talent, and scaling its operations. With growth, however, came complexity. The agility that once defined Innovatech began to weaken under the weight of its own size. Processes became more structured, decision-making layers multiplied, and the once nimble giant found itself grappling with the inertia that often accompanies large organizations.

Despite these challenges, the heart of Innovatech Solutions still beats with the spirit of its early days. The leadership, aware of the creeping rigidity, is deeply committed to rekindling the startup culture that fueled the company's initial success. Senior staff recognize that, in the fast-paced world of technology, adaptability is not just an advantage; it is a necessity. Efforts are being made to streamline processes, encourage open communication, and empower employees to make decisions. Innovation labs and think tanks dot the Innovatech landscape – small oases where the startup spirit thrives, nurturing new ideas and approaches.

The Project

One of these oases within the walls of the tech giant is its latest venture: the GreenTech Integration System. This project is not just another feather in Innovatech's cap; it is a bold statement of its commitment to sustainability and innovation. The GreenTech Integration System was born from a simple yet powerful idea: to harmonize technology with environmental responsibility. Innovatech, once a nimble startup and now a global powerhouse, has set its sights on a new kind of challenge – to drastically reduce its carbon footprint and lead the way in corporate environmental stewardship. Beyond its internal benefits, Innovatech harbored the hope of monetizing this investment in the future, transforming the GreenTech

Integration System into a product that could benefit other companies seeking sustainable solutions.

The Team

At the forefront of Innovatech's ambitious GreenTech Integration System was Mihai, a project lead as adept at navigating the complexities of large-scale initiatives as he was at managing the nuances of corporate dynamics. Respected for his strategic insights and dedication to sustainable progress, Mihai's role was pivotal in shaping the project's trajectory. However, Mihai's responsibilities extended beyond the operational aspects of the project. The company had presented him with a tantalizing offer: the leadership of Innovatech Solutions' European branch, contingent on the successful completion of the GreenTech Integration System. The proposition was more than a vote of confidence; it was a high-stakes opportunity that placed Mihai in a position where his professional success was intertwined with personal advancement. This new dynamic introduced an additional layer to Mihai's decision-making. Known for his humorously reflective yet sometimes cynical nature, Mihai often mused over the ironies and contradictions of the corporate world. This disposition, which oscillated between light-hearted observations and sharp, critical insights, allowed him to navigate the intricate web of corporate motivations and project demands with a unique perspective.

Today, Mihai was in a light-hearted mood and, as he leaned back in his chair, he couldn't help but smile at the thought of his core team for the GreenTech Integration System. Each member was a character in their own right, bringing a unique flavor to the mix.

> There's Sabina, our lead data scientist. Brilliant as a supernova and just as likely to explode with ideas. She can find a data solution to a problem we didn't even know we had. But sometimes, I'm sure she sees the world in binary – ones and zeros, with little room for the gray areas of ethical dilemmas.
>
> And then we have Andrei, the sustainability team coordinator. His pragmatism is as solid as the Earth he's trying to save. He's all about practical solutions, even if it means bending the rules a bit. I sometimes wonder if his middle name is "Compromise."
>
> Ioana, our environmental analyst, is the team's conscience. She's got a heart as green as the Amazon and a mind as sharp as a thorn. She'll call out an unsustainable practice before you can say "carbon footprint." But flexibility? Not her strongest suit.
>
> And, of course, there's Bogdan, the IT team coordinator, the young gun. Fresh from a newly acquired startup, with enough ambition to fuel a rocket. His ideas are as bold as his coffee, which is strong enough to be classified as a new element on the periodic table. But I worry his eagerness to impress might sometimes cloud his judgment on what's right for the project.

Mihai's thoughts were a blend of affection and amusement. He knew that leading this diverse and vibrant group would be as challenging as it was rewarding. Their varied perspectives, strengths, and, yes, even their quirks, were what would drive the GreenTech Integration System forward. As a unit, they had the potential to not merely innovate but to revolutionize the way Innovatech, and perhaps the world, approached sustainability. After contemplating the unique mix of personalities in his team, Mihai's thoughts naturally drifted towards his own role in this intricate tapestry. He leaned back in his chair, eyes tracing the familiar contours of his office, a space that had witnessed many pivotal moments in his career. "There's a thin line I'm walking here," Mihai mused to himself, a hint of seriousness seeping into his usually light-hearted demeanor. The offer to lead Innovatech Solutions' European branch was a crowning achievement, a testament to his years of dedication and hard work. Yet, it was more than just a promotion; it was a mirror reflecting his deepest aspirations and the complex web of decisions that brought him here.

Mihai was abruptly pulled from his thoughts by the entrance of his team, gathering for the preparation of the kick-off meeting. In the meeting room, the whole team grouped around the table, each member scrutinizing the project management plan for the GreenTech Integration System. Mihai, ever focused, initiated the session. "Let's ensure everything's in order before the kick-off meeting. We need this plan to be watertight," he said, scanning the room.

Bogdan, flipping through the pages of the plan, paused. "I notice we don't have anything about ethics in here. At my old startup, we developed our own code of ethics and professional conduct. Shouldn't we consider something similar?" The room fell silent for a moment, as everyone considered his point.

Mihai nodded thoughtfully. "That's a good catch, Bogdan. Integrating the company's values into our project plan could reinforce our commitment to ethical practices. Let's add a section on this." Sabina chimed in, "It could guide our decision-making, especially in gray areas." Andrei agreed, "It's a proactive step to maintain integrity throughout the project's lifecycle."

Mihai concluded, "Alright, let's draft this section. We'll weave in Innovatech's core values and ensure our project aligns with these principles."

Six Months Later

Six months into the GreenTech Integration System project, the once-vibrant energy of Mihai's team had begun to wane. The diverse personalities that had initially synergized to propel the project forward were now showing signs of strain, each facing their unique challenges.

Sabina, the team's brilliant lead data scientist, had encountered several technical roadblocks. The data her team needed to push the project on was muddled with inconsistencies and gaps, leading to frequent setbacks. Her frustration was palpable in team meetings, where her usual spark of enthusiasm had dimmed.

Andrei, the sustainability coordinator, found himself in a tight spot. His practical solutions, often involving bending the rules, started to compromise the project's integrity. His tendency to find the middle ground was now creating more problems than solutions, leading to suboptimal outcomes that only partially aligned with the project's sustainability goals.

Ioana, the environmental analyst, remained steadfast in her principles, refusing to budge on sustainability standards. Her rigidity started to clash with the rest of the team, especially Andrei. Their debates, once constructive, now turned into tense standoffs, hindering progress.

Bogdan, the young and ambitious coordinator of the IT team, had gradually become disenchanted. The reality of corporate hurdles and the complexity of the project had started to erode his initial enthusiasm. His bold ideas, once a source of inspiration, were now met with skepticism or mired in red tape. Feeling undervalued and stifled, Bogdan's engagement with the project dwindled. As a result, his team started to miss deadlines, their participation in meetings became minimal, and Bogdan's once-vibrant presence faded into the background.

To further aggravate the situation, an incident subtly altered the team's high regard for Mihai. Andrei, in his bid to maintain project momentum, had bypassed key sustainability protocols. Though his intentions were to keep the project on track, this action starkly deviated from the project's core values and risked serious repercussions for both the team and the project. Aware of the precarious situation, Mihai made a decision aimed at preserving the project's continuity. He chose to discreetly address Andrei's lapse, negotiating with senior management to prevent escalation.

However, Mihai's intervention, intended to be unobtrusive, did not go unnoticed by the team and set off a ripple effect. Team members, already dealing with individual challenges, started sensing favoritism in Mihai's leadership. Sabina, who took great pride in her meticulous commitment to data integrity, felt especially betrayed. She perceived Mihai's action as a compromise of the team's dedication to excellence and integrity, a sentiment she shared with Ioana. Both felt that this intervention was a setback to their collective efforts. Bogdan, witnessing these developments, became even more disenchanted. His enthusiasm and sense of belonging, already diminishing, were further eroded by what he perceived as the triumph of corporate politics over genuine talent and effort. This experience prompted him to seriously consider leaving Innovatech to join a new and dynamic startup where he hoped to find an environment more conducive to his ambitions and values. The incident, though seemingly minor, added a layer of tension and mistrust within the team. It contributed to the reluctance of team members to speak openly and honestly about the challenges they faced.

Mihai, observing the unfolding challenges, felt a deepening concern. The high-stakes opportunity of leading Innovatech Solutions' European branch intensified his pressure to steer the project to a successful conclusion. He recognized that the team's struggles mirrored the broader issues faced by Innovatech as it continued its transition from a nimble startup to a corporate giant. The agility and creativity that once defined the company now conflicted with its new structured, process-driven approach. Although Mihai was aware of the operational challenges, he did not connect them to his own leadership style. Unaware of the growing discontent among his team members about his leadership, particularly in how he handled the situation with Andrei, Mihai remained blinkered to the undercurrents of doubt and skepticism. This lack of awareness caused a blind spot in his management style, leaving him unable to address the brewing concerns and the subtle shift in the team's perception of his decision-making.

Nevertheless, with the project's success and his own career advancement at stake, Mihai knew he had to act. He needed to reignite the team's passion, streamline communication, and foster a balance between innovation and practicality. As the challenges mounted, Mihai realized the need for a pivotal meeting to address the growing concerns within his team. He scheduled a gathering, hoping to foster open communication and collaborative problem-solving.

On the day of the meeting, Mihai looked around the conference room at his team. The atmosphere was tense, a stark contrast to the vibrant discussions that once filled this space. He began with a candid overview of the project's status, highlighting the setbacks and the urgent need to realign their efforts. "Today, I want us to speak openly about the challenges we face," Mihai said, his tone serious yet encouraging. "This project is not just about Innovatech or our careers; it's about making a real impact. I believe in this team's ability to turn things around, but we need to be honest with each other and work together to find solutions."

A heavy silence fell over the room. Mihai's words, intended to inspire, seemed to weigh heavily on the team members. Each of them was lost in thought, contemplating the risks of speaking up.

Sabina was the first to break the silence, but her words were cautious, lacking her usual analytical sharpness. She spoke of general challenges with data but steered clear of addressing the deeper issues that hindered her work. Her fear of exposing the gaps in her expertise overshadowed her desire to seek help.

Andrei, once pragmatic and outspoken, now seemed hesitant. He knew his approach of bending rules had backfired, but admitting this could jeopardize his standing in the team. Instead, he chose to focus on minor operational issues, avoiding the core problems that stemmed from his compromises.

Ioana, usually the voice of uncompromising standards, remained silent. She was aware that her inflexibility had caused friction, but acknowledging this felt like betraying her principles. Her internal conflict kept her from contributing meaningfully to the discussion.

Bogdan, who had once brimmed with ideas, sat quietly, almost invisible. The disillusionment he felt had sapped his confidence. He had ideas that could potentially help the project, but the fear of further rejection held him back.

Mihai observed the dynamics, realizing that the team's reluctance to speak up was rooted in self-preservation. Each member, wrapped up in their insecurities and personal interests, was unwilling to expose their vulnerabilities or challenge the status quo.

The meeting ended with a few half-hearted suggestions, far from the collaborative breakthrough Mihai had hoped for. As the team dispersed, a sense of unease lingered in the air. Mihai reflected on the challenges ahead. It was clear that the issues ran deeper than just professional disagreements; they were a manifestation of the team's loss of trust and fear of taking risks. Determined to keep the project from faltering, Mihai knew he had to find a way to rebuild the team's confidence and sense of unity. He needed to create an environment where speaking the truth was not only encouraged but celebrated. The path ahead was uncertain, but Mihai was resolute in his mission to steer the GreenTech Integration System, and his team, back to the spirit of innovation and collaboration that once defined them.

DISCUSSION QUESTIONS

1. Identify and discuss the key issues presented in the text regarding team dynamics, leadership challenges, and ethical decision-making in a corporate setting. Consider how these issues impact the project's progress and the team's overall effectiveness.
2. Analyze how Mihai's leadership style contributed to the team's perception of favoritism and mistrust.
3. Evaluate the effectiveness of Mihai's strategy to call a team meeting for open communication in resolving the underlying issues.
4. Reflect on the reasons why Mihai's team might have been unwilling to openly discuss the issues during the meeting. Consider factors such as team dynamics, psychological safety, leadership style, and personal insecurities.
5. Given the challenges in his team, what additional strategies could Mihai employ to enhance his leadership effectiveness in this complex situation?
6. If the project management plan included the ethical values of Innovatech Solutions, shouldn't these values have prevented situations like the one faced by Mihai's team? Reflect on how the inclusion of ethical guidelines in project planning can influence team dynamics and decision-making processes.

ACTIVITY: SOLVING GREENTECH TEAM DILEMMAS

1. Task and research:
   - Download and read the Practitioner Ethics Toolkit provided by the PMI, from www.pmi.org/about/ethics/resources/toolkit
   - Carefully examine the various tools within the toolkit, understanding their purpose and applications.
   - Choose the tool you believe is most suitable for addressing the ethical challenges presented in the case study.
2. Argumentation: Write a detailed argument explaining your choice of tool. Your argument should include:
   - an explanation of why this tool is appropriate for the GreenTeach team scenario
   - how you envision the tool being applied to the case study to effectively address the ethical issues identified.
3. Submission: Present your findings in a structured report or essay format, supporting your argument with specific references from both the toolkit and the case study.

REFERENCES AND FURTHER READING

Agarwal, U. A., Jain, K., Anantatmula, V., & Shankar, S. (2023). Ethics in projects. In *Managing people in projects for high performance*. Springer.
Blanchard, K., & Peale, N. V. (1988). *The power of ethical management*. William Morrow and Company.
Clarke, N., D'Amato, A., Higgs, M., Vahidi, R. (2018). *Responsible leadership in projects: Insights into ethical decision making*. Project Management Institute.
Kliem, R. L. (2012). *Ethics and project management*. Auerbach Publications.
Müller, R. (2014). Guest editorial. *International Journal of Managing Projects in Business, 7*(4).
Project Management Institute (PMI) (n.d.-a). *PMI Code of Ethics and Professional Conduct*. Retrieved on December 26, 2023, from www.pmi.org/about/ethics/code
Project Management Institute (PMI) (n.d.-b). *PMI Ethics Toolkit*. Retrieved on December 26, 2023, from www.pmi.org/about/ethics/resources/toolkit
Wiese, J. (2023). *Ethics in the workplace*. Emtrain. Retrieved on December 20, 2023, from https://emtrain.com/blog/code-of-conduct/ethics-in-the-workplace

APPENDIX A9.1: PMI PRACTITIONER ETHICS TOOLKIT

The **Practitioner Ethics Toolkit,** available online at www.pmi.org/about/ethics/resources/toolkit includes various tools designed to assist PMI practitioners in understanding, identifying, and managing ethical issues. The following are brief descriptions of the tools included in the toolkit.

The **Ethics Self-Assessment** is an ethics tool for practitioners to apply the PMI Code of Ethics to their daily activities, helping them reflect on their ethical leadership and actions (PMI, n.d.-b).

This tool is useful for practitioners to reflect personally on their adherence to the PMI Code of Ethics in their daily activities. It is particularly beneficial in helping to identify areas for ethical improvement and reinforcing ethical practices. This tool can be used periodically, especially when faced with ethical dilemmas or when seeking to enhance ethical leadership and decision-making skills. It serves as a self-check mechanism to ensure alignment with ethical standards and promotes continuous personal and professional ethical development.

The **Team Ethics Assessment** is an ethics tool which aids increasing awareness about ethical perspectives and supports teams in improving their internal functionality and ethical culture (PMI, n.d.-b).

This is valuable for enhancing self-awareness about ethical perspectives within a team. It is useful when a team aims to improve its ethical culture and functionality. This tool should be employed in team settings, particularly when forming a new team, during periods of change, or when facing ethical challenges. It facilitates discussions on ethical norms and behaviors, encouraging team members to align on ethical standards and practices. The process involves team members completing the assessment individually, followed by group discussions to explore and reconcile any differences in ethical understanding and expectations.

The **Project Bully Identification** is an ethics tool to distinguish between normal workplace conflict and bullying, providing guidelines to identify and address workplace bullying (PMI, n.d.-b).

This tool is designed to distinguish between normal workplace conflicts and bullying. It is useful when there are concerns about potential bullying behaviors within a project team. The tool helps in identifying, understanding, and addressing workplace bullying, ensuring a respectful and professional environment. It should be used when team members experience or witness behavior that may constitute bullying, providing guidelines for recognition and subsequent steps to address the issue effectively. This proactive approach helps in maintaining a healthy, productive, and ethical workplace.

The **Ethical Decision-Making Workshop Guide** offers guidelines for conducting interactive workshops to enhance awareness of the value of ethical behavior in project success (PMI, n.d.-b).

This guide is designed for conducting interactive workshops focused on ethical behavior in project management. It is beneficial when there is a need to enhance awareness and understanding of ethical practices within and among project teams. The tool is particularly useful for facilitating discussions and activities that help participants recognize the impact of ethics on project success. It should be used in training sessions or team meetings, providing a structured approach to explore ethical scenarios and reinforce the importance of ethical decision-making in a collaborative environment.

The **Code of Ethics & Professional Conduct** outlines the values of honesty, responsibility, respect, and fairness as ethical conduct drivers in project management (PMI, n.d.-a).

The Code is essential guide to the PMI's ethical values: honesty, responsibility, respect, and fairness. It serves as a foundational resource for practitioners, reinforcing the importance of these values in professional conduct. This tool is useful for both new and experienced project managers, providing a clear ethical framework to guide their decisions and actions in various project management scenarios. It helps ensure that project management practices are carried out with integrity and professionalism.

The **Code Values Card** is a resource affirming the four foundational values of the PMI Code of Ethics, serving as a reminder for PMI members (PMI, n.d.-b).

This is a quick-reference guide affirming the four foundational values of the PMI Code of Ethics: honesty, responsibility, respect, and fairness. It is especially useful for PMI members as a daily reminder and a concise summary of these ethical principles.

The **Ethical Decision-Making Framework** is a practical resource to guide practitioners towards ethical choices and accountability in decision-making (PMI, n.d.-b).

The framework guides practitioners in making ethical choices in their project management roles. It is useful when facing complex decisions where ethical implications are a concern. The framework helps in systematically evaluating the ethical aspects of a decision, considering factors such as the stakeholders involved, potential outcomes, and alignment with ethical standards. It provides a step-by-step approach to ensure decisions are made with accountability and in accordance with ethical principles.

10
Leveraging work readiness to develop a professional identity

Jessica Borg

OPENING PARAGRAPHS

This case is unique in that it will ask you to reflect on your professional development and professional identity in light of the knowledge you have gained throughout your project management courses. That said, we will take a little bit of creative licence to help you begin to craft your professional identity – think of this chapter as a 'build your own adventure' segment. The case study will involve several tasks to prompt reflection, each with a set of corresponding questions and tasks to help craft your professional identity and work-readiness reflections.

This case focuses on: establishing an awareness of the work-readiness attributes project management graduates need to thrive in their early careers; encouraging students to reflect on the work-readiness attributes they gained in their project management degree and/or courses; helping them identify their work-readiness areas of strengths and weaknesses for continuous professional development; and providing guidance on how students can leverage those work-readiness attributes to pitch themselves to prospective project management employers.

Project management professionals continue to be in high demand globally (Vaz-Serra & Mitcheltree, 2020), with organisations recognising that 'most modern work requires significant project management skills and capabilities' (Konstantinou, 2015, p. 21). Approximately a fifth of global economic activities are project-based (McKevitt et al., 2017), making project management graduates valuable resources for organisations worldwide. Despite being in such great demand, research shows that many project management graduates are not 'work ready' upon completing their tertiary education. Indeed, successfully completing a project management degree is not enough to render a graduate work ready (Masole & van Dyk, 2016). In recent years, scholars (e.g., Borg & Scott-Young, 2021; Burga et al., 2020; Ekstedt, 2019) have started to pay more attention to the skills development and work readiness of early-career PM professionals, calling for more research in this area.

Work readiness is a concept encompassing values, behaviours and skills that enable individuals to perform successfully in their professional roles and contribute to their organisations

(Business Council of Australia, 2016; Prikshat et al., 2018). As such, work-ready project managers are those who possess the work-readiness attributes (values, behaviours and skills) that enable them to contribute positively to projects and their project-based organisations. Ensuring that graduates possess the work-ready attributes that allow them to thrive in their early careers is fundamental to ensuring a healthy pipeline of PM professionals.

This chapter aims to help PM students' achieve these objectives, and gain awareness of their own work readiness and develop their *professional identity.*

BODY OF THE CASE

In the Shoes of an Early-Career Project Manager

Imagine you are working as a junior project manager at a consultancy called Projectify. The company is a client-side PM firm, which means that, as part of the PM team, you will act as the client representative on a range of projects. This is your first job after graduating from university and you are very excited to get into the workforce and start putting everything you learned in your degree into practice. It is only your first week, and as you start getting ready for your day at the office, you reflect on the last few months.

Over the last six months, you have achieved some incredible milestones to kickstart your project management career (Figure 10.1):

- In December, you graduated from your degree programme with a focus on project management – congratulations!
- In January, you received a phone call that you were shortlisted for an interview at the PM consultancy you really wanted to work at.
- A few weeks ago, you received the welcome news that you were successful in getting the role of junior project manager at Projectify.
- Today marks one week in your role – well done!

Over the last week, you have been familiarising yourself with the company policies, practices and processes. You have mastered the art of filing emails, looking (and dressing) the part, and you have attended your first project control group (PCG) meeting. You are excited to be working on real projects at last. Having a job like this in the field is what you and your friends dreamed about when you were sitting in lecture theatres trying not to worry about all the assignments that were due.

The problem is that, at times, you feel a little bit out of your depth. You want to do everything perfectly and impress your senior project manager, Vincent, but you know you still have a lot to learn, yet are a bit hesitant to ask questions in case you ask the wrong ones or come across as inexperienced. You thought you would be hitting the ground running after finishing your degree, but maybe you are not 100 per cent work ready...

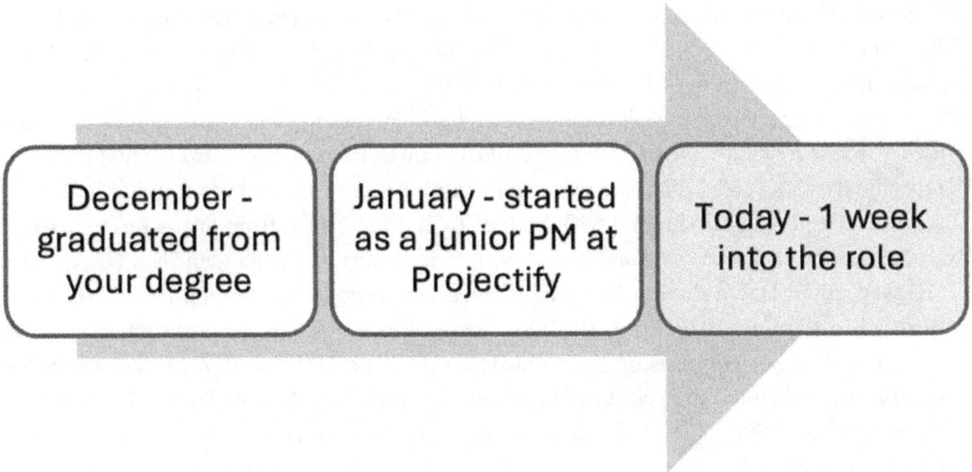

Source: Author.

Figure 10.1 Timeline of events for becoming a junior project manager

Section 1: Evaluating Your Own Work Readiness

As you are on the train home from work, you get a call from your friend Naomi. You went to university together, and Naomi is now working as a graduate project manager at another company. You tell her that your first week went well but that you are not entirely confident that you have all the skills for the job. Naomi confides that she shares a similar feeling. She has spoken to another mutual friend, Adon, who is having a similar experience at the job he started a month ago. You call Adon, and it seems he sometimes has the same feelings as you and Naomi. He reveals that, "Starting this job feels like being thrown in the deep end and you need to sink or swim."

Knowing you are not alone in feeling a little unprepared for the world of work makes you feel a bit better, but you know you need to do something about it. In fact, knowing that your friends are feeling the same way empowers you to do something about it. You decide that you are going to explore this further – as your mother says, you always were the determined type!

Later that evening, you remember that one of your lecturers, Dr Jessica Borg, researches in the area of work readiness of PM professionals. You feel more comfortable asking her for help than going to your manager, so you send an email asking her what project managers need to be work ready and whether there are certain skill sets that you and your friends should work on to make you feel more work ready.

The next morning, there is an email from Dr Borg. It includes the following:

> It's lovely to hear from you, and congratulations again on your project management role! It's great to hear that you are enjoying working at Projectify. I have heard great things about the company.

I understand where you're coming from with regard to feeling a little out of your depth. It's important to remember that it's completely normal to feel like this as a graduate following your transition from university to the workplace.

Work readiness is a complex concept, and scholars across many disciplines (not just project management) have tried to pinpoint the values, behaviours and skills that make an individual 'work ready'. In response to your question on what makes an individual work ready, I'm attaching a document with a table [Table 10.1]. This is from my research on work readiness and it illustrates some key work-readiness attributes, as identified by scholars (Harvey, 2000; Dacre Pool & Sewell, 2007; Cavanagh et al., 2015; Lippman et al., 2015; Borg & Scott-Young, 2020; Borg, 2020) in the education as well as the project management literature. The two columns on the rightmost side identify the work-readiness attributes specifically embedded in project management degrees (Borg & Scott-Young, 2020) as well as the attributes that key stakeholders (including employers, educators and professionals) (Borg, 2020) consider to be key work-readiness skills for graduating project management students.

Hopefully this will give you a better understanding of what work-readiness attributes are considered key for project management professionals. Perhaps you can use it to self-evaluate where you stand.

Remember, these skills may change as the workforce changes, so don't be scared to ask your managers and mentors their thoughts as well.

Have a wonderful week and let me know how it all goes.

You decide to follow Dr Borg's suggestion and self-evaluate your own work-readiness attributes in line with the attributes identified in the table as important for project managers.

Section 2: Building Self-Efficacy – Practising 'Performance Accomplishment'

You have now been in your role for a month (Figure 10.2). You are happy with the projects you have been assigned, and they are all progressing well. Your company has an in-house mentoring programme. Your mentor, Frer, is a project manager and has been with the company for three years. Just like you, she joined the company after graduating from university, and, just this year, was promoted from junior project manager to project manager. As part of the mentoring programme, you are invited to reach out to Frer with any work-related questions. At the human resources meeting last week, all the junior project managers were encouraged to have a catch-up with their mentor once a month or as needed.

You met with Frer for your first mentor meeting yesterday and had a great chat about how you are finding the company and project management in general. You told her a little bit about your first month and how, at the start, you felt like you were thrown in the deep end a little bit (or a lot). You confided in her about feeling unprepared to deal with certain tasks at

Table 10.1 Work-readiness attributes as identified by education and project management researchers

Education literature	**Project Management literature**
Work-readiness attributes valued by employers:	WR attributes embedded in PM undergraduate bachelor's degrees
Harvey (2000)	
• Communication	Borg and Scott-Young (2020)
• Teamwork	• Critical analysis
• Interpersonal skills	• Knowledge
• Intellectual abilities	• Globally aware
• Ability to learn	• Collaborative
Dacre Pool & Sewell (2007)	• Literacy
• Adaptable	• Technical skills
• Independent	• Business literacy
• Cooperative	• Digital technology
• Manage and lead others	• Problem solving
• Communicate effectively	• Respect
• Manage time	• Work ethic
• Utilise new and emerging technologies	• Business minded
Cavanagh et al. (2015)	• Self-aware
• Effective communication	• Data analysis
• Adaptability	• Customer focused
• Commitment	• Continuous improvement
• Will to learn	
• Time management	• Adaptable
• Interpersonal skills	• Numeracy
• People skills	• Communication
	• Cultural awareness
WR attributes linked to employment performance in 15 to 29-year-olds)	**WR attributes considered essential for project management graduates (perspectives of employers, educators, professional bodies, project management students and professionals)**
Lippman et al. (2015)	Dacre Pool & Sewell (2007)
• Social skills	• Knowledge
• Higher order thinking skills	• Respect
• Self-control	• Authentic
• Positive self-concept	• Collaborative
• Hard working	• Self-aware
• Teamwork	• Resilient
• Positive attitude	• Digital technology
• Self-motivation	• Literacy
• Integrity/ethics	• Problem solving
	• Technical skills
	• Communication

Source: Adapted from Borg 2020, pp. 115.

work until you had gained a little more experience, and started telling her about the work-readiness attributes you think you possess and the ones you think you need to work on.

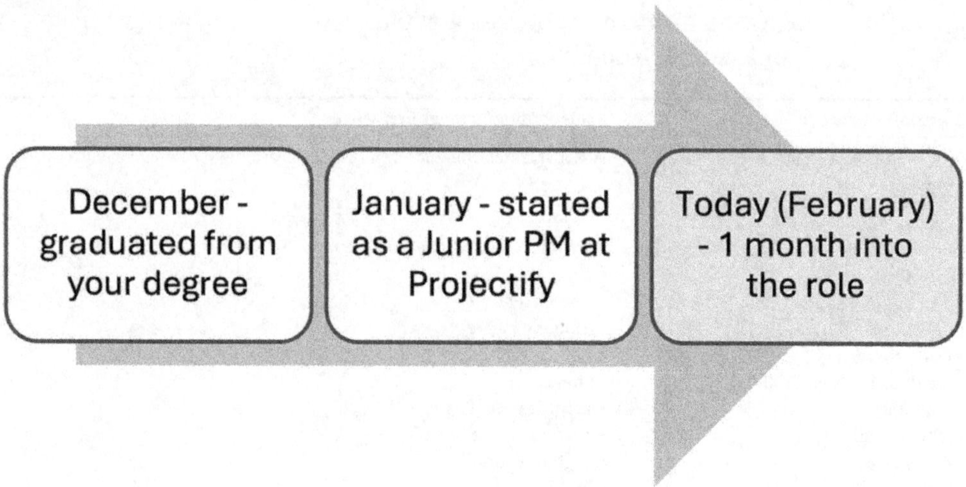

Source: Author.

Figure 10.2 Timeline of case study events, one month into role

Frer mentions the concept of self-efficacy and says that it is a helpful theoretical lens for understanding graduate work readiness (e.g., Henderson et al., 2016; Spanjaard et al., 2018). She suggests you might want to read up a little on self-efficacy in the context of work.

Later that evening, you research self-efficacy and find that it is 'concerned with people's beliefs in their capabilities to produce given attainments' (Bandura, 2012, p. 15). Self-efficacy is considered to be 'a major determinant of people's choice of activities and how much effort they will expend' (Bandura, 1977, p. 194). There are four major sources for developing self-efficacy: i) performance accomplishment, ii) vicarious experience, iii) verbal persuasion, and iv) emotional arousal (Bandura, 1977). Drawing on Bandura's (2012) work, PM graduates' beliefs about their own self-efficacy will influence whether they consider themselves prepared for their early careers in project management. Moreover, as work readiness is indicative of the potential for career advancement (Caballero & Walker, 2010), it is imperative that PM graduates have a clear appreciation of their own work-readiness attributes.

In the office the next day, you run into Frer while collecting your copies of the PCG meeting minutes from the printer. You mention that you had read up a little on developing self-efficacy. Frer suggests that focusing on the area of 'performance accomplishment' and reflecting on your achievements in your role to date can help boost your self-efficacy and, by extension, make you feel more work-ready and confident in your role.

Section 3: Work Readiness – a Function of Self-Awareness and Continuous Improvement

You have now been in your junior project manager role at Projectify for six months (Figure 10.3). Time certainly flies when you're having fun! Today, Antony from human resources

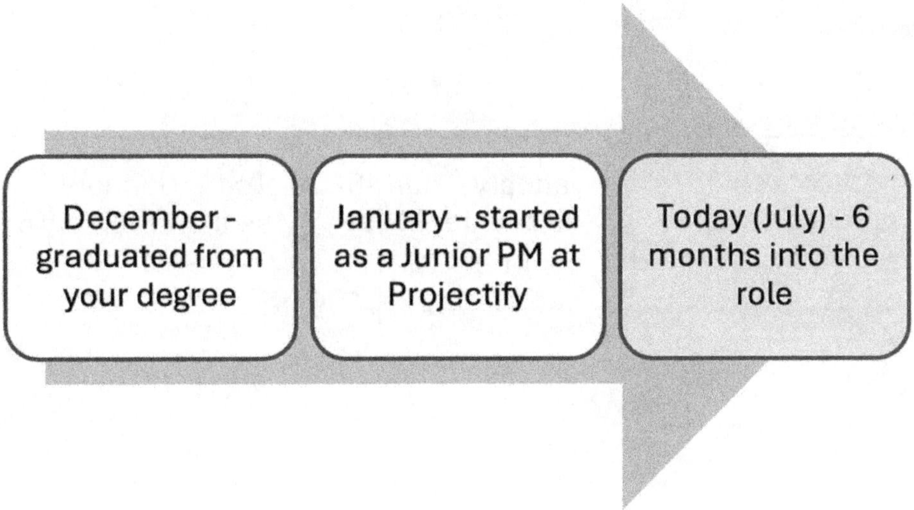

Source: Author.

Figure 10.3 Timeline of case study events, six months in role

calls to remind you that you are due for a performance review with your manager Vincent as part of your probation requirements. He suggests that you take some time to reflect on your progress and your skill development over the last six months in preparation for the meeting.

You start to reflect on your projects and what you have accomplished. As you think about how successfully you have been leading the PCG meetings and liaising with stakeholders lately, you realise you have indeed come a long way from that first week in the job. You bring up the work-readiness table on your screen and notice how you have continued to build these skills and attributes within the last six months.

After lunch, Vincent drops by to let you know he has scheduled your probation review meeting for Wednesday next week. He explains that the meeting is not only about reviewing how you have performed over the last six months but also to help you identify the areas you need to improve on and how the organisation can support your ongoing professional development. So, he asks you to reflect on your strengths and weaknesses and how you can develop these through the projects you are working on.

Section 4: Looking Ahead - Enhancing Work Readiness

Congratulations! Today is your anniversary in your junior project manager role at Projectify (Figure 10.4). Over the past year, you have worked across three projects, successfully seeing two delivered and one going well, three months away from projected completion. You have learned a lot, grown a lot and have definitely found your feet as an early-career project manager.

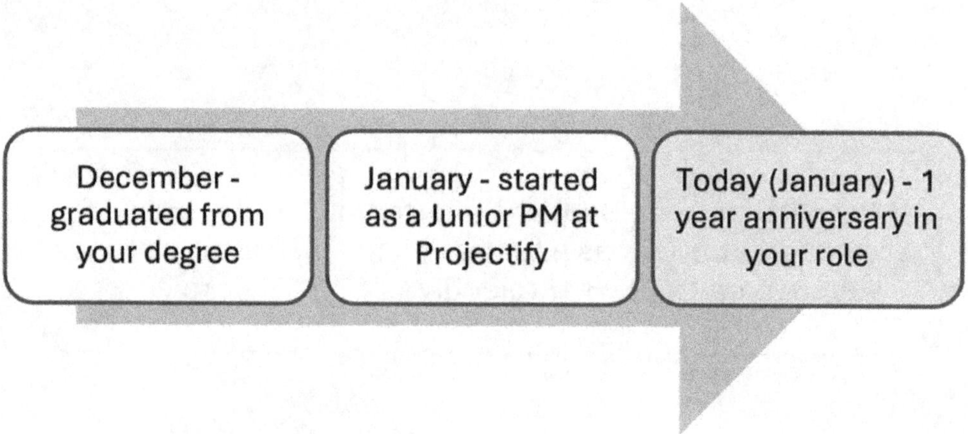

Source: Author.

Figure 10.4 Timeline of case study events, one year in role

The company has employed three graduates this year, and they all start next week. You have been asked whether you could mentor one of them, just as Frer did when you started. You are happy to, and are excited to share your experiences with someone who is new to the company. You remember what it was like to be the new person, and would love to help someone settle into the role.

You have been assigned to mentor Thomas and are meeting him for your first catch-up. He confides that one of the things he is struggling with is thinking ahead about his career progression:

> "When I was at uni, all I was aiming for was good grades to get a position like this one. Now that I'm here, it's great, but I'm not sure what I should focus on next. I feel nervous about how I need to progress in the role and actually managing real projects."

Thomas shares that, while he was talking with the other two newly appointed graduates, he noticed that they all had a similar feeling of not knowing how to plan for their careers. He asks you what your career plan looks like and whether you could share it with the new graduates.

CONCLUSION

This chapter introduced work readiness and work-ready attributes. Work-ready professionals are those who, through learning, have gained the skills and knowledge that allow them to make meaningful and positive contributions to their organisations, industry and communities. We want you to be a work-ready project manager, to thrive in your transition from university into the professional world and to grow into a future leader in the field. Moreover, work-ready individuals are better prepared to respond positively to workplace challenges and, as we know, the current workplace is littered with challenges – from emerging technologies and AI to innovative industry practices (Schwab 2016).

The objective of this chapter was to give you a deeper understanding of your own work readiness as a PM professional and to help set the foundational self-awareness and self-efficacy that you can draw on as you advance in your PM career.

Most importantly, remember too that, just as you have a lot to learn, you also have a lot to give. It is great to commit to a continuous improvement cycle when it comes to your work-readiness attributes, but also remember to celebrate your skill strengths and achievements throughout your career. Too often, we get so caught up preparing for the storm that we forget to appreciate the silver linings (and the sunshine). You are the future of the project management profession. Go out there and give it your best!

DISCUSSION QUESTIONS AND TASKS

Section 1

Self-identification of personal work-readiness attributes

Read through the work-readiness attributes in Table 10.1 and make your own list of:

- the attributes you think you possess
- the attributes you think you need to improve upon
- any other attributes you think should be on the list.

Understanding work readiness strengths and weaknesses

From your list, select your five key areas of strength and your five key areas of weakness. Rank these in relation to how important you think they are for your early career as a project manager.

Section 2

Work readiness personal reflections

For this task, the focus is on 'performance accomplishment' as a factor for developing self-efficacy pertaining to work readiness. According to self-efficacy theory, successful performance of a task raises an individual's personal expectations of mastery in that task; whereas, repeated failures in a task lower them (Bandura, 1977). We can say that successful past performance of project-related tasks (e.g., via education and classwork, as well as through work experience) is expected to increase confidence in that task, and this, in turn, will help successfully complete similar work tasks in future.

Reflect on the list of work-readiness attributes identified in Table 10.1 and identify the three attributes that you believe you possess and which you ranked as being most important for your early career as a project manager. Now reflect on how you have demonstrated your possession of these attributes, either through assessments at university or work experience.

Write a short (about 200 words) reflection for each of the three attributes, explaining with an example how and when you demonstrated this attribute. Use the STAR method to structure each response:

- Identify the Situation – in this case, the work-readiness skill/attribute (e.g. problem-solving skills).
- Explain the Task – describe the situation in which you obtained or demonstrated the attribute.
- Explain the Action – give detailed information on what specific actions you took that demonstrated the work-readiness attribute.
- Detail the Result – give information about the results or accomplishments you achieved through exercising the work-readiness attribute.

For class discussion and peer feedback, practise another key work-readiness attribute, 'communication', and share your best response with your class (either in a small group or with the whole class, as guided by your instructor). Provide feedback to other students and be prepared to receive feedback on your response.

Work-readiness signalling to employers

You had an informal meeting with Moira and Christian - two Directors at the company. They informed you that earlier that day, they were was discussing project scheduling. There are a few project tenders coming up and Moira and Christian were wanting to know how you feel about being included as part of the proposed team to work on a project if the tender is successful. You think this is a great idea as you would love to be put on a project from start to finish. You ask if there is anything they need from you for this. Moira informs you that as part of the tender process, the company will need to provide an updated Curriculum Vitae (CV) for all of the proposed project members. She asks you to please send her and Christian a copy of your latest CV as well as a cover letter of approximately 500 words about your project management skills and what you can bring as a project management team member on a new project. She tells you that the CV should not be more than 3 pages long. "It's a great way for our potential clients to get to know the team they will be working with if our tender is successful!", she reminds you.Later on, while making yourself a cup of tea in the office, you bump into Christian and you start talking about the upcoming projects and which ones you would be interested in being a part of. "Your CV and experience is very important," says Christian, "but so is working on projects you are passionate about! Don't be scared to highlight your passions and interests in your cover letter!" You head back to your desk ready to start preparing a stellar CV and cover letter to send to Moira and Christian. After all, you need to impress your Directors!

1. For this exercise, use your own experience to compile your CV. Accurately list your tertiary qualifications, previous work experience (even if in another field) and any awards you might have or professional certifications and courses you have obtained. Your CV should be two to three pages and include:

- your full name
- contact details
- education history
- employment history
- professional certifications/awards
- referees (two, ideally).

2. Having practised the STAR method, and with your new-found understanding of work-readiness skills, write a 500-word cover letter about your project management skills and what you can bring as a project management team member on a new project. In your cover letter, as a guide, you can use the STAR method to illustrate at least three key work-readiness attributes hat you can bring to the team. Remember to be professional in your communication (literacy and communication are key work-readiness skills after all).

3. In peer discussion and feedback, practise the key work-ready attribute 'collaboration'. In a pair, swap your CV with a partner and provide feedback, paying close attention to professional format, professional communication and how well work readiness is articulated in the CV. Provide your partner with:

- two key pieces of positive feedback (what works really well in their CV)
- two key pieces of constructive feedback (what you recommend they do to improve their CV).

4. Revise your own CV in line with the peer feedback and comments discussed.

Section 3

Work-readiness skills encompass personal attributes (Artess et al., 2017) and in this way, you have both responsibility and power when it comes to enhancing your own work readiness. As evident from Table 10.1, which is by no means an exhaustive list of work-readiness attributes, there are many personal attributes (i.e. values and behaviours) that constitute work readiness. In this task, and in line with advice from both Vincent and Antony to reflect on your skill strengths and weaknesses, focus on two key work-readiness attributes – self-awareness and continuous improvement. This task is designed to help you reflect on your areas of weakness (thereby enhancing self-awareness) and identify steps for improving your competency of these attributes (hence promoting continuous improvement). This should help you in your probationary review meeting and demonstrate to your manager that you are self-aware when it comes to your work-readiness attributes and that you are serious about continuous improvement.

1. Work-readiness skills enhancement: Consider the five work-readiness attributes that you noted as areas of weakness for you in Section 1. For each of these attributes, write a 200-word reflection in which you:

- explain why this is an area of weakness
- identify how you can improve/enhance this work-readiness attribute
- develop a plan for how you will improve this attribute over a period of three to six months
- set some goals for yourself and identify how you will measure your improvement in that particular attribute.

Section 4

Career plans are important in helping individuals map out their career goals, aspirations and, most importantly, how they are going to achieve them. Research finds that someone's level of work readiness is indicative of their future career advancement (Caballero & Walker, 2010), therefore, career education is considered to be critical in ensuring that graduates are prepared not only for the transition into their careers (Jackson 2019), but also for their ongoing career development.

1. Career plans are a great way to communicate your career goals and set some objectives to achieve in the short-medium term. For this task, you will be setting a five-year career plan. Start the career plan from when you graduated university and finish it five years after graduation.
   a) Class discussion and peer feedback: Practice 'communication' and 'collaboration' again and share your career plan (either in a small group or with the whole class, as guided by your instructor). Provide feedback to other students and be prepared to receive feedback on your response. Share ideas on what is and is not an achievable goal in the short to medium term and what can be done to achieve set career goals.
   b) Revise your career plan in line with the feedback received.
   c) Remember to present your career plan creatively and to include colour. You should keep a copy of this career plan and revise it as necessary over the next five years.
2. As you progress in your career, set yourself the challenge of continuously assessing your own areas of strengths and weaknesses:
   a) For areas of strengths, continue to note down examples of demonstrating your competencies in those particular attributes. Keep a record of these, as they will come in handy in any future job applications.
   b) For areas of weakness, continue to plan ahead for how to build up these areas through the reflection and goal planning in Section 3.

Remember, just like most things in life, careers are dynamic. So too is work readiness. Your attributes will change and evolve as you obtain more experience and confidence in your early career after graduation.

REFERENCES AND FURTHER READING

Artess, J., Mellors-Bourne, R., & Hooley, T. (2017). Employability: A review of the literature 2012–2016. In Higher Education Academy (Ed.), *Transforming teaching, inspiring learning*. Higher Education Academy.

Bandura, A. (1977). Self-efficacy: Toward a unifying theory of behavioral change. *Psychological Review, 84*(2), 191–215.

Bandura, A. (2012). On the functional properties of perceived self-efficacy revisited. *Journal of Management, 38*(1), 9–44.

Borg, J. (2020). *Work readiness of project management graduates in construction: A multi-method multi-vocal qualitative study* [PhD Thesis]. RMIT University, Melbourne.

Borg, J., & Scott-Young, C. M. (2020). Priming the project talent pipeline: Examining work readiness in undergraduate project management degrees. *Project Management Journal, 51*(2), 165–180.

Borg, J., & Scott-Young, C. M. (2021). Supporting early career project managers in construction: A multi-vocal study. *Engineering, Construction and Architectural Management, 29*(10), 3830–3846.

Burga, R., Leblanc J., & Rezania, D. (2020). Exploring student perceptions of their readiness for project work: Utilizing social cognitive career theory. *Project Management Journal, 51*(2), 154–164.

Business Council of Australia (2016). *Being work ready: A guide to what employers want*. Business Council of Australia. Accessed 9 June 2025 at www.bca.com.au/being_work_ready_a_guide_to_what_employers_want

Caballero, C. L., & Walker, A. (2010). Work readiness in graduate recruitment and selection: A review of current assessment methods. *Journal of Teaching and Learning for Graduate Employability, 1*(1), 13–25.

Caballero, C. L., Walker, A., & Fuller-Tyszkiewicz, M. (2011). The work readiness scale (WRS): Developing a measure to assess work readiness in college graduates. *Journal of Teaching & Learning for Graduate Employability, 2*(2), 41–54.

Cavanagh, J., Burston, M., Southcombe, A., & Bartram, T. (2015). Contributing to a graduate-centred understanding of work readiness: An exploratory study of Australian undergraduate students' perceptions of their employability. *The International Journal of Management Education, 13*(3), 278–288.

Dacre Pool, L., & Sewell, P. (2007). The key to employability: developing a practical model of graduate employability. *Education and Training, 49*(4), 277–289.

Dacre Pool, L., Gurbutt, D., & Houston, K. (2019). Developing employable, emotionally intelligent, and resilient graduate citizens of the future. In A. Driver (Ed.), *Employability via higher education: Sustainability as scholarship* (pp. 83–97). Springer.

Ekstedt, E. (2019). Project work, a challenge to traditional work life institutions. *International Journal of Managing Projects in Business, 12*(2), 267–281.

Harvey, L. (2000). New realities: The relationship between higher education and employment. *Tertiary Education and Management, 6*(1), 3–17.

Henderson, A., Rowe, J., Watson, K., & Hitchen-Holmes, D. (2016). 'Graduating nurses' self-efficacy in palliative care practice: an exploratory study'. *Nurse Education Today, 39*, 141–146.

Jackson, D. (2019). Student perceptions of the development of work readiness in Australian undergraduate programs. *Journal of College Student Development, 6*(2), 219–239.

Konstantinou, E. (2015). Professionalism in project management: Redefining the role of the project practitioner. *Project Management Journal, 46*(2), 21–35.

Lippman, L. H., Ryberg, R., Carney, R., & Moore, K. A. (2015). *Workforce connections: Key 'soft skills' that foster youth workforce success: Toward a consensus across fields*. Child Trends.

Masole, L., & van Dyk, G. (2016). Factors influencing work readiness of graduates: An exploratory study. *Journal of Psychology in Africa, 26*(1), 70–73.

McKevitt, D., Carbery, R., & Lyons, A. (2017). A profession but not a career? Work identity and career satisfaction in project management. *International Journal of Project Management, 35*(8), 1673–1682.

Prikshat, V., Nankervis, A., Priyono, S., Salleh, N., Connell, J., & Burgess, J. (2018). Graduate work readiness challenges in the Asia-Pacific region and the role of HRM. *Equality, Diversity and Inclusion: An International Journal, 37*(2), 121–137.

Schwab, K. (2016). *The fourth industrial revolution.* World Economic Forum.

Spanjaard, D., Hall, T., & Stegemann, N. (2018). Experiential learning: helping students to become 'career-ready'. *Australasian Marketing Journal, 26*(2), 163–171.

Vaz-Serra, P., & Mitcheltree H. (2020). Understanding the key master of construction project management graduate competencies required to meet industry needs in Australia. *International Journal of Construction Education and Research, 17*(3), 222–241.

11
Half Double methodology in a large EU-funded research and innovation project: half-way there or double trouble?

Liv Juul Nielsen, Ulrik Bak Kirk and Per Svejvig

OPENING PARAGRAPHS

Suppose you have been hired as a project management (PM) consultant for the EU-funded research and innovation project FEMaLe (Finding Endometriosis using Machine Learning). With your background of ten years' experience in leadership and organizational development positions, you have extensive knowledge in both traditional project management methodologies and the more agile approaches that are increasingly shaping the field. Prior to establishing your own consultancy firm, you have been employed in several large international companies and organizations. These roles have brought you into close collaboration with diverse sectors, including the technological industry, healthcare, and various research groups. In addition, your previous employments have given you personal experience of having low motivation in a project, and you have experienced first-hand how it affects performance in a project. With these insights, you are therefore considered to be the ideal candidate to tackle the challenges that the FEMaLe project is currently facing.

Until now, and already more than halfway through, the project has been running smoothly. However, results from the latest first- and second-quarter stakeholder and staff satisfaction survey, known as Pulse Checks, revealed problems with a lack of motivation and morale among project members, raising concerns about possible consequences of the low scores. Already, it has impacted on collaboration challenges and suboptimal service delivery, which are starting to threaten the stakeholder satisfaction and overall performance. To overcome this setback, the project management office (PMO) has initiated several mitigation actions to combat the negative trend. Among these initiatives, the FEMaLe coordinator has conducted individual evaluation meetings with key project participants, providing a space for honest feedback and concerns. Furthermore, the problem has been addressed in group meetings, encouraging open dialogue and the sharing of potential solutions. There has also been a heightened focus on the individual project participants' personal satisfaction and well-being. So far, however, the initiatives have not had the desired effect on the project members' satisfaction.

Therefore, the FEMaLe project needs fresh eyes, ears, and expertise to guide it through its final and most important phase. As a result, the PMO has decided to hire you as a PM consultant for three months. Your role will involve becoming an integrated part of the PMO team and assessing and evaluating the project's challenges as seen from an external position, as well as to provide recommendations to guide next steps, in close collaboration with the FEMaLe PMO. Over the next three months, you will conduct an in-depth analysis of the project's initiatives, establish an evaluation framework to assess their impact, and propose changes aimed at boosting motivation and morale among project members.

BODY OF THE CASE

Project Background

Finding Endometriosis using Machine Learning (FEMaLe) is an EU-funded research and innovation project, under the auspices of the Horizon 2020 program.[1] The project runs over a four-year period, from January 2021 to December 2024. In June 2023, the project was just over halfway through. FEMaLe involves 17 partners across nine European countries, and is coordinated by the Department of Public Health at Aarhus University in Denmark.

Key figures of the FEMaLe project (2023)

- Employee count: 40.
- Seventeen partners across nine European countries (Figure 11.1).
- Project coordinator: Aarhus University, Denmark.
- Total budget: €5,944,134.50

The FEMaLe project is researching the disease endometriosis, a chronic inflammatory disease characterized by lesions of endometrial-like tissue outside the uterus (Taylor et al., 2021; Zondervan et al., 2020). Living with endometriosis is, for many, associated with debilitating symptoms, such as pelvic pain, severe menstrual pain, and infertility (Seear, 2009). It is estimated that endometriosis affects one in ten of all individuals assigned female at birth worldwide (Fedele, 2021). This represents 190 million globally, making its prevalence similar to diabetes (MOGA, 2022). The World Health Organization recognizes the importance of endometriosis and its impact on people's reproductive health, well-being, and quality of life (World Health Organization, 2023).

Despite its high prevalence, the diagnosis of the disease can be delayed by up to 11 years from the first symptoms until the time of diagnosis (Agarwal et al., 2019). In addition, delivery of effective therapy and care is prolonged: a recent Danish study demonstrated that endometriosis is under-diagnosed, with only (up to) 2 percent of women receiving the correct

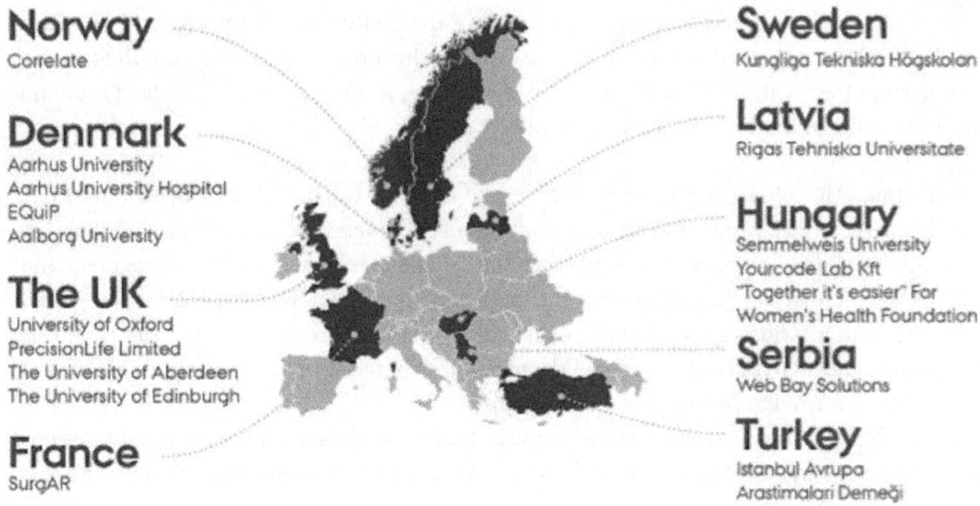

Source: Nielsen et al. (2023a).

Figure 11.1 FEMaLe partners

diagnosis, and a follow-up study revealed that people with endometriosis use the healthcare system 19 percent more than people without endometriosis, even ten years before they are diagnosed (Melgaard et al., 2023).

The diagnostic delay may be due to the societal normalization of pain and the stigmatization of women's health, which meanwhile leaves people with endometriosis living with significant physical (Hållstam et al., 2018), social (Fedele, 2021) and psychological (Gallagher et al., 2018; Rowlands et al., 2016) consequences.

Due to the severe pain, endometriosis is associated with significant absences from education as well as loss of productivity in the workplace, averaging 11 absent hours per week (Graaff et al., 2013). This has a major economic impact on society, with healthcare costs (surgery, monitoring tests, hospitalization, and doctor visits) and the annual cost of lost productivity estimated to be €9,579 per person with endometriosis (Simoens et al., 2012).

Despite this, endometriosis remains an under-recognized, under-prioritized, under-studied, and under-mentioned condition, and is highly affected by a lack of awareness from healthcare providers, families, and friends (Mirin, 2021; Nielsen et al., 2023b; Young et al., 2014). This is mainly due to a severe lack of research funding, in line with that for women's health in general (Smith, 2023).

To improve the overall quality of life of individuals living with endometriosis, the FEMaLe project will deliver a scalable multi-omics platform that converts multidimensional population datasets and feeds the information into an individualized predictive model, enabling a personalized pathway in primary and secondary care. The intention is to design, validate, and implement a comprehensive model for the detection and management of people with endometriosis to facilitate shared decision-making between the patient and the healthcare provider, enable the delivery of precision medicine, and drive new discoveries in endometriosis treatment to deliver novel therapies and improve the quality of life for patients (FEMaLe, 2023). Moreover, the project seeks to raise awareness, improve menstrual health literacy, and aiding empowerment, with the ultimate objective of improving the quality of life of individuals living with endometriosis. To achieve this, the project aims to:

1. Estimate the actual prevalence, incidence, and geographical distribution of endometriosis.
2. Identify, validate, and refine genetic subtypes of endometriosis to stratify individuals into high- and low-risk patient groups, contributing to the realization of precision medicine.
3. Develop an advanced period-tracker mobile health app (Lucy), designed for individuals with endometriosis to track their menstrual cycles and learn more about the condition; collect and analyze citizen-generated and patient-shared data to identify possible lifestyle patterns related to subtypes of endometriosis.
4. Develop a computer vision-based software tool for real-time augmented reality-guided surgery for endometriosis that enables automatic detection of endometriosis during laparoscopy when operating.
5. Produce a validated digital version of the mindfulness- and acceptance-based program MY ENDO to empower patients to gain knowledge and develop coping strategies to improve their mental health.

The FEMaLe project includes ten work packages (WPs), shown in Figure 11.2, each focusing on different areas and fields of research and innovation, including epidemiology, genetics, digital mental health, machine learning, augmented reality in surgery, responsible research and innovation, open science and data, communication, policy, project management, dissemination, and exploitation of results. To support this, the FEMaLe project team is diverse in expertise and experience. It includes interdisciplinary researchers, patients, surgeons, software engineers, advanced computer scientists, and more.

Together, this contributes to a high level of complexity in the FEMaLe project, which is why the Half Double methodology (HDM), a hybrid PM framework, was selected and implemented from the beginning of the project. This choice was made to ensure dynamic project leadership and promote an agile approach across different disciplines. To maintain the effectiveness of this methodology, dedicated funds have been allocated for the entire duration of the project. This means that throughout the project, the impacts of the tools and practices used from HDM will be continuously tracked, monitored, and evaluated. HDM serves as a robust foundation to navigate the complex journey of the project, promoting agility and flexibility as it progresses and ensuring that the project stays on the path to success.

The Half Double Methodology

For decades, research projects have been dominated by traditional project management. The focus and goals have centered around delivering outputs and products (Atkinson, 1999), with an emphasis on timely delivery, within a specified budget, and with a certain level of quality, also known as the "iron triangle" (Andersen, 2008). However, we now know that

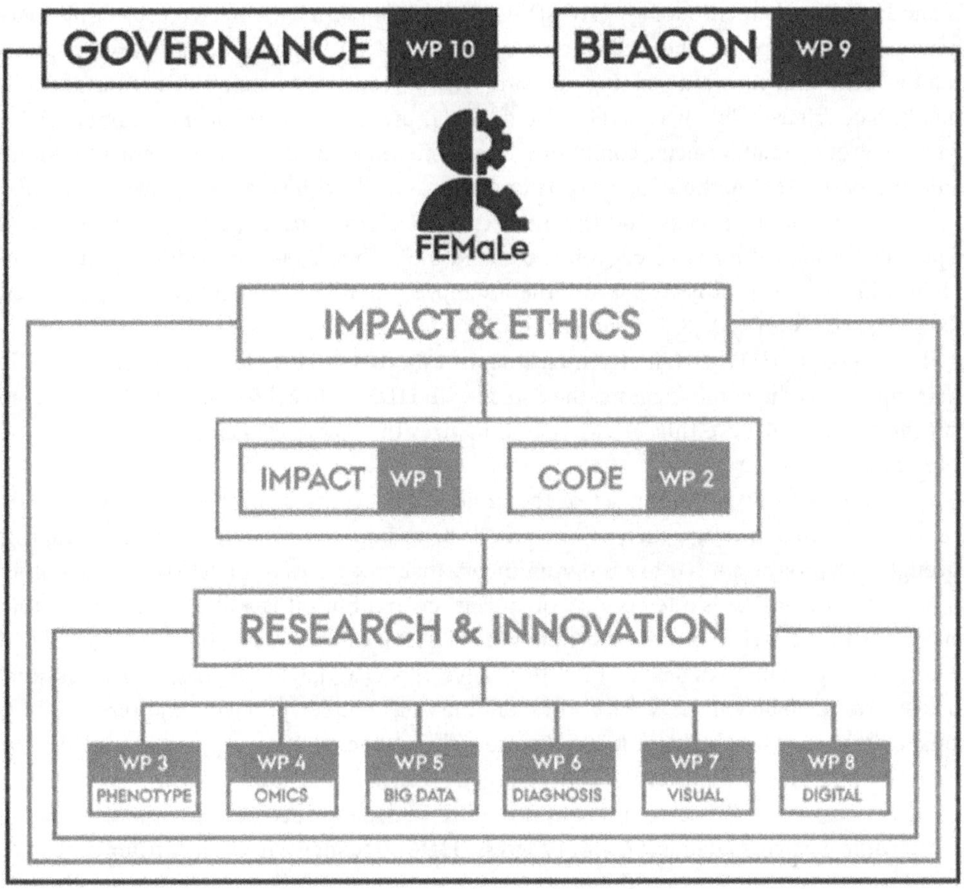

Source: Nielsen et al. (2023a).

Figure 11.2 The ten FEMaLe work packages

delivering a product does not necessarily create value for an organization or project (Winter & Szczepanek, 2008), which makes it problematic to focus solely on product creation.

Today's projects have become more complex, with no immediately obvious solutions, and unpredictable outcomes (Svejvig et al., 2019). We see an increasing expectation to deliver results faster, and projects are expected to bring major change within strict time frames (Svejvig et al., 2019). Therefore, traditional project management, based on the iron triangle, is rarely considered sufficient to address these challenges alone. It is essential to adapt to a new understanding of our society and project management (Half Double Institute, 2022). Innovative solutions are needed to manage the complexity of research projects today. In recent years, we have seen a shift in focus from delivery to impact, rapid learning, and responsiveness, as well as certification and competency development of project managers and employees (Olsson et al., 2019).

The Half Double methodology (HDM) is an example of an agile hybrid project management model that supports the realization of a project with an emphasis on early value creation in a turbulent and constantly changing world, where focusing on stakeholder satisfaction is the ultimate criterion for success (Half Double Institute, 2022). HDM offers a framework for complex project management, combining classic methods of project management with an agile approach. As a methodology, HDM attempts to work with rather than against the new understanding of our society and the projects we work in. Building on solid research and experience from several large organizations and more than 2,000 practitioners, the methodology aims to help projects capture the untapped potential through concrete principles, methods, and tools (Rode & Svejvig, 2023).

The purpose of HDM is to find a model that can shorten project lifespans while increasing their impact. As the name suggests, the core idea in HDM is to achieve *double* the impact in *half* the time. To achieve this, HDM operationalizes three core elements: *impact*, *flow*, and *leadership*.

The primary focus is the impact of the project: what impact and behavioral change do we want to realize through the project? HDM views impact as a series of smaller impacts throughout a project, similar to a program theory that progresses from deliverables to output to impact.[2] The project is a temporary organization, and impact is realized after the output has been handed over to operations (Ehlers et al., 2018). Consequently, impact is considered to be more important than deliverables. To achieve impact as quickly as possible, it is essential to ensure a stable flow in the project. Responding to a complex problem requires creativity, collaboration, and fast feedback loops. The flow element acts as the engine that provides the motivation to drive and realize the desired impact (Ehlers et al., 2018). This flow is created by the project manager's leadership. Projects require leadership that embraces societal uncertainty while ensuring adaptation and progress. HDM operates with a shift from control to trust, involvement, and ownership for all project members as well as employing a collaborative leadership approach (Olsson et al., 2022).

Therefore, impact, flow, and leadership serve as the three core elements of the methodology, and each core element is supported by three dedicated tools that can be implemented into the project. The nine tools are further elaborated in Table 11.1.[3]

To fully comply with HDM, the nine tools should be utilized as widely as possible across the project. Each tool comes with a set of methods that can be adapted to the organization's own needs, that is, local translation (Olsson et al., 2022). There is no one-size-fits-all, which is why it is necessary to think and act in terms of a project approach that includes the influence and impact of the environment and can adapt accordingly. When implementing HDM, local translation holds paramount importance, ensuring that the hybrid agile approach, together with the organization, contributes to realizing early value. Local translation is an integrated part of the HDM framework; it surrounds the three core elements, as illustrated in Figure 11.3. Thus, it helps a project tap into what is already there, such as existing language, practices, and tools, to ease implementation (Half Double Institute, 2022).

Table 11.1 Description of the nine HDM tools

Core element	Tool	Description of tool
Impact	Impact Case	A road map of the project's business and behavioral impacts, serving to establish a shared understanding of the specific impacts the project aims to achieve, along with their logical interdependencies.
Impact	Impact Solution Design	The tool is human centered, learning focused and hypothesis driven, aiming to help projects achieve early impact and reduce uncertainty through a series of workshops with key stakeholders.
Impact	Pulse Check	An electronic questionnaire of six questions, distributed regularly to key stakeholders, serving as a foundation for continuous feedback dialogue. The tool is used to monitor satisfaction levels in real time, which enables proactive adjustments of the project's processes, based on important insights and emerging learnings.
Flow	Co-Location	The core team should allocate at least 50% of their time to the project and ensure co-location to reduce complexity in both time and space, as this will free up time to solve complex problems.
Flow	Visual Planning	Utilize visual planning for rapid prototyping, facilitating group sessions, and sprint planning to increase project tangibility. Can be created physically and/or virtually.
Flow	Rhythm in Key Events	Establish and adhere to a set rhythm of six key events: sprint planning, daily visual status updates, weekly solution feedback, planning for the next week, reviewing the sprint solution, and gathering pulse check feedback.
Leadership	Active Ownership Approach	The active project owner works closely with the PM and steering committee to ensure the project's success, dedicating at least half a day every two weeks.
Leadership	Collaborative Leadership Approach	Collaborative project management entails leading a complex system of people, embracing the inevitable uncertainty, and making the project successful.
Leadership	Reflective and Adaptive Mindset	To function and succeed in an unpredictable and chaotic environment, the PM and project owner must be able to say yes to the mess and adapt to the changing environment. The focus is on understanding and acting on changing stakeholder behavior on an ongoing basis.

Introducing HDM to the FEMaLe Project

The introduction of HDM to the FEMaLe project aimed to establish a shared and standardized methodology while reducing the time required to produce results and outputs. As stated, the HDM was designed to assist project members to complete tasks more effectively, reduce complexity, and foster collaboration with others through a common language. Moreover, the aim was to realize faster impact and support employees with creating clear structures and keeping an overview.

To kick-start the implementation of HDM, a handful of FEMaLe project members became certified at the Half Double foundation level. They took part in an intense three-day training

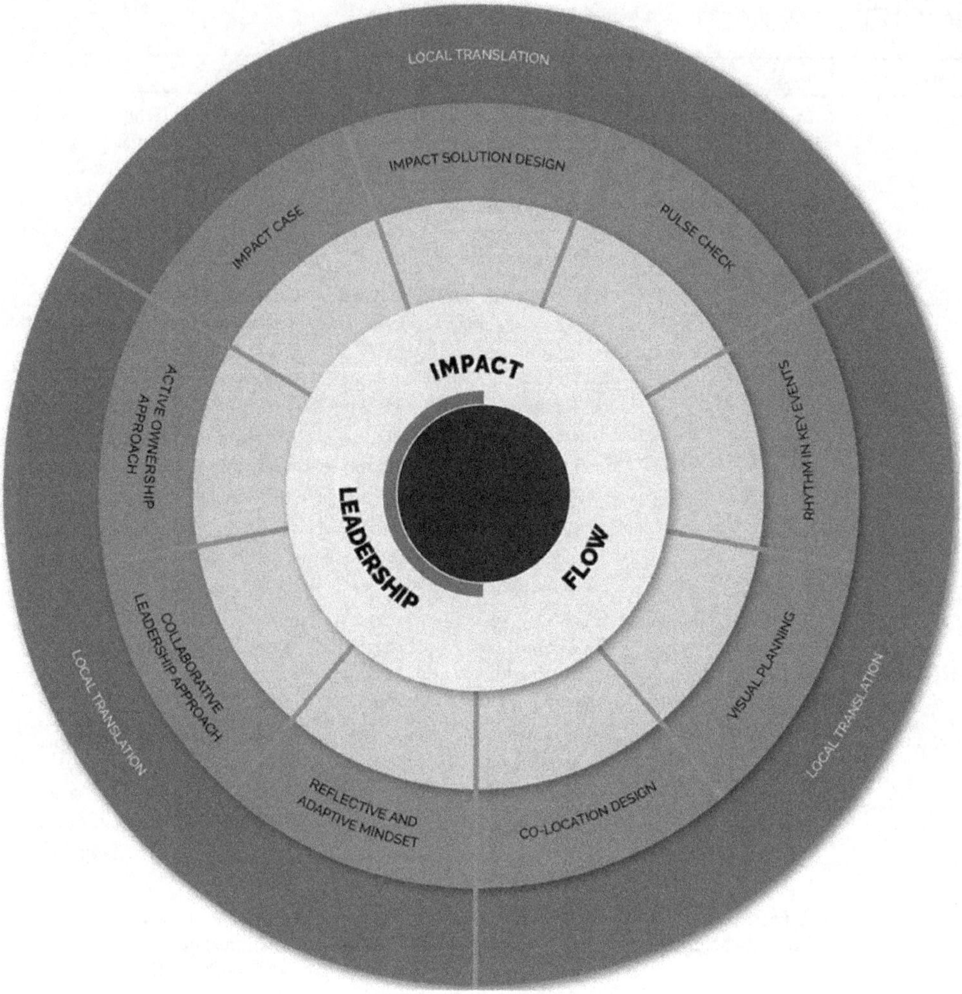

Source: Svejvig P. (2025).

Figure 11.3 The Half Double methodology

course and were introduced to the three core elements as well as the nine methods and tools of HDM. After this, all 17 project partners were introduced to HDM from the very beginning of the FEMaLe project in online workshops as well as WP-level-specific training sessions to increase capacity.

Further, the FEMaLe coordinator undertook Half Double practitioner training, which included a one-day booster course. As part of the certification process, the FEMaLe coordinator compiled a reflection report, documenting real-life experiences and insights gained from working with the Half Double methodology in the FEMaLe project. The final certification exam involved a one-hour interview, based on the report, with an external assessor.

Following the introduction of the theories and principles of HDM to the project, the FEMaLe's flow was established, based on the tool Rhythm in Key Events, by inviting each of the ten WP teams to individual online workshops at the beginning of each new cycle (ranging from six months to a year), where they co-produce their Impact Case. During these workshops, relevant sub-goals and KPIs (key performance indicators) were defined together to keep an overview and to ensure that they would only perform, target, and track value-creating activities. Further, the Impact Case workshops contributed to building shared understandings of HDM as well as offering a safe space for discussing terms and concepts, which required local translations to the research context in particular.

At the end of each cycle, starting with Impact Case workshops per WP, Constructive Evaluation is conducted in the shape of structured online interviews to track the progress of the individual WP and evaluate the use of the HDM tools and methods. The evaluation draws on a multidimensional framework (Rode et al., 2022) and includes 17 questions related to the three core HDM elements (impact, flow, and leadership). At each constructive interview, participants discuss the questions and indicate, with a score from 1 to 4, the extent to which they have applied each of the nine HDM tools. The evaluation involves participation from both the WP leader and the FEMaLe coordinator, and each session lasts approximately two hours (on Zoom).

Between the Impact Case workshops and the Constructive Evaluations, the rhythm of the FEMaLe project consists of alternating bi-monthly consortium meetings and executive board (EB) meetings. The FEMaLe EB serves as the governance body responsible for project-related matters, and it comprises the ten WP leaders, the project manager, the project owner, additional members of the PMO, and any relevant FEMaLe advisory board members upon request.

During the consortium meetings, a WP representative for each of the ten WPs gives a short status update on the KPIs, as defined in the Impact Case. Possible mitigation actions are discussed in a plenary whenever needed. During the EB meetings, all the appointed representatives discuss project-related matters, such as the deployment of strategies, the involvement of stakeholders, reallocation of resources, and so on.

To data-guide the ten WP leaders in EB decisions, Pulse Checks (one of the three Impact tools) is used regularly. Pulse Checks allow project members to monitor the satisfaction level of key stakeholders each month, enabling them to proactively adjust processes in real time. Pulse Checks have been conducted using an online questionnaire with five (later expanded to six) standard questions, which forms the basis for an ongoing feedback mechanism, followed by dialogue. The questions are aligned with the recommendations from the Half Double Institute, where participants respond, on a Likert scale from 1 to 5, to the following questions:

1. Are you confident that your current work is creating impact for the project?
2. Do we deliver and collaborate effectively on the project?
3. Do you have good fun and energy working on the project?
4. Are you getting the support and feedback you need?
5. Are you developing personally and professionally working on the project?

6. All in all; are you convinced that this project is executed more effectively and with more focus on impact than other projects?

Through the results of these six questions, the "pulse" of project members can be followed over time. This approach facilitates timely adjustments to project workflows, based on the feedback and needs of the stakeholders. The use of the remaining tools is described in Table 11.2.[4]

How to get Project Members' Motivation and Energy Back on Track

In the first half of the FEMaLe project (2021–2022), stakeholder satisfaction overall was very high and steady. Participants in project meetings displayed positivity as well as high levels

Table 11.2 Description of the local translations of the nine HDM tools

Tool	Local translation	Local transition
Impact	Impact Case	Annual workshops are held with all ten WPs to collectively co-produce the Impact Case. This offers a prioritized overview of the project's business and behavioral objectives aimed to create project value.
Impact	Impact Solution Design	FEMaLe runs a series of workshops with each of the ten WPs to monitor impact. Moreover, progress on agreed tasks and KPIs are presented at bi-monthly consortium meetings as well as FEMaLe's executive board meetings.
Impact	Pulse Check	A monthly online questionnaire is shared with key stakeholders, and the results are the basis for ongoing feedback dialogue, creating an opportunity to proactively adjust the project according to actual needs.
Flow	Co-Location	The FEMaLe coordinator works 50% in the project and shares workspace with the other leaders of WP1, WP3 and WP8 at Aarhus University. In general, most FEMaLe project members work less than 50% in the project.
Flow	Visual Planning	Due to geographical distances and cross-border activities, visual planning is highly utilized in the project, including conducting online meetings, workshops, and interviews.
Flow	Rhythm in Key Events	The rhythm is primarily driven by the 65 deliverables and 21 milestones required for submission to the European Commission. Further, the project adheres to a fixed rhythm during project meetings.
Leadership	Active Ownership Approach	The regular rhythm in meetings facilitates interaction between the PO, the PM, the PMO, and the entire team, establishing a foundation for active participation.
Leadership	Collaborative Leadership Approach	A people-first approach is used to drive the project forward in close collaboration. The FEMaLe coordinator has regular one to one dialogue with key FEMaLe members.
Leadership	Reflective and Adaptive Mindset	The project has been heavily impacted by Covid-19, posing challenges to workspaces.

of energy and motivation, both in their own tasks and those set by the FEMaLe PMO group. These observations were supported by Pulse Check results, which maintained an average mean score of at least 4 out of 5 points in the first half of the project. The baseline 2021 average mean was 3.96, followed by four 2021 Pulse Checks ranging from 4.14 to 4.26 on average, in addition to the six 2022 Pulse Checks ranging from 4.26 to 4.30 on average for the first version with five questions.

However, there was a new trend in the data in the first half of 2023, with a significantly lower average mean Pulse Check score, ranging from 4.13 to 4.17 for six questions. FEMaLe project participants reported that delivery and collaboration felt less effective as a whole, they had less fun and energy working on the project, and they were not receiving the support and feedback they needed. This trend was also reflected in the project's group meetings, where some WPs were making less progress, there were cancellations at FEMaLe meetings, and people were less active and asked fewer questions at meetings.

This emerging trend raised concerns, as demotivated members are very likely to affect the project's ability to create value and drive impact. Indeed, some effects of this situation were already being witnessed. Likewise, we know from literature that lack of motivation in a project affects employees' performance, even though they are skilled (Vo et al., 2022). In fact, lack of motivation among project members can determine whether or not a project will succeed or fail (Wallström et al., 2012).

Following the identification of this negative trend, the PMO initiated a series of mitigation actions to get project members' motivation and energy levels back on track. As the project enters its second half and final phase, the project members take great pride in their commitment to delivering efficiently to maximize impact, based on research results and innovations. To foster positive relations and collaborations, drive early value creation and lasting impact, it is vital that project members find pride and joy in their work as well as regain motivation and maintain high levels of energy.

Based on the poor Pulse Check results of March 2023 (4.13 on average), the FEMaLe coordinator organized individual evaluation meetings with all project participants in April 2023 to create space for honest feedback and concerns. Afterwards, problems were discussed in group meetings, encouraging open dialogue and the sharing of potential solutions. There has further been a heightened focus on individual project participants' personal satisfaction and well-being.

Despite these efforts, however, the many meetings and dialogues have not had the desired short-term effect, as seen in the Pulse Check results of May 2023 (4.17 on average), indicating still-low satisfaction levels. Thus, innovative external expertise is required to change this course and guide the project safely through its final and most important phase.

CONCLUDING PARAGRAPHS

This case stems from a real-world problem in the research and innovation FEMaLe project, which is characterized by its complexity due to its difficult area of research (endometriosis), the divergent project team, and the interdisciplinary research and innovation actions carried out. To navigate this complexity, an agile, hybrid project management framework (HDM) was implemented from the beginning, to continuously guide and support the project in the right direction.

One HDM tool has been particularly utilized, namely Pulse Checks, enabling project members to provide regular feedback, using a Likert scale from 1 to 5. This allows FEMaLe's PMO to continuously track the overall satisfaction levels of key stakeholders in the project. Now, at the halfway point of the project, the monthly Pulse Checks have revealed a negative trend that project members are less motivated working on the project, and they perceive that the delivery and collaboration effectiveness has declined. Thus, the PMO is concerned about the impact on the overall performance and success of the project.

Therefore, the FEMaLe project needs fresh eyes, ears, and expertise to guide it through its final and most important phase. As a result, the PMO has decided to hire you as a consultant for a duration of three months. You will assess and evaluate the project's challenges as seen from an external position, as well as provide recommendations to guide next steps, in close collaboration with the PMO. As the new PM consultant for the FEMaLe project, your responsibility will be to recommend strategies to improve the motivation of project members and ensure the effective delivery of project results during the final period. During this period, you are required to develop a plan for conducting an in-depth analysis of the project's initiatives, establishing an evaluation framework to assess their impact, and proposing changes aimed at boosting motivation and morale among project members.

DISCUSSION QUESTIONS

1. What effective strategies can regain motivation in a project? Are there specific tools you are aware of that could be relevant to introduce to the FEMaLe project? How can we improve the level of energy and motivation of project members working in a complex project?
2. Drawing from your previous expertise, how would you consider the impact of the initiatives that the FEMaLe project's PMO has already implemented? Do you deem them sufficient, or should they be supplemented or replaced by other initiatives?
3. Based on your previous reflections, you are asked to conduct an in-depth analysis of the project's existing initiatives and propose new initiatives. Your initiatives should consider the following:

   - What is the intended purpose of each initiative?
   - Who will be responsible for implementing each initiative?
   - In what context(s) will each initiative be most effective? (Consider this from the perspective of program theory or impact case theory.)
   - Which project participants will be affected by these initiatives?
   - Are there any external or internal partners required to execute these initiatives?
   - How will you introduce and implement each initiative within the FEMaLe project? (Outline a step-by-step plan.)

4. Following the implementation of these initiatives, consider how you will establish an evaluation framework at the end of your three months' consultancy. What are the potential advantages and disadvantages of the initiatives you have proposed? As a consultant, how will you evaluate the impact of these initiatives?

NOTES

1. ID: 101017562. https://findingendometriosis.eu
2. For further literature on program theory, please refer to Rogers & Funnell (2013).
3. For a further explanation of the tools, please refer to Ehlers et al. (2018).
4. For a more detailed description of the project's implementation of Half Double, please see Nielsen et al. (2022).

REFERENCES AND FURTHER READING

Agarwal, S. K., Chapron, C., Giudice, L. C., Laufer, M. R., Leyland, N., Missmer, S. A., Singh, S. S., & Taylor, H. S. (2019). Clinical diagnosis of endometriosis: A call to action. *American Journal of Obstetrics and Gynecology, 220*(4), 354.e1-354.e12.

Andersen, E. S. (2008). *Rethinking project management: An organisational perspective*. FT Prentice Hall.

Atkinson, R. (1999). Project management: Cost, time and quality, two best guesses and a phenomenon, its time to accept other success criteria. *International Journal of Project Management, 17*(6), 337–342.

Ehlers, M., Adland, K. T., Olsson, J. R., & Ahrengot, N. (2018). *Half Double: Projects in half the time with double the impact* (2nd ed.). Implement.

Fedele, F. (2021). An overview on the psychological impact of endometriosis on adolescent girls' life. *Women's Health Bulletin, 8*(4).

FEMaLe. (2023). *FEMaLe project*. https://findingendometriosis.eu

Gallagher, J. S., DiVasta, A. D., Vitonis, A. F., Sarda, V., Laufer, M. R., & Missmer, S. A. (2018). The impact of endometriosis on quality of life in adolescents. *The Journal of Adolescent Health: Official Publication of the Society for Adolescent Medicine, 63*(6), 766–772.

Graaff, A. A., D'Hooghe, T. M., Dunselman, G. A. J., Dirksen, C. D., Hummelshoj, L., Simoens, S., Bokor, A., Horne, A. W., & Wullschleger, M. (2013). The significant effect of endometriosis on physical, mental and social wellbeing: Results from an international cross-sectional survey. *Human Reproduction, 28*(10), 2677–2685.

Half Double Institute. (2022). *Half Double Methodology Foundation Guide & Handbook Set*. Van Haren Publishing. www.vanharen.store/half-double-methodology-foundation-guide-handbook-set

Hållstam, A., Stålnacke, Bm., Svensén, C., & Löfgren, M. (2018). Living with painful endometriosis – a struggle for coherence: A qualitative study. *Sexual & Reproductive Healthcare, 17*, 97–102.

Melgaard, A., Vestergaard, C. H., Kesmodel, U. S., Risør, B. W., Forman, A., Zondervan, K., Bech, B. H., & Rytter, D. (2023). Utilization of healthcare prior to endometriosis diagnosis: A Danish case-control study. *Human Reproduction*, dead164.

Mirin, A. A. (2021). Gender disparity in the funding of diseases by the U.S. National Institutes of Health. *Journal of Women's Health, 30*(7), 956–963.

MOGA. (2022, March 31). *Raising endometriosis awareness*. Memphis Obstetrics & Gynecological Association. https://mogamd.com/raising-endometriosis-awareness

Nielsen, L. J., Kirk, U. B., & Zhu, T. (2022). *Project Half Double case study: Project FEMaLe*. Half Double Institute. https://halfdoubleinstitute.org/sites/default/files/2024-08/20220324%20Case%20study%20-%20FEMaLe%20project.pdf

Nielsen, L. J., Kirk, U. B., Zhu, T., & Svejvig, P. (2023a, June 14). *How agile practices change over time in a large EU-funded research and innovation project* [Conference presentation]. EURAM 2023 Conference, Trinity Business School, Dublin.

Nielsen, L. J., Poulsen, K., Funch, A. L., & Petersen, K. S. (2023b). The lived experiences of endometriosis in adolescence: A critical hermeneutic perspective. *Scandinavian Journal of Caring Sciences*, scs.13176.

Olsson, J. R., Adland, K. T., Ehlers, M., Ahrengot, N., Aalbæk, J., Ruth, T. K., & Kærn, E. F. (2022). *Half Double methodology foundation guide: Version 1.0.* Half Double Institute.

Olsson, J. R., Ahrengot, N., & Attrup, M. L. (2019). *Power i projekter og portefølje* [Power in projects and portfolio] (4. udgave). Djøf.

Rode, A., & Svejvig, P. (2021). *Designing a project evaluation framework.* [Conference paper]. European Academy of Management, Montréal.

Rode, A. L. G., & Svejvig, P. (2023). *Project Half Double: Evaluation of Phase 3 and consolidation of Phases 1, 2, and 3.* Aarhus University.

Rode, A. L. G., Svejvig, P., & Martinsuo, M. (2022). Developing a multidimensional conception of project evaluation to improve projects. *Project Management Journal, 53*(4), 416–432.

Rogers, P. J., & Funnell, S. C. (2013). *Purposeful program theory: Effective use of theories of change and logic models.* Jossey-Bass.

Rowlands, I. J., Teede, H., Lucke, J., Dobson, A. J., & Mishra, G. D. (2016). Young women's psychological distress after a diagnosis of polycystic ovary syndrome or endometriosis. *Human Reproduction, 31*(9), 2072–2081.

Seear, K. (2009). The etiquette of endometriosis: Stigmatisation, menstrual concealment and the diagnostic delay. *Social Science & Medicine, 69*(8), 1220–1227.

Simoens, S., Dunselman, G., Dirksen, C., Hummelshøj, L., Attila, B., Brandes, I., Brodszky, V., Canis, M., & Colombo, G. L. (2012). The burden of endometriosis: Costs and quality of life of women with endometriosis and treated in referral centres. *Human Reproduction, 27*(5), 1292–1299.

Smith, K. (2023). Women's health research lacks funding: These charts show how. *Nature, 617*(7959), 28–29.

Svejvig, P., A. Kock and L. K. Hansen (2025). "How Successful Are Principles-Based Project Management Methodologies?" IEEE Transactions on Engineering Management 72: 2831-2847.

Svejvig, P., Geraldi, J., & Grex, S. (2019). Accelerating time to impact: Deconstructing practices to achieve project value. *International Journal of Project Management, 37*(7), 784–801.

Taylor, H. S., Kotlyar, A. M., & Flores, V. A. (2021). Endometriosis is a chronic systemic disease: Clinical challenges and novel innovations. *The Lancet, 397*(10276), 839–852.

Vo, T. T. D., Tuliao, K. V., & Chen, C.-W. (2022). Work motivation: The roles of individual needs and social conditions. *Behavioral Sciences, 12*(2), 49. https://doi.org/10.3390/bs12020049

Wallström, H., Ridderheim, Y., Påhlson, E., Åkesson, E., & Landgren, H. (2012). *Motivational triggers in projects: A comparative study of the construction and consulting industries.* [Conference paper]. PMI® Research and Education Conference, Limerick. Newtown Square, PA: Project Management Institute. www.pmi.org/learning/library/motivational-triggers-projects-6365

Winter, M., & Szczepanek, T. (2008). Projects and programmes as value creation processes: A new perspective and some practical implications. *International Journal of Project Management, 26*(1), 95–103.

World Health Organization. (2023). *Endometriosis—Fact sheets.* www.who.int/news-room/fact-sheets/detail/endometriosis

Young, K., Fisher, J., & Kirkman, M. (2014). Women's experiences of endometriosis: A systematic review and synthesis of qualitative research. *Journal of Family Planning and Reproductive Health Care, 41*(3), 225–234.

Zondervan, K. T., Becker, C. M., & Missmer, S. A. (2020). Endometriosis. *New England Journal of Medicine, 382*(13), 1244–1256.

PART III
BUSINESS ACUMEN

12
Navigating the tides of transformation: Natalia's quest for a project management office

Sanaa El Boukri and Monique Aubry

OPENING PARAGRAPHS

The pandemic context, which significantly affected the progress of projects within the local health care system, much like elsewhere in the world, must be taken into account from the outset (Lavoie-Tremblay et al., 2022). For example, those authors found that nurses caring for Covid-19 patients experienced high levels of chronic fatigue and perceived a decline in the quality of care they were able to provide to patients, lower job satisfaction, and a higher intention to leave their organization. For almost all countries, Covid left health care organizations in a worse state than before the pandemic: suffering from the lack of personnel along with the increase in the aging and vulnerable patients. The pandemic also meant that many urgent constructions or modernization projects were delayed, if not abandoned. Eventually, in the fall of 2022, many activities in the health sector were resumed, including projects.

The projects for health care company REORG, for example, were very much affected by Covid (especially in construction), as many of the people involved in these projects were required elsewhere in the clinical units. These projects had been started before the pandemic and were responding to urgent needs at that time. After the pandemic, the urgency became even greater. For example, one of the construction projects was a care home for older residents. The "House for the Elderly" was a cutting-edge facility designed to provide older individuals with a conducive environment for receiving health care services. This project, conceived prior to the onset of the Covid pandemic, gained heightened relevance in the wake of global health challenges, underscoring the imperative of modernizing health care infrastructure to meet evolving demands.

BODY OF THE CASE

Introduction to the Organization

REORG has a total of 18,000 employees and 20 departments. Its mission is to provide local, integrated, and accessible health and social services to individuals and their families in North America. It aims to contribute to improving the overall health of the population in its territory. Focused on quality, safety, and performance, care and services are grounded in best practices, innovation, and the involvement of users and their families. It mobilizes and coordinates local networks to meet the needs of its entire population.

Affiliated with a university and in collaboration with educational institutions, it ensures high-quality education and develops cutting-edge knowledge and practices. It also promotes the sharing and dissemination of scientific and clinical knowledge to contribute to the improvement of the quality of care and services provided.

REORG aspires to be a recognized leader for the excellence and accessibility of its care and services, to earn the trust of its partners and the population, and to be an inspirational academic organization for staff, physicians, and researchers. REORG is grounded in its actions by the following five organizational values: benevolence, respect, collaboration, empowerment, and audacity. Benevolence is exemplified through relationships guided by the pursuit of the well-being of all individuals involved. Respect is characterized by recognizing the capacity for action in every person, treating them with dignity, and esteeming their worth. Collaboration is demonstrated by the commitment of individuals working at REORG to engage within work teams and to include users, their loved ones, and partners as fully fledged members, all working towards a common objective. Empowerment is evident through diligence and accountability, contributing to the realization of the institution's mission while remaining focused on the user's experience and the needs of the user and their loved ones. Finally, audacity is manifested through a proactive attitude towards change and the ability to seize opportunities while displaying creativity, innovation, and courage.

REORG has in its portfolio approximately 600 projects in three categories: large projects, regular projects, and IT projects (see Figure A12.1). The IT projects are under the direct responsibility of the IT department, while the other two categories are under the technical department, where project directors and project management are grouped.

The Call to Action

It's 5:30 p.m., Natalia sits at her desk. Everyone else is back home. While Natalia is reflecting on the future of the PMO (project management office), she reminds herself of all the steps she made over the last year.

Natalia has been a project director in her technical department since 2015. She began her career as a nurse. Her interest in management, particularly project management, emerged over a decade ago. Since then, she has held various positions in the health care system, almost always in the field of project management. Her primary focus lies in coordinating project portfolios and PMOs.

After the Covid pandemic, a new general director (Jamie) was very much focused on the organization's performance in line with the health ministry's orientations. Recognizing the potential for significant improvement in current project management practices to enhance overall strategic performance, Natalia finds herself in a bustling organization with 20 departments and a workforce of 18,000. Over the past two years, she has served as the project director, seeing major projects through numerous challenges. Her journey has been punctuated by a seemingly insurmountable number of projects, a lack of efficient project management, and an organizational structure where chaos and confusion often trumped clarity and progress.

The myriad of questions that plagued Natalia's mind fuelled her desire for change. Her organization was at a critical juncture,[1] and the absence of a PMO only added to the conundrum. "We can do better," Natalia thought, as she was unable to ignore the need for an organization overhaul. The lack of competent project managers became evident as she observed that the current human resources processes were not yielding the right profiles. In fact, Natalia clearly recognized the technical and clinical skills of her colleagues, their sensitivities, and expectations regarding project objectives. However, what was primarily lacking were the essential project management skills necessary, among other things, to break down silos, communicate effectively, enhance project visibility, and facilitate collaboration between departments.

The existing project tracking and monitoring systems were inadequate. Color-coded indicators were used to gauge progress, but they provided little informative substance. There were no retrospectives, no feedback loops, and escalations to the steering committee were met with deafening silence. The situation begged the questions: "How could they manage a sprawling portfolio of projects? How could they align these endeavours with the overarching strategic goals?"

These questions have highlighted new needs relating to the processes and ways of doing project management and the project governance components. Natalia was aware of the skills that exist in terms of project planning, but did they reflect the appropriate profiles in project management? Through these questions, new reflections arose, notably in the necessary roles and responsibilities and the limits of their decision-making scope.

Seeking Guidance from the Wise

Determined to bring about transformation, Natalia embarked on a journey of self-improvement. This quest led her to two experts in the realm of project management –Kate and Joanna. Kate is a project management professor with over 25 years' professional and extensive research experience, renowned for her prominence within the scientific community. Similarly, Joanna is a project management professor in the health care field, also recognized for her research in project management and involvement in clinical settings. These individuals, with their wealth of experience, became Natalia's lifelines in a world where she had little formal training.

Encountered in fall 2020, during presentations on project management in a health care environment, Kate and Joanna shared their knowledge, which caught Natalia's attention. Convinced of the value and opportunity to participate in the process of improving internal project management practices, she later said, "They helped me go further with their experience in project management."

From 2020 to 2023, Kate and Joanna, her newfound mentors, were instrumental in guiding Natalia. She shared with them the progress of her discussions with her boss regarding the establishment of the PMO. The outcome of these discussions pertained to the form, structure, positioning, and functions of the PMO in alignment with REORG's intentions and its strategic mission, encompassing possible project governance modes, executive committee challenges, and the requirements of other departments. In the summer of 2023, with the assistance of her mentors, Natalia prepared a presentation to move forward with this concept (see Table A12.1).

They instilled in her the significance of the PMO – a dedicated entity that could oversee project portfolios, streamline decision-making, and improve PM practices (facilitate coordination between portfolios, programs, and projects; develop and implement a standard management cycle, methodology, and tools; foster the development of competencies, their capitalization, and an increase in project management maturity, following standards and best practices; promote PM within the organization; provide support to the entire hierarchical structure of the organization, from senior management to day-to-day operations).

While Natalia lacked formal project management education, she quickly realized the tremendous potential that a PMO could offer. As she delved into the world of PM, she gained a deeper understanding of the various PMO types and roles, and their impact on an organization. She understood the importance of aligning projects with strategic objectives, governance significance, and the need to prevent power struggles and conflicts arising from inadequate planning.

Using knowledge she had learned from Kate, Natalia grasped that the PMO's responsibilities can range from supporting project management functions to directly managing one or more projects; a structure that standardizes project governance processes and facilitates the sharing of resources, methodologies, tools, and techniques among projects. Kate emphasized the variety of functions that a PMO can have (support, center of excellence, passive, advisory, centralized, services). Natalia would remember it for a long time: "As Kate said, the PMO is the power."

It becomes increasingly apparent that the success and effectiveness of the organization's portfolios, programs, and individual projects are intricately linked to the role of the PMO. Beyond mere oversight, the PMO serves as the linchpin that connects strategic objectives with on-the-ground project execution. By strategically aligning portfolios and programs with overarching organizational goals, the PMO ensures that every project undertaken contributes meaningfully to the broader mission and vision of the organization. This alignment not only optimizes resource allocation and enhances risk management, it also fosters a cohesive and synergistic approach to project delivery.

Natalia took on more significant projects and, along with the newly appointed senior management, started discussing the establishment of a PMO. This involved negotiations regarding responsibilities, positioning, decision-making, and alignment with strategic goals.

At REORG, projects are managed via the quality and performance evaluation and ethics departments. Establishing the PMO could be a complex process that involved clarifying roles, approval processes, and alignment with the organization's strategic objectives. It required the organization's top management to believe in the concept, which Natalia considered a stroke of luck due to the allocation of $350,000 for an upcoming portfolio management system which would go out to tender in the coming weeks. Natalia considered herself fortunate to be allocated this amount, especially in this challenging context.

In the following weeks, Natalia was allocated three senior advisors to assist her in advancing her project. They worked on establishing the PMO's service offering (see Figure A12.2), which is a work in progress at the same level as the acquisition of the project portfolio management system; the development of the official portfolio tracking and update process; the establishment of the project steering committee; the implementation of key performance indicators for organizational projects; and the communication plan.

In this service offering, Natalia promises that the PMO would be able to deliver an organizational project portfolio planned for the short, medium, and long term (based on the duration of selected projects and the capacity of the departments), and scheduling of projects over time, based on capacity with an overview of the teams involved in the implementation of selected organizational projects.

Initiating the Transformation

Eight months later, armed with new knowledge and perspectives, Natalia knew it was time for change. Jamie, the general director, who shared her enthusiasm for project management, arrived on the scene. A discussion ensued about the possibility of establishing a PMO, particularly keeping in mind the internal stakeholders expected to accept this project. By leveraging her credibility and influence with the REORG departments, Jamie continued to support Natalia, opening the doors to discussions with other management and helping to convince them to accept and join the project. In fact, Natalia prepared the content, which was reviewed by the coaches, while Jamie paved the way. Natalia approached directors and their deputies, as well as stakeholders involved in or dedicated to the projects. The purpose was to seek complementarity, gather their comments, perceptions, and impressions, initiate a dialogue, and collect their expectations to introduce the PMO as an entity that enhances collaboration, especially concerning departments with high expectations. To demonstrate effectiveness, Jamie dedicated additional project managers to Natalia's team.

In the wake of these events, Natalia realized the impact and complexity of the multiple hierarchical layers where various stakeholders interact: the ministry, contractors, professionals, and public infrastructure organizations. The establishment of the PMO was a journey waymarked with challenges, adjustments, and the need to continually adapt. The transition phase was marked by a transfer of responsibilities, and, and as we shall see, convincing departments to relinquish control of their projects would be a formidable task.

The journey was far from straightforward… Establishing a PMO was not a mere decision; it required extensive negotiations. The proposed framework continually evolved, adapting to the needs and requirements of various departments and stakeholders. The PMO was seen as an entity that could oversee tactical projects, leaving strategic and organizational endeavors to other departments. To avoid power struggles and ensure alignment with strategic objectives, it was essential to define roles, approval processes, and decision-making instances. Natalia was regularly challenged by management to show the effectiveness and usefulness of her PMO. She had to fight to prove that this new entity was not synonymous with administrative burden (a perception of certain actors in the organization who also believed that it might reinforce silo functioning by separating functions and tasks).

This phase of transformation involved multiple challenges. The establishment of a PMO was an intricate process that demanded clear roles, instance definitions, and strategic alignment. The top management had to be convinced of the PMO's worth, but, as mentioned, Natalia was fortunate to secure financial support in the form of $350,000 for an upcoming portfolio management system. With the foundations laid, the next step was the transition of existing projects into the PMO's purview. This phase proved to be more complex than Natalia initially anticipated. It involved the delicate task of persuading departments that their projects should be transferred to the PMO, leading to resistance and power conflicts.

Natalia realized that she needed to demonstrate the value of the PMO to skeptical stakeholders in order to gain acceptance. She proposed a plan to improve project capacity management, which was met with resistance. However, the establishment of this committee was developed in consultation with the Innovation & Business Intelligence Department. The process began by guiding individuals with project ideas towards the appropriate resources. Over time, it evolved into a more concrete calibration of capacity. At each stage of evolution, there were visits to different departments (for example, Physical Disability Department, Intellectual Disability Department). Natalia made efforts to persuade colleagues of the PMO's importance by prompting them to reflect on the operational impacts of poor project management, such as affecting the quality of patient care and the ability to meet their needs.

Subsequently, Natalia continued her journey by assisting staff in clinical departments in project prioritization and aligning the annual project portfolio process with strategic planning. Meanwhile, senior advisors focused on revising mission documentation, refining the vision, and adjusting the value of the service offering. In a recent follow-up meeting with her team, Natalia felt things were still somewhat theoretical and abstract; that there is much work ahead. She acknowledged: "We need to mature the service offering to establish the PMO's vision effectively, and it's true that we have a long way to go."

Convincing departments to entrust their projects to the PMO's management was a challenge that required patience and persistence. REORG has project offices connected to other departments, including IT and technical services, which coordinate operational projects but not organizational and strategic ones.

In the meantime, Natalia began to set up the project referral committee to reduce the ambiguity around which door to knock on to get support for the project. The committee must bring together members of departments to guide project applicants according to the project objectives and direct them to the appropriate office or entity (PMO or other innovation office or another department). As she continued her work, Natalia recognized the importance of integrating the PMO into the organization's functions. The collaboration and alignment between the PMO and various departments was crucial in achieving success. By providing centralized oversight and support, Natalia was convinced that the PMO will enhance project visibility, accountability, and transparency, thereby instilling confidence among stakeholders and fostering a culture of continuous improvement. However, the journey was far from over. After Jamie's arrival, she decided to reorganize the team structure (see Figure A12.3). She took the opportunity for a meeting with Jamie, Kate, and Joanna to gather feedback. Several changes were implemented; for instance, the coordinator, who previously reported to management, is now part of the PMO to prevent the senior management from assuming PMO responsibilities.

During the PMO implementation, Natalia was also supported by a change management team. This team was established following a workshop conducted by the organizational development department to address Natalia's needs and expectations for guidance. However, it proved to be less effective than hoped because Natalia soon realized that she needed to take charge of driving the change throughout the PMO deployment, as she and her team had already anticipated in defining the PMO roles.

Overcoming Challenges and Planning for the Future

Natalia's journey was a testament to the complexities of introducing a PMO in a large organization. It underlined the importance of effective stakeholder management, streamlined decision-making processes, and continuous improvement in project management practices. Despite facing challenges, Natalia aimed to create a multidisciplinary team within the PMO. She sought to standardize practices across the organization while maintaining flexibility. Her leadership was essential in bringing the PMO into existence, and she had the support of a senior manageer who understood the importance of project success in the clinical setting. The road ahead was still uncertain, but Natalia aimed to put in place a governance framework for the PMO, focusing on roles and responsibilities, strategic alignment, and capacity configuration. Her determination to ensure that the PMO's vision was embraced across the organization was unwavering.

Natalia continued to conduct meetings with the directors (see Table A12.1) gaining a better understanding of this structure within their specific contexts and to communicate its added value. It has been a significant journey of organizational learning. She firmly believed that the current capacity management and project prioritization tools were not effective: "The effort put into the decision grid is no longer meaningful because, in the end, it's the political importance that prevails if a project is deemed obligatory by a powerful stakeholder, such as a public organization."

Furthermore, Natalia would like the PMO to have its dedicated space within the REORG zone (similar to other departments) to make all the necessary project-related information readily available. "The challenge is that we have 18,000 employees, and the tools we've been using to have been in place for eight years. We aim to standardize our practices without becoming overly rigid."

She has been told several times that "people will create project charters and many other documents, but for them, it's not a walk in the park. The PMO won't make them happy with it. What they want is for projects to work in clinical operations." To this, Natalia responds: "Well, then we will show them that we will support them to make it work for them, and they will come to embrace it and say, 'Yes, it works!'."

Natalia looked back at her journey with a mix of pride and humility. She had encountered myriad challenges – from convincing stakeholders of the PMO's worth to transitioning projects and overcoming stubborn resistance. The process of change was dynamic and demanding. She acknowledged that, although her vision and perseverance were successful, she should have sought support and collaboration earlier. Building a robust foundation and ensuring that everyone understood the significance of the PMO early would have streamlined the journey. The need for an action-oriented approach to foster a culture of project management within the organization became clearer with each passing day.

Natalia's journey was far from over, and she remained determined to see it through. She knew that a brighter, more organized future awaited her organization, and she remained resolute in her determination to bring it to fruition.

The Path Forward

It is October 2023, one month after the implementation of the PMO, and the objective remains to sustain the effort to convince other departments to re-evaluate their portfolio management practices. The current capacity is insufficient to handle all project requests, especially with the existing portfolio of 600 projects. Developing understanding among other departments is proving to be a challenge. Natalia is committed to enhancing and integrating project management and coordination. It is true that one month after the PMO implementation is quite early to list the achievements, but some progress has been made. Natalia takes pride in it:

> I've now dedicated five resources to project coordination, with three of them operational and two in the recruitment process. Together, we've been cleaning up the project list and actively engaging in portfolio management. Now, the results aren't stellar, but we're working on it. Only 1 percent of the projects have been discontinued, which is quite low, just six projects out of a hundred!

Two weeks earlier, Natalia began receiving phone calls from other regions of the state. Through word of mouth, news of the PMO quickly spread. Several people reached out to share their experiences. There are discussions about establishing a Community of Practice for the benefit of other regions.

Natalia had learned that change was not a sprint but a marathon. She was determined to continue on the path she had forged, ensuring that the PMO became an integral part of her organization's culture. The challenges she had faced were stepping stones to success, and she was ready to tackle whatever lay ahead. The implementation of the PMO was a complex and arduous process, but it was a journey that would shape the future of her organization, transforming it into a well-oiled machine where projects aligned seamlessly with strategic goals, and chaos gave way to clarity and progress.

At this point, after a year of efforts, Natalia is happy with the PMO implementation. As REORG embarked on its transformation journey, Natalia sees the integration of portfolios, programs, projects, and the strategic role of the PMO as the cornerstone of organizational success, driving innovation, resilience, and sustainable growth in the ever-evolving health care landscape. The next step is to execute and enforce the transition plan with the previous project management department. This department will continue to provide information for one year. Subsequently, this will be taken over by the PMO, which will then need to review and refine the information for the senior management to select the top-priority projects, with a target of 20, based on available capacity. Additionally, there is the need to develop a communication plan, with ongoing adjustments to the service offering to enhance its visibility. Following this, the focus will shift to the collaborative establishment of a comprehensive project management framework.

During the latest PMO progress meeting, the PMO coordinator suggested evaluating maturity. However, Natalia postponed the assessment via a questionnaire, opting to wait until the PMO was firmly established:

> Why don't we discuss this in a year? Let's wait a bit. Maturity is about how it's measured, not just through a questionnaire, but when elements of culture and maturity are observed in action, something we're all actively doing. It's about people saying, "Hey, you can reach out to the committee for help with your project," and regarding capacity, "the PMO will assist you, you'll see!"

In the medium term, Natalia intends to establish a project governance framework with a focus on roles and responsibilities, a blend of tactical and strategic oversight, operational mechanisms, strategic alignment, and capacity configuration. It is not something to be expected in the coming weeks. The key now is to stay on course regarding what the PMO can genuinely deliver with the current resources and capabilities.

Recognizing the ever-changing dynamics, Natalia acknowledges that the current service offering is evolving and will continue to change over the coming months. The PMO will remain in flux for the next one or two years. What concerns her is strengthening the buy-in for this service offering because, for the time being, people continue to submit their project requests, despite the hundreds of projects already in the queue. For this, she relies on PM expertise and a dedicated multidisciplinary team to support the PMO's focus. Currently, the predominant skills are deeply rooted in clinical practice. This, in itself, is not a hindrance, but Natalia is aware of this limitation. Without skilled professionals and profiles trained in PM, it will be challenging to establish the PMO and achieve its objectives. She knows that doing it alone would be a lost effort.

One month later, sipping her coffee and reflecting on her journey, Natalia contemplates what she might have done differently if she could start over:

I would have liked to revisit my preparation phase before the initial presentation, even before kicking off everything. I wish I had conducted a thorough diagnostic at the very beginning, perhaps even before what we referred to as Step 0. This diagnostic would have delved into organizational peculiarities, the prevailing culture, and deeper expectations. What exactly did we want to achieve? Taking more time to push the organization further in considering the "why" of a PMO. More time for a reflective diagnostic involving all stakeholders would have made things easier down the road. Investing time in a greater challenge to reduce the hours lost in discussions about the vision or unrelated topics, as it can be quite draining. Going beyond justifying its existence or how internal project processes work. Internal research to uncover if there were any genuine PMOs within the organization would have been beneficial. Ensuring a shared understanding of what a PMO is for internal stakeholders, as it's not a straightforward concept. I would have delved deeper into the PMO's vision, emphasizing that its success doesn't rely solely on proficiency in project management techniques and methods. Instead, it hinges on the ability to mobilize people. When sitting down with a nurse or a doctor, it's not, understandably, the technical aspects that capture their interest.

Following this moment of reflection, and fuelled by her passion for project management, Natalia persists in her quest to find answers to a series of questions. She is wondering how this PMO will evolve. How to maintain the momentum of delivering "good" projects efficiently? How to integrate the PMO into current organizational functioning while avoiding silo operation and ensuring alignment with the organizational strategy? How to ensure that colleagues are fully committed? How to anticipate signs of resistance, address them, and reduce their impact on the project, ensuring a smooth transition for another team to take over?

DISCUSSION QUESTIONS

1. How did Natalia effectively engage and manage various stakeholders during the implementation of the PMO in the organization? What strategies or approaches could have been used to increase stakeholder alignment and support?
2. Given the evolving nature of the PMO and its services, what key components should be included in Natalia's action plan for the next two years to ensure the PMO's continued success and impact? How can the PMO adapt to changing organizational needs and goals?
3. What challenges did Natalia encounter in the decision-making process related to the PMO implementation, and how did she address them? What strategies or methods could be used to improve the decision-making process for project management initiatives in complex organizations?
4. The organization faced challenges in managing its project portfolio. How can the PMO contribute to better portfolio management practices, especially in prioritizing projects and aligning them with the organization's strategic goals? What actions can be taken to improve the efficiency and effectiveness of the project portfolio?

NOTES

1. In 2020, health care spending in the country reached a peak, at 13.2 percent, due to additional funding allocated for increasing health care system capacity, testing, vaccination, and other pandemic-related interventions. Simultaneously, measures implemented to curb the spread of the virus (including travel restrictions, lockdowns, closure of non-essential businesses) had a detrimental effect on the economy, causing a 4.5 percent decline in GDP. According to forecasts, the national economy is expected to recover. Budgetary restrictions are expected, which could have a moderating effect on the growth of health care expenditures Canadian Institute for Health Information, 2022).
2. Turner, R. (2016). *Gower handbook of project management.* Routledge.

REFERENCES AND FURTHER READING

Aubry, M. (2024). PMO Toolbox: Fundamentals and implementation of a project management office (PMO). In J. R. Turner & M. Huemann (Eds.), *Gower Handbook of Project Management.* Gower.

Aubry, M. (2015). Project management office transformations: Direct and moderating effects that enhance performance and maturity. *Project Management Journal, 46*(5), 19–45.

Aubry, M., & Hobbs, B. (2010, April). *Project management office (PMO): A quest for understanding.* Project Management Institute.

Bianchi, C., Nasi, G., & Rivenbark, W. C. (2021). Implementing collaborative governance: Models, experiences, and challenges. *Public Management Review, 23*(11), 1581–1589.

Canadian Institute for Health Information. (2022). National health expenditure trends, 2022.

Darling, E. J., & Whitty, S. J. (2016). The project management office: It's just not what it used to be. *International Journal of Managing Projects in Business, 9*(2), 282–308.

De Lucca, T. A., Hinnig, M. P. F., & dos Santos, N. (2020). PMO as a tool for the organizational knowledge management: Case study in a project-based company of the sanitation service sector. *International Journal of Project Management, 4*(1), 10–35.

Bredillet, C., Tywoniak, S., & Tootoonchy, M. (2018). Exploring the dynamics of project management office and portfolio management co-evolution: A routine lens. *International Journal of Project Management, 36*(1), 27–42.

Lavoie-Tremblay, M., Aubry, M., Cyr, G. (2017). Innovation in health service management: Adoption of project management offices to support major health care transformation. *Journal of Nursing Management, 25*(8), 657–665.

Lavoie-Tremblay, M., Aubry, M., Richer, M. C., & Guylaine, C. Y. R. (2018). A health care project management office's strategy for continual change and continuous improvement. *The Health Care Manager, 37*(1), 4–10.

Lavoie-Tremblay, M., Gélinas, C., Aubé, T., Tchouaket, E., Tremblay, D., Gagnon, M. P., & Côté, J. (2022). Influence of caring for COVID-19 patients on nurse's turnover, work satisfaction and quality of care. *Journal of Nursing Management, 30*(1), 33–43.

Too, E. G., & Weaver, P. (2014). The management of project management: A conceptual framework for project governance. *International Journal of Project Management, 32*(8), 1382–1394.

Tsaturyan, T., & Müller, R. (2015). Integration and governance of multiple project management offices (PMOs) at large organizations. *International Journal of Project Management, 33*(5), 1098–1110.

Ziek, P., & Anderson, J. D. (2015). Communication, dialogue and project management. *International Journal of Managing Projects in Business, 8*(4), 788–803.

APPENDIX

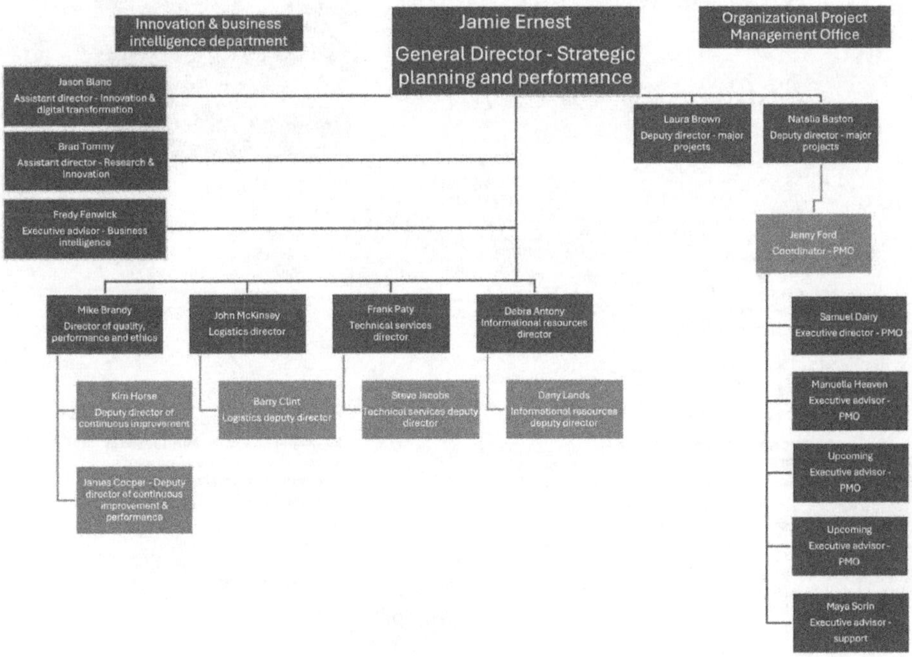

Source: Authors.

Figure A12.1 REORG organigram

Source: Authors.

Figure A12.2 PMO REORG service offering

Table A12.1 The content presented by Natalia during the meeting with senior management, organized according to four axes

Postulates / PMO observations	Configuration / types and functions	Organizational proposal and approach	Interest for directions
According to Turner (2016),[2] more than 90% of all projects are executed in a multi-project management context, often involving competition between projects. • 75% of projects do not adhere to their budget and delivery date. • 61% of projects do not meet the original quality specifications. • Only 19% of cross-functional projects with a cultural change component are successful.	The PMO is an organizational structure that standardizes project governance processes and facilitates the sharing of resources, methodologies, tools, and techniques among projects. The responsibilities of the PMO can range from supporting project management functions to directly managing one or more projects. PMO's functions: • Support • Center of excellence • Passive • Advisory • Centralized services • Responsible or organizational.	• Strategic thinking. • Understand what we need to resolve and correct within REORG. • Analyze our performance in carrying out projects. • Establish a portrait of the existing structures in REORG. • Mandate to write and strategic thinking. • To have a management framework or charter regarding PM (approach and process). • Identify the required expertise. • Have a BP organization chart and cross-functional coordination. • Determine roles and responsibilities. • Identify the decision-making structure, the units and organizational offices. • Carry out an inventory of pending, current, and future projects in various units. • Determine the management and coordination of the project portfolio(s).	• An organizational vision. • Other entities manage their sector. • An overview of interdependencies / comprehensive analysis. • All projects with clinical focus. • Ensure collaboration and mobilization towards the common objective. • Constant competition between operational management and projects and between the PMs of different departments. • According to needs analysis, consider a resource consolidation model for each department. • PMO must be aligned with the strategic objectives and located near decision-making areas.

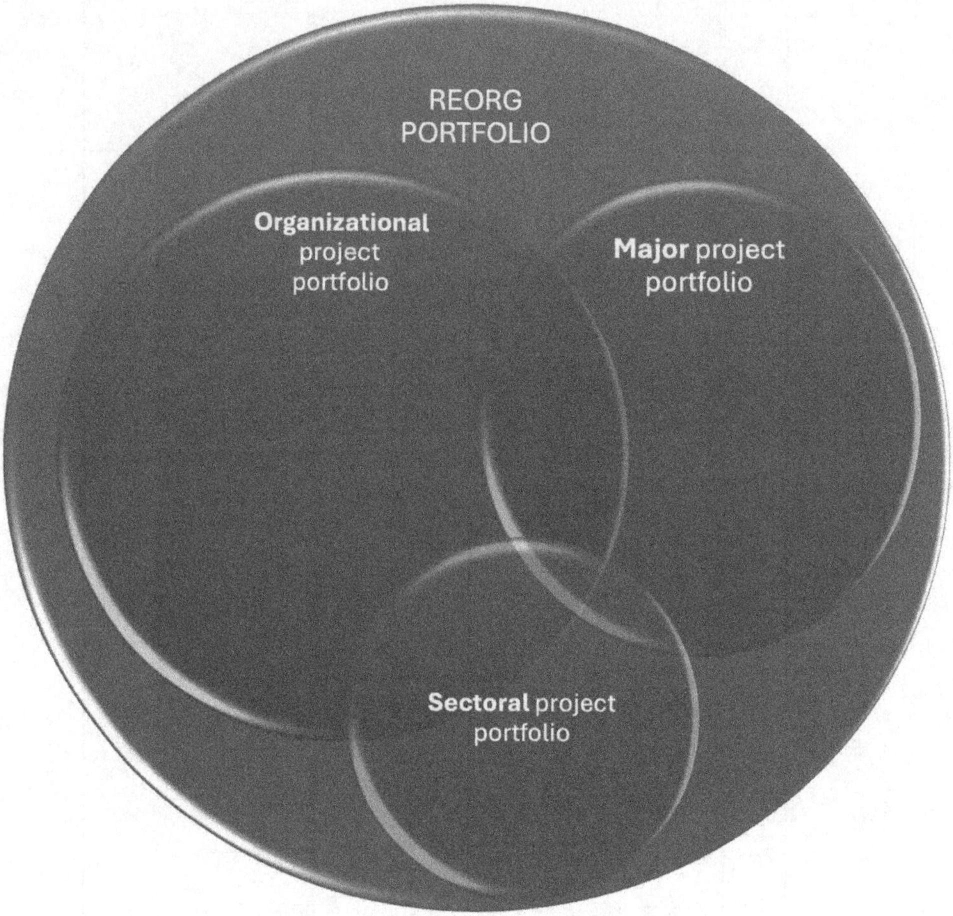

Source: Authors.

Figure A12.3 REORG project portfolio

13
Making the decision of project termination during the delivery stage: the Keystone XL pipeline

Jose Rodrigo Juarez Cornelio

OPENING PARAGRAPHS

Infrastructure investment plays a pivotal role in shaping economic development, competitiveness, job creation and improved quality of life for every nation. Infrastructure encompasses a broad range of essential sectors, ranging from transportation and energy systems to communication networks, water supply and public facilities. Recent years have seen a revitalisation of infrastructure investment mainly due to ageing infrastructure, escalating urbanisation, and evolving environmental conditions. It is estimated that, in 2017, the world spent over $10 trillion on new infrastructure. Nations worldwide continue to invest to address deficiencies and adapt to modern challenges, such as enhancing sustainability, combating climate change and improving resilience against natural disasters.

A relevant example of the infrastructure investment boom is the United States. With an increasing population exceeding 340 million people, and mainly concentrated in major cities such as New York, Los Angeles and Chicago, the country has been increasingly investing in maintaining, improving and delivering complex infrastructure projects. Despite the significant investments made in high-profile projects, such as the JFK Airport expansion, the Hudson Tunnel and California high-speed rail, there have been relevant instances of major projects that have been terminated during the delivery stage.

A noteworthy infrastructure project that has been terminated in the US is the fourth stage of the Keystone XL Pipeline Project (KXL), causing political and social polarisation. Due to the variety of stakeholders involved, encompassing the national government, regulatory agencies, contractors, environmental groups, First Nations, labour unions, investors, local communities, suppliers, NGOs and financial institutions, there have been divergent views on the project. Due to the resources already invested, the environmental impacts associated with the project and multiple changes in strategic priorities, the future of the KXL project is under review. In response to the ongoing debates, successive governments have intervened to determine its future, and now, in collaboration with the project owner, a decision must be made on whether the project is needed or not. A reflexive approach must be taken by students to solve this case.

BODY OF THE CASE

A Global Perspective of the Oil and Gas Sector

The oil and natural gas industries represent one of the most important sectors in the energy market, and they typically play an influential role in the global economy as primary fuel sources around the world. Just in 2021, it is estimated that over $650 billion was invested worldwide in projects including pipelines, refineries, drilling platforms, storage facilities and processing plants.

Oil and gas production is the multistage process of discovering a resource, transporting it to a refinery, and converting it into a finished product that is readily available for sale. The oil and gas industries are often divided into three segments:

- Upstream, which refers to the exploration and production of oil and gas.
- Midstream, which refers to transportation and storage facilities.
- Downstream, which refers to the refining and marketing activities.

These industries are highly complex and require capital-intensive, state-of-the-art technology and defined processes and systems, and are usually a highly regulated environment.

Downsides of the Oil and Gas Sector

Despite the relevance of the oil and gas sector in the worldwide economy, it is a sector that continues to spark controversy. This includes negative impacts across environmental, social and economic dimensions.

From an environmental point of view, the release of greenhouse gases from burning fossil fuels is a major contributor to climate change. The extraction, transportation and refining processes often result in air and water pollution, as well as the destruction of natural habitats destruction. Oil spills pose a significant threat to biodiversity and ecosystems, particularly marine life. Deforestation and the disruption to wildlife and biodiverse environments are having long-lasting ecological consequences. Furthermore, as oil and gas are finite resources, their constant extraction contributes to the depletion of non-renewable reserves.

From a social point of view, the oil and gas sector typically requires large areas of land. This leads to the displacement of local communities, disrupts their traditional ways of life, causes social opposition and leads to conflicts over land rights. This sparks further controversies, as, in most cases, First Nations and local communities are not often able to capitalise on the economic benefits that the project organisation usually generates.

From an economic point of view, countries heavily reliant on oil exports can face economic instability due to fluctuations in oil prices. Sharp declines in prices can impact government revenue, leading to economic downturns and budgetary challenges.

Oil and Gas Sector in the United States

Oil is one of the most relevant sources of energy in the US. At the end of 2022, the US was the world's largest producer of crude oil, followed by Saudi Arabia, Russia, Canada and China. Crude oil extracted from underground reservoirs is the basis for all petroleum products, such as gasoline and diesel. It is estimated that, as of 2022, the average daily consumption of oil in the US was 18,000,000.[1]

By the end of 2021, the surface area of the US was reported at 9,831,510 square kilometers. Due to the vast land-mass of the country, pipelines remain the most efficient and reliable way to transport crude oil. Goveernment statistics indicate that, by the end of 2021, there were 190 crude oil pipelines either active or under construction in the country. Just as a comparison, Russia has 61, China has 55, Canada 48, Saudi Arabia 39, Venezuela 27, and Algeria 18.[2]

The US is heavily dependent on crude oil. By the end of 2022, the oil and gas industry had contributed nearly 15 per cent of the GDP of the country (estimated to be $31.259 trillion). Because of this, states such as Texas, North Dakota, New Mexico, Alaska or Colorado have low unemployment rates. The oil and gas industry is estimated to directly support over 12 million jobs, close to 6.5 per cent of the total US employment force, and to indirectly support over 3 million jobs in other sectors within the value chain.[3]

Context of Crude Oil Pipelines in the United States

Statistics from 2020 indicate that, before Covid-19, approximately 75–85 per cent of the crude oil pipelines in the US were in use, with multiple projects and proposals coming along due to an expected production boom. However, after the global health crisis, the net use of pipelines reduced to an estimated 55–60 per cent, and the global demand for oil and gas crumbled, with production and prices reducing drastically to below $20 per barrel, the lowest for over 20 years. Oil companies have struggled to recover losses, are having to rethink their investment strategies, and are pausing investment for the future.[4]

Due to other external factors, such as the war in Ukraine, oil and gas prices are back on the rise, at around $85 per barrel, which is closer to pre-pandemic levels. However, the outlook is still pessimistic. Recovering the original levels of production and keeping up with the significant demand is not easy for the oil companies, as the cost of maintenance of the pipelines is expensive and not all the companies are equipped for this. At the beginning of 2023, new pipelines had not been much needed or wanted in the US, as they were not expected to help reduce the costs of crude oil extraction, transportation or production/refining. Building new pipelines is now much more economically feasible than in previous years. However, it is estimated that around 23 per cent of the existing pipelines require significant investment for refurbishment and care, which would have a long-term impact if there were a need for further increases in capacity.[5]

By the end of 2022, the US had seen a significant decline in the construction of crude oil pipelines. It is estimated that there was a decline of 15 per cent compared to the previous year, and then an estimated 20 per cent decline in 2023. At the time, the country was focusing on the implementation of new environmental policies that made the construction of new pipelines much more complex. Oil companies face significant pressure to obtain permits on time for their projects, but the main barrier has been complying with environmental restrictions, which has significantly increased construction costs. However, the overall construction of crude oil pipelines has not decreased worldwide. It is estimated that over 20,000 km of new oil pipelines are being built, with efforts being driven by the US, Russia, China and India.[6]

The US Political System

US politics function within the framework of a constitutional federal republic and a presidential system, in which there are three distinct branches that share power: the legislative branch, composed of the House of Representatives and the Senate; the executive branch, headed by the president; and the judicial branch, composed of the federal courts and the Supreme Court. Each branch has distinctive faculties. For instance, the House of Representatives and the Senate approve all bills. The president can appoint ambassadors, ministers, judges of the Supreme Court and all other officials of the country and has the power of veto, which can be overturned by two-thirds of the votes in the legislative branch. The Supreme Court is responsible for interpreting and applying the laws of the constitution.

The US political system is particularly sensitive to environmental issues. It is often considered to be highly fragmented at the national, state and local levels. The Environmental Protection Agency (EPA) is an independent agency of the government, established for environmental protection. It has the responsibility to maintain and enforce national standards under environmental laws, in consultation with stakeholders and states, First Nations and local government. The president appoints the Administrator of the EPA, who is approved by the Senate. While maintaining independence, the president has the power to veto legislation and regulate the behaviour of the administrator. The EPA has faced controversies regarding a less-than-satisfactory review of its programmes, policies and activities towards environmental justice. Because of this, it is often seen that the EPA is still influenced by the president and is guided by the environmental issues and administrative goals of the government.

Project Background: the Keystone XL Pipeline

The KXL project is a crude oil pipeline system that begins in Canada and ends in the US. Crude oil is extracted from bituminous sand in the western part of Canada. This type of crude oil involves one of the most polluting extraction techniques.

The project was originally initiated by OilCanada in 2005 and approved by the National Energy Commission of Canada in 2007. In March 2008, the US Department of State issued a presidential licence that granted permission to OilCanada to develop, maintain and operate the project at the border between the US and Canada. Both governments agreed that the KXL system was of strategic interest for both countries and had sufficient support to proceed with its development. The project had the full support of President Bush.

The development of the KXL system is one of the major infrastructure endeavours that were attempted shortly after the US financial crisis of 2008. Infrastructure investment, energy saving, improvement of medical care and economic stability were some of the main priorities of President Obama when he came to office in 2009. The Ministry of Labor reported that, by the end of December 2008, the unemployment rate in the US was as high as 10 per cent of the total population (over 30 million individuals).

In June 2008, OilCanada formally began construction of the first phase of the project. In June 2010, it became operational. The first phase runs from Hardisty in Canada to Illinois in the US. The total length of the first phase is 3,375 km, consisting of the reconstruction of 796 km of existing natural gas pipelines in Canada, a brand new 395 km pipeline in Hardisty, and 2,184 km of new pipelines in the US. The first phase has a total capacity of 450,000 barrels per day. The second phase of the project was operational by February 2011. It runs from Steele in Nebraska to Oklahoma, with a total length of 460 km. This expanded the capacity of the keystone pipeline system to 600,000 barrels per day. The third phase of the KXL system was approved by President Obama in March 2012 and completed in January 2014. This segment runs from Cushing in Oklahoma to Nederland in Texas, with a length of 784 km. This phase increased the capacity of the system to 720,000 barrels per day.

Once the whole system was operational, consideration for a fourth phase came into action. The fourth phase of KXL was planned from Hardistyto Nebraska. The total length of this new section of pipeline is 1,897 km. It was expected to add an additional 800,000-barrel daily capacity.

Change of Direction and Opposing Views of the Project

The energy strategies of President Bush and his successor President Obama were different. Obama was an advocate of environmental protection and renewable energies. His energy strategy included initiatives such as the integration of solar, wind and geothermal energy into the existing power grid. This implied redirecting resources into more sustainable sources of energy production to reduce dependence on fossil fuels and diverting the use of taxpayers' funds away from oil and gas projects.

However, among the strategic priorities of the Obama administration was to invest in major infrastructure projects to boost the economy of the country. Just the first phase of KXL required an investment of over $12 billion, which falls within the strategic interests in terms of economic recovery. The project did not align with the government's environmental and energy policies, which led to serious questioning, but official data from the Ministry of Labor indicated that, between 2008 and 2010, KXL phases one and two provided over 43,000 direct jobs, boosting the US economy and reducing welfare needs. So, despite conflict over the environmental issues, the positive social and economic impact persuaded President Obama to approve phase three of the KXL construction, mentioning that it was a way of curbing the rising cost of natural gas and had further potential for employment generation, directly contributing to a more stable economic environment. Support for KXL phases two and three remained constant until their completion, but phase four did not have the same luck.

Multiple reports suggested that KXL phase four had the potential to generate over $20 billion in commercial activities and create at least 25,000 direct jobs. While such numbers were questioned and suspected to be inflated, even conservative studies estimated that the project, with a forecasted cost of $8 billion for phase four, could still create around 5,000 direct jobs. Meanwhile, President Obama argued that the project would only be of strategic interest for the US if it did not have a significant impact in terms of carbon pollution, which was one of his renewed priorities in the environmental and energy strategy.

During the early months of 2015, the Ministry for Environmental Protection issued the final environmental impact assessment (EIA), in which it stated that KXL phase four would significantly increase greenhouse gas emissions. Because of this EIA, Obama vetoed the permit to approve the construction of the next phase of the project, despite it being approved by the Senate. The Department of State declared that, since the project was no longer a matter of national interest, it rejected any permit applications that could grant contractors permission to proceed with the construction of the project.

Also during 2015, a significant environmental milestone was reached. The Paris Agreement, a legally binding international treaty on tackling the climate crisis, was signed with the objective of substantially reducing activities that cause climate change. The US was one of the nations that signed this agreement, which served as guidance for the development of other strategic priorities for the government in the coming years. KXL had been initiated before 2015, and the early perspective from the government was of support and praise for the benefits it generated in terms of economic development. After the Paris Agreement, however, there was no further support, and the government's priorities shifted to environmental protection and energy transition.

Furthermore, following the new strategic priorities of the government, and given the fact that KXL phase four could be restarted in the future, multiple NGOs (non-governmental organisations), environmental protection bodies and social movements were motivated to obstruct and protest the development of the project. So, due to such increased pressure and the administration's new priorities, for the remainder of Obama's presidential term, KXL phase four remained suspended.

The two-party political system (Democratic and Republican) and fixed four-year presidential terms mean that there is a constant battle for power in the US. Typically, there is significant polarisation and opposing views regarding the strategies that the government follows. Often, opponents deny or minimise the accomplishments of previous administrations. In 2015, for example, President Obama believed that "the keystone pipeline project occupies a role that I think has been exaggerated in our political discourse. It has become a symbol that both sides often use as a campaign stick, rather than a serious policy issue." This simplifies the complexity that the future of the KXL project has.

One of the first activities that President Trump undertook during his first days in office in 2017 was to revoke Obama's veto of the KXL phase four construction permits, allowing the project to be resumed. This again indicates that the project was an object of polarisation in the political sphere.

Further into his presidential term, Trump made the decision that the US would cease all participation in the Paris Agreement, making the US the first country to withdraw from it. President Trump argued that, by being part of the agreement, the US economy was undermined and at a permanent disadvantage. This received huge support from Republicans but was highly criticised by Democrats, environmentalists, scientists and many business leaders, and much of the US population disapproved of the withdrawal.

In November 2018, requests to reassess the original EIA were made. There had been several reports suggesting that the original EIA was outdated and unreliable. A new report claimed that there were an estimated 170 million metric tons of carbon emissions generated by the KXL system. Furthermore, additional information suggested that emissions would occur even without new pipelines being developed, as there was still a market for oil so it would come into the country through other means. This led to further assessments in which the District Judge of Montana noted that the global decline of oil prices and the reduced costs of transportation would lead to an over-exploitation of the pipeline, significantly increasing greenhouse gas emissions. So, the construction permit of KXL phase four was again revoked and an updated EIA was requested to supplement the original from 2014.

Because of the extensive delays in resuming the construction of the project and the difficulties within government, President Trump issued a new licence for KXL with the updated EIA. The EIA indicated that there would be no significant differences in terms of greenhouse gas emissions in this new phase, which meant that the project could proceed as planned. Construction continued until April 2020, when environmental agencies complained that the project had not been properly authorised, and construction was again suspended.

During his first days in office in 2021, new president Joe Biden mandated re-joining the Paris Agreement and cancelling all construction licences for KXL phase four. It is estimated that, up to this point, approximately 53 per cent of the project had been completed, and over $4 billion already invested. This figure does not include any potential additional costs for termination, such as the costs of cancelling contracts, national and international litigations, repayment of loans, bonds or other types of structured finance, or the costs of proceeding with a different project. By the end of 2023, there had been no further construction activities on the project. At the time of writing, President Trump, in his second term, has yet to decide on the future of the project..

The constant power struggles and differing opinions within government often cause difficulties for the population, investors, and other stakeholders in the country. There are major differences in strategic priorities between Democrats and Republicans, and each new administration tends to cancel or suspend their opponents' projects. Thus, there is often no sense of accountability and ownerships, as projects are often seen as "someone else's". This has sometimes sparked concern in international markets, seeing the US as a fragile investment environment. Investors are cautious about making significant capital investments in large infrastructure projects in the US, aware that, if a transition comes during the delivery stage, key permits might not only be denied but revoked altogether. This puts US infrastructure developments at significant reputational risk. This lack of decision and repeated back and forth show that successive administrations take different approaches to developing projects and have different priorities. There is no clarity or consistent strategic direction.

Decision Point

The first three phases of the KXL system are functioning normally, and there have never been plans to revoke any operational permit. However, there are multiple opposing views about the final phase. A major concern is associated with the proposed route of the pipeline, through the dunes of Nebraska, which is a natural protected area. The controversial project has been challenged by environmental groups and First Nations. The following sections describe the views of relevant stakeholders.

National government (neutral towards termination)

The new government has been trying to act as a neutral party by balancing the overall benefits and impacts of the project on society, the environment and the economy, including potential termination costs. It is concerned to prioritise the welfare and long-term interests of the local population while assessing whether the project aligns with the broader public interest, economic development strategies, and infrastructure needs. Key considerations for include potential cost overruns, environmental concerns, safety risks and changes in public opinion. Terminating the project could significantly impact public finances, as a significant amount of the project's funding comes from taxpayers.

Investors (against termination)

Investors in the project include a consortium of private companies and financial institutions from the US, Canada, UK and Saudi Arabia, as well as a First Nation alliance from Alberta in Canada. They are primarily concerned with the return on their investment and want the project to proceed as planned to realise the anticipated financial gains. From their perspective, terminating the project can result in significant financial losses from which they believe it will be impossible to recover. They have committed substantial amounts of resources and capital, expecting future profits once the project is complete and full production capacity is in place. The investors argue that any issues or challenges encountered can be addressed through modifications to the existing project or mitigation strategies, without scrapping the project entirely. They emphasise the importance of honouring contractual agreements and protecting the interests of those who have provided finance.

Local population (mixed views)

The local population, which includes First Nations, other residents and businesses in the project's vicinity, have mixed perspectives. Their primary concerns are the immediate and long-term impacts and benefits of the project on their legacy and culture, their community, environment, and quality of life. The First Nations groups are divided by two perspectives: the First Nations alliance from Canada, and the First Nations residents in the US.

- The alliance from Canada invested over US$1 billion with OilCanada. Because the Canadian component of the project has been completed, they argue that their investment will be lost, affecting all the First Nations in Canada because of economic development plans that would no longer be achieved. They see the project as a means to reduce the wealth gap between the general population and the First Nations in Canada.
- The First Nations from the US are completely opposed to the development of the project. They argue that, if the project continues, a significant amount of land will be taken away from them. They contend that the project will cause them to be displaced and be an unnecessary destruction of their ancestral lands and their identity, and a reinforcement of the historical and current injustices they face due to colonialism.

Other residents have mixed views on the project. Some welcome the financial benefits, but many are in favour of terminating it, mainly due to environmental degradation, climate effects, reduced property values, increased traffic and health and safety risks. Many feel that the project is not in their best interests and do not see any social value being delivered to them in the short, medium or long term. They first manifested their opposition through self-organised protests. Once these movements began attracting more attention, in coordination with the First Nations, they joined forces with a political advocacy group to mobilise greater public opposition and legal challenges in the district courts. They argue that the project's drawbacks outweigh its benefits and advocate for alternative solutions or mitigation measures. These social movements have been well supported by environmental defence organisations.

Local business owners in the project's vicinity are against terminating the project, mainly due to the potential economic growth, opportunities for employment creation and potential increased value of their businesses and properties. Most of them feel that, if the project does not materialise, the government will choose to invest in other parts of the country instead, potentially leading to high unemployment rates and even 65–80 per cent of existing businesses having to close. They believe the project is an opportunity they must capitalise on.

Regulatory agencies (neutral towards termination)

The regulatory bodies, such as the Ministry of Infrastructure and the Environmental Protection Agency, are responsible for enforcing and upholding legal and safety standards. Their role is to be neutral and objective in their assessments. They must ensure that projects and programmes comply with all relevant laws, regulations and safety standards. If it meets these criteria, they must remain neutral and allow the project to proceed, albeit under close supervision and monitoring processes. Social movements organised by the general publicand First Nations, although not binding, attract the attention of regulatory agencies, encouraging them to monitor the project closely. If the project violates regulations, poses environmental risks or threatens public safety, the agencies have the capacity to impose fines, sanctions or other measures, which can include modifications to the project, notices of suspension, or termination of the project to protect the public interest and ensure compliance with legal requirements.

These opposing views of key stakeholders must be balanced, as their different perspectives can significantly impact the outcome of the project. There are extensive negotiations, consultations and transparent communication strategies that must be undertaken to address the different concerns of the multiple stakeholders.

Some Additional Figures

The continuation or termination of the project is open to many discussions and views. According to the US Department of State, the first three phases of KXL provided up to 45,000 indirect jobs and 5,000 direct jobs. This was a significant justification to continue with the project, despite differing opposing views. Continuing with the development of KXL phase four is estimated to generate a maximum of 2,300 direct jobs and up to 30,000 indirect jobs.

Key Milestones of the KXL Phase Four Project

- Approval of the third phase of the KXL project was given by President Obama in March 2012.
- The USs Department of State issued the project's final environmental impact assessment (EIA) in January 2014. The document stated that, due to the market dynamics of the logistics system of North America, the crude oil transportation (upstream and downstream) would not have a significant environmental impact, whether the project was completed or not.
- The Supreme Court of Nebraska approved the construction of KXL phase four in January 2015.
- President Obama vetoed the bill to approve the construction of KXL phase four in February 2015. This was despite the House of Representatives and the Senate having approved the bill.
- The Secretary of State declared that the project was no longer in the public interest in November 2015. The justification for this was the negative public perception due to the expected increase in greenhouse gas emissions and the country's aim of combating climate change.
- Following the declarations of the Secretary of State, President Obama announced that KXL phase four was no longer feasible due to economic and environmental concerns. This was mainly related to the levels of domestic oil production being at their lowest point since 1985 (and therefore existing systems were sufficient), and the project was suspended.
- During the first week of his term in office in January 2017, President Trump mandated that the construction of KXL be resumed.
- President Trump declared that KXL is of national interest, and the Department of State issued a new statement in March 2017 reiterating that the project could be resumed.
- During January 2017, First Nation leaders and environmentalist groups mobilised to protest against KXL and other fossil fuel projects.
- The District Judge of Montana revoked the construction licence of the KXL phase four project in November 2018.

- In March 2019, President Trump directly issued a new construction licence for the KXL phase four project, superceding the previous licence, and construction promptly resumed
- A month later, the project was again provisionally suspended by the District Judge of Montana due to environmental concerns, invalidating the new construction licence issued by President Trump.
- In July 2020, the US Supreme Court confirmed suspension of the KXL phase four project and all activities related to the construction.
- During October 2020, the First Nations Alliance of Canada signed a Memorandum of Understanding to facilitate equity investment in the project.
- On the first day of his presidential term in January 2021, President Biden revoked the construction licence for KXL phase four, and the project was suspended.

FINAL REMARKS

This case study focuses on the concept of project termination or cancellation. Termination is the premature discontinuation of a planned project before its intended completion and before its objectives have been achieved. Project termination can occur during any phase of a project's life cycle, from the initial planning and design stages to the later stages of construction or implementation. This case focuses on potentisl termination during the delivery stage.

Project termination is one of the most difficult challenges that decision-makers face, as it is often associated with failure and high levels of reputational risk. It concerns situations where internal or external forces cause the project to become irrelevant, unsuitable, unprofitable or even harmful and, even when these are good reasons, is often associated with failure. Project termination may result from various factors, such as changes in strategic priorities, regulatory issues or a reassessment of the project's feasibility or benefits, to mention a few. Project termination is associated with sunk costs, loss of potential economic gains and disruptions to stakeholders' plans and expectations. Despite the negative connotations associated with project termination, contrasting views argue that just because a project is being well developed does not mean that it should continue to be supported.

Understanding the termination of construction projects is relevant for the project management discipline for several reasons. It provides valuable insights into complex decision-making involving both public and private stakeholders, and assesses multiple perspectives that are not always clear or straightforward.

The termination of a project can occur because of multiple reasons that are present during development, which include:

- Social opposition or acceptability: There may be social movements in favour of or against the project, and this oppositon or support can be measured at national, state, local or territorial level through polls, for example.
- Environmental considerations: Endangerment of protected resources that jeopardises or exploits the environment, flora or fauna, protected areas and Indigenous people;

misrepresentation of environmental impact assessments that arise from failure to identify or assess proper impacts and mitigation measures; or transition to cleaner sources of energy as part of a worldwide effort to contribute to the fight against climate change can all indicate the need for a shift in strategic priorities to terminate a project.

- Cost analysis: The termination of a construction project can result in significant financial losses. Understanding the implications, where resources can be reallocated or when to stop can guide adequate financial planning and risk management.
- Biases in decision-making: Behavioural biases in project management play a central role in the decision to continue or terminate a project. Optimism bias, strategic misrepresentation and escalation of commitment are examples of biases that lead decision-makers to persist with a project because of the resources invested, and the belief that there is too much at stake to quit. Further research on biases such as the reverse escalation of commitment provides novel insights to identify when to terminate a project from a rational point of view.
- Risk mitigation: Identification of factors that are conducive to termination can help in risk assessment and mitigation. By recognising pitfalls or issues, project stakeholders can implement strategies to avoid or address these challenges in future projects.
- Accountability and transparency: The termination of a construction project requires accountability in project management. It ensures that stakeholders, including project owners, contractors and regulators, are accountable for their roles in the project's outcome. Transparency in decision-making is essential for maintaining public trust.
- Improved decision-making: Making the decision of termination is not easy. However, learning from terminated projects can improve decision-making in future endeavours to make more informed choices.
- Resource allocation: Understanding why and when to terminate projects can help allocate resources more effectively. By recognising patterns or recurring issues, governments, organisations and investors can allocate resources to projects with a higher likelihood of success.
- Legal and regulatory compliance: If a project is terminated, there are rules and regulations that need to be followed before, during and after termination. Knowing what happened in the project can ensure that all legal and regulatory requirements were met while the project was under execution. This is crucial to prevent legal issues, disputes or the consequences of non-compliance.
- Data for research and analysis: Understanding and gathering data from similar projects or historical projects is valuable to understanding common causes, patterns and trends that are conducive to the termination of projects. This can ultimately lead to improved practices and policies.
- Stakeholder communication: Engaging with stakeholders and explaining the reasons behind project termination is essential for maintaining trust and relationships. This includes government agencies, investors, contractors and the local community. It demonstrates transparency and a commitment to responsible project management.
- Continuous improvement: Understanding and analysing projects that have been terminated is integral to the concept of continuous improvement. By learning from past

experiences, stakeholders can adapt and enhance their practices and decision-making processes to increase the likelihood of success for future projects.

This case study highlights the importance of making timely decisions based on the different types of information available and allows the reader to understand the contextual factors that affect a project's development, helping them to decide whether to terminate the project. Understanding the termination of construction projects is a useful example that helps organisations and government agencies learn from past experiences, make informed decisions and improve their project management practices. It ultimately contributes to better resource allocation and risk management, and the successful execution of future projects.

DISCUSSION QUESTIONS

For the purpose of this case study, assume that the date is 1 February 2024. A new US president has recently been elected. The new administration is aware of the back and forth that has been occurring with the project, but wants to avoid any further controversies around it. A decision must be made regarding the future of the project. The decision will be final.

1. Assume that you are the CEO of OilCanada. The President of the USA has asked you to explain what you will do. You need to decide the future of the project:
   a. The project continues to be delivered.
   b. The project is terminated.

Explain why you chose a or b. Include any relevant assumptions and support your rationale for the decision. Consider that your response will be an official answer to share with the press. Your investors, the governments (USA and Canada) and the public are listening.

2. What are some of the causes that led to the termination of the project?
3. What are some of the financial implications of terminating a project?

NOTES

1. https://www.eia.gov/tools/faqs/faq.php?id=33&t=6
2. https://marketrealist.com/p/how-many-oil-pipelines-are-in-the-us/
3. https://tradingeconomics.com/united-states/gdp
4. https://blog.fenstermaker.com/how-many-oil-pipelines-are-in-the-united-states/
5. https://countryeconomy.com/raw-materials/brent?year=2022
6. https://www.offshore-technology.com/data-insights/top-ten-active-oil-and-gas-pipelines-north-america/?cf-view

REFERENCES AND FURTHER READING

Brockner, J. (1992). The escalation of commitment to a failing course of action: Toward theoretical progress. *Academy of Management Review, 17*(1), 39–61.

Cantarelli, C. C., & Flyvbjerg, B. (2013). Megaprojects cost performance and lock-in: Problems and solutions. In H. Priemus & B. Van Wee (Eds), *International handbook on megaprojects*. Edward Elgar Publishing.

Denicol, J., Davies, A., & Krystallis, I. (2020). What are the causes of poor megaproject performance? A systematic literature review and research agenda. *Project Management Journal, 51*(3), 328–345.

Drummond, H. (2014). Escalation of commitment: When to stay the course? *Academy of Management Perspectives, 28*, 430–446.

Flyvbjerg, B. (2021). Top ten behavioral biases in project management: An overview. *Project Management Journal, 52*(6), 531–546.

Juarez Cornelio, J. R., Sainati, T., & Locatelli, G. (2021). What does it take to kill a megaproject? The reverse escalation of commitment. *International Journal of Project Management, 39*, 774–787.

Juarez Cornelio, J. R., Sainati, T., & Locatelli, G. (2023). Digging in the megaproject's graveyard: Why do megaprojects die, and how to check their health? *International Journal of Project Management, 41*(6), 102501.

Ross, J., & Staw, B. M. (1993). Organizational escalation and exit: Lessons from the Shoreham Nuclear Power Plant. *Academy of Management, 36*(4), 701–732.

Winch, G. M. (2013). Escalation in major projects: lessons from the Channel Fixed Link. *International Journal of Project Management, 31*(5), 724–734.

Zhang, Q. (2019). Legal options to stop the revival of Keystone XL Pipeline. *Environmental Claims Journal, 32*(3), 201–220.

14
Digital innovation strategy at a construction company's project business

Eleni Papadonikolaki, Bethan Morgan and Issam El-Asbi

OPENING PARAGRAPHS

It was the evening of July 29, 2019. Ahmed Shalhoub, chief innovation officer (CIO) at the Main Contractors Company (MCC), had just arrived in Athens, Greece from San Francisco. Shalhoub had participated in a conference at Stanford University on the latest developments in digital technologies in construction and spoke about MCC's groundbreaking digital approach. He was committed to bringing exciting new digital technologies such as building information modelling (BIM) and virtual reality to the construction industry, but a dark shadow was hanging over him, as his transformation strategy was under attack from the MCC board.

The day before, Shalhoub had taken a call from the chair of the board, who asked him to explain, again, the details of his digital innovation strategy. The build contract for the New Airport Terminal Building (NATB) in the Middle East that MCC had been awarded was the spearhead of MCC's digital innovation strategy. However, things were bleak. In a recent meeting with the MCC chief executive officer (CEO), Shalhoub had been loudly complained at: "We told you from the beginning that digitalization won't work for construction. You insisted that it is worth it, and now we have problems…" Shalhoub knew that he would be asked to lose or give back some of his department's achievements. He was trying to work out what concessions to make to satisfy the board: sacrifice resources, people, infrastructure, or digital processes.

Shalhoub was convinced that data and digital technologies could make MCC more competitive by optimizing construction, one of the most traditional industries worldwide and least digitized.[1] He had been granted resources for digital innovation in 2012 to support the Middle East project. That was a big success because, in such a project-based business, research and development (R&D) resources are scarce and only through successful and profitable projects could he negotiate for more power and independence. Now the NATB project was facing its own challenges that were affecting the digital innovation strategy he had developed.

BODY OF THE CASE

Company Background

The Main Contractors Company has been on a journey towards digital innovation since its early background. It was a top construction company in the Middle East region, on the ENR list of top 250 international contractors carrying out construction, engineering and procurement works (see Figure A14.1). Founded in the early 1950s, this private company offered commercial project management, engineering, procurement, construction services and investment activities internationally, according to Bloomberg. MCC had offices and projects in over 40 countries, and a workforce of more than 100,000 employees.

MCC is an example of a project-based firm[2] and a significant player in the construction industry. As construction is a project-based sector, companies in the sector develop their business models around projects, typically their only source of income. Top-tier contractors in construction, such as MCC, usually rely on investing the free working capital from projects, together with other profits and loans, to finance new project developments. In April 2020, MCC was engaged in 40 ongoing projects globally, including in the Middle East, Africa and East Asia from private capital and oil companies (Figure A14.2 and Figure A14.3). Some 80 per cent of its sales were in the Middle East region (Figure A14.4). Most projects of MCC were in mainstream construction, but they also worked on engineering procurement construction projects, which are common contracts for large-scale and complex infrastructure projects, such as oil and gas projects (Figure A14.5).

This temporary nature of projects results in fragmentation in resources, social capital, knowledge and finances for R&D and innovation. For example, a project may be delivered by different firms located across different regions or countries, so the social capital and knowledge base of projects are also fragmented since these inter-organizational constellations have diverse cultures, operating principles and strategies. Innovation in projects is scarce and of secondary importance as there is a lack of overarching strategy and dedicated budget for experimenting with and trying new ideas. Any funding tends to come from some of the profit accumulated by earlier projects. A few projects may have a dedicated innovation budget if the client is innovative. Nonetheless, the interdisciplinarity of projects offers fertile ground for experimentation, creativity and innovation.

MCC has been a pioneer in digital innovation since 2012, focusing on optimizing construction, one of the least digitized industries worldwide. As a CIO, Shalhoub was always attuned to the latest developments in digital technologies and keen to bring new ideas to the company. With his background in the early stages of digitalization in construction in the 1990s and his important position in MCC, he could usually negotiate with the leadership team as a champion for digital change. Shalhoub's belief in the potential of data and digital technologies to enhance MCC's competitiveness led to the allocation of resources for digital innovation in

2012, supporting the Middle East project. MCC invested various types of resources in being an innovative company as, early on, the directors saw the benefits of digital technologies in dealing with changes in design. "We needed a better way to manage change in projects. For every small change, we needed to recalculate everything again," said Shalhoub, explaining how MCC became an innovator and invested in digital tools.

Digital Innovation in Project Environments

Digital innovation in project-based industries such as construction is distinctive. The construction sector shapes the built environment and surrounds all aspects of our life, work and recreation. The sector is one of the largest in the world economy. Construction consistently produces 7–11 per cent of gross domestic product in many national economies. However, while other sectors, from retail to manufacturing, have transformed their efficiency, boosted their productivity and embraced the digital age, construction still underperforms in terms of efficiencies.

McKinsey identified major causes of this poor performance as the extensive regulations, its dependence on public-sector demand, and its highly fragmented nature. It found that contracts had mismatches in risk allocations and rewards, leading to poor project management, insufficient skills and underinvestment in R&D and innovation. McKinsey[3] identified seven ways to tackle the root causes of construction's poor productivity:

1. Reshape regulation and raise transparency.
2. Rewire the contractual framework.
3. Rethink design and engineering processes.
4. Improve procurement and supply chain management.
5. Improve on-site execution.
6. Infuse digital technology, new materials and advanced automation.
7. Reskill the workforce.

As the construction industry worldwide undergoes an inevitable transition towards digitalization, various efforts have been made to induce change in the sector and push digital methods. Across different countries, such efforts come from clients and owners of built assets. For example, in the US, the use of intelligent building design methods, whose benefits would spill over to asset maintenance, began as early as 2007. Other countries followed this approach, including the UK, where the public sector accounts for around 40 per cent of the construction market and is the largest construction client. In 2011, the UK government set up a task group and announced the mandated use of digital tools, such as building information modelling, in all public projects from 2016.[4] Later, the UK government developed the BIM Framework[5] to direct and assist the industry in both domestic and international markets in adopting the International Organization for Standardization (ISO) 19650 series, addressing a broader spectrum of information management.

A wealth of data can be generated, managed and shared through BIM applications, an ecosystem of digital platforms that has been gaining traction worldwide since the early 2000s.

In many countries, such as the UK since spring 2016, the use of BIM in public sector projects has been mandated.[6] Although MCC was active in the Middle East and not in the UK, this trend is relevant as it was followed by many countries. While MCC does not typically work on public projects (Figure A14.2), it was aware of the developments and wanted to keep up if not be one step ahead. Unlike the latecomers who reactively addressed such mandates, MCC went beyond the mandated requirements for digital construction and investigated how to make the most of the opportunities that digital transformation could bring to shape its digital journey.

The global trend of digital transformation across different sectors, including construction, involves the use of BIM, an approach in three-dimensional space for designing built assets that uses and organizes a variety of data across various project life cycle phases. Despite the industry's slow take up of digital technologies, MCC has been an early adopter, investing in digital tools to become more efficient since the early 2000s. As advanced digital technologies and data-driven analytics have become increasingly important in improving construction, MCC's extensive experience in developing and using digitization workflows to share data and optimize its processes and projects has been a significant advantage. This data was shared through common data environments, digital platforms for storing, sharing and managing data generated by commercial BIM solutions.

Strategizing for Innovation in a Project-Based Business

In June 2019, MCC completed the New Airport Terminal Building (Figure A14.6). In a joint venture with the Middle East Airports Company, MCC led the digitalization of the project. This landmark transportation project consisted of the construction of a terminal building with a capacity of 27 million passengers per year and a very complex form (Figure A14.7 and Figure A14.8). This terminal building and its surroundings had a massive scale, could accommodate 106 aircraft, serve 8,500 passengers per hour and handle 19,000 packages per hour. The baggage handling system's conveyor belt length was, at the time of writing, about 27 kilometres (Figure A14.7).

On the way to this point, Hanin Al-Zubi was one of Shalhoub's mentees at MCC. Shalhoub had given the reins to Al-Zubi to act as an internal consultant at MCC and open the BIM centres integrated into MCC's strategy (Figure A14.9). In 1997, MCC completed its first BIM-based estimation project. This was a turning point for its digital approach and the development of digital evangelists such as Al-Zubi.

Al-Zubi's role in MCC was to manage the three BIM centres in MCC: in Europe (the first one created) Egypt and Palestine. MCC was proud of its three BIM centres on three different continents. Al-Zubi would also oversee and supervise the implementation of digital technologies such as BIM in various projects concurrently and offer various digital services (Figure A14.10). As well as the BIM centres, Al-Zubi was the managing director of the BIM Academy, the educational arm of MCC. He explained:

> We were about to be awarded this project, and this is a huge, eight-year project, that was required to be delivered using BIM. Back in 2009, we could not find in the market core

> resources to answer our requirements and demands. The market did not have properly educated resources. We had to develop our own resources.

Before bidding for the NATB project, MCC knew that, since BIM was a contractual requirement for the client, it had to be very proficient in digital technologies. The company's competitive advantage from working with these methods since 1997 was invaluable. "Actually, one of the reasons we were selected for that project was because of our capabilities with BIM, because we were the only contractor who had such BIM capabilities back in 2012 when the tender was opened," Al-Zubi stated. After winning the bid, MCC worked for six months to create its BIM Academy, which was ready eight months before the start of the NATB project. It started teaching 40 engineers the digital methods and workflows, and continued during the project, when 204 engineers were trained.

Along with its own staff, MCC trained its partners and collaborators in the NATB project. As the project was huge, MCC entered into a joint venture with two other companies. MCC led the initiative as it was the most experienced party in digital technologies within the joint venture. When the project started, and MCC began to recruit subcontractors and vendors, it realized that, at that time, only two out of 120 companies could really meet the client requirements. Al-Zubi stated: "We educated them, and they managed to deliver the work. Some of them, we had to sit with for days and days to show them the process and to write data exchange policies with them. For some of them, we had to do all the work on their behalf."

MCC developed its digital innovation strategy to become a leader in the global market of digital construction and used the NATB as a vessel to unveil and test their digital innovation strategy. As a system integrator, MCC helped to upskill the entire supply chain and deliver the NATB using digital technologies, without which, it believes, it would have been impossible. Sarah Hamadani, project manager of the NATB, stated: "We don't know how we would ever have built this project without BIM." Like Shalhoub and Al-Zubi, Hamadani was passionate about digital technology, and believed that it was vital for fast decision-making and knowledge-driven operations.

MCC took a risk in bidding for such a complex project. According to Hamadani, it managed to deliver because of the support from Shalhoub, who drove a very clear strategy, including education, preparing resources, providing expertise and educating the supply chain, so that everybody would be in total sync despite the massive size of the project. After winning the bid, MCC smoothly began work on the NATB, "thanks to Al-Zubi, who took an early decision to build the digital model six months earlier, before the award – a high-risk decision to build a model of $2.5 million before even getting the award," reflected Hamadani. MCC laser-scanned the whole site and consolidated the 3D point-cloud information with the ready model (Figure A14.11). Hamadani continued: "This gave us a kind of readiness of knowing how to build our early logistic plan, how to build a truly reliable baseline schedule on true quantities and true figures that will give you the right key performance index to measure your progress."

A Resilient Digital Innovation Strategy

Shalhoub, CIO at MCC, was trained as a civil engineer. Unlike most of his fellow students, who quickly entered the job market, he chose to pursue further studies in the US. He was thirsty for knowledge and eager to keep learning. At Stanford University, he met his mentor and dissertation supervisor, Raymond Levitt, Kumagai Professor in the School of Engineering. Thirty years ago, Shalhoub, a civil engineering graduate, studied under Levitt on information technology (IT) modelling applications on construction sites. After his time in the US, Shalhoub steadily rose in the hierarchy of MCC, from graduate engineer to site engineer, to project manager, to head of IT and, most recently, CIO.

MCC's digital innovation strategy was resilient, driven by Shalhoub's leadership and vision. Influenced in the US by value chain thinking, the manufacturing sector and operations improvement, Shalhoub developed a strategy that included investment in BIM centres, in-house applications and state-of-the-art systems. The strategy emphasized integration between different functions, systems and workflows on construction sites.

MCC's digital innovation strategy is exemplified in the NATB project. The project's complexity and scale necessitated the extensive use of digital technologies, including BIM. MCC's experience in digital methods was invaluable in winning the bid and executing the project. Its BIM centres around the world and its BIM Academy trained engineers, partners and collaborators in digital methods, ensuring that the entire supply chain was aligned with the digital approach.

During the transition to digital ways of working, Ahmed Shalhoub developed a digital innovation strategy. Hamadani explained:

> We spent a long time investing in our BIM capabilities and BIM strategies, starting with, of course, computerization. When I say computerization, I am including networking, robust networking, in-house application, fetching the latest market capabilities, and then drilling such new workflows, policies and procedures into the whole organization, which is what we've tried to do actually since 1998. Showing the benefits in terms of cost, as time saving, as quality.

The digital strategy included investment in state-of-the-art hubs of knowledge in the form of the BIM centres, where the company's expertise in BIM was shared internally and externally. Since their launch, the MCC BIM centres have accumulated extensive experience and skills in the field of BIM and relevant digital technologies. Through these hubs, the company continuously innovates to be at the forefront of the industry. For Al-Zubi, digital tools such as BIM are not just pretty 3D digital models: "It is the integration between the different functions, different systems, different workflows on a construction site with the model, with the scope generated from the model." Along with training for MCC staff and their supply chain partners, the BIM centres were at the forefront of MCC's R&D, pushing the boundaries of existing digital applications and workflows.

In terms of investment in resources, MCC developed its own state-of-the-art systems where readily available commercial solutions did not meet its requirements. A document interface management system was designed based on MCC's business rules and its daily trends in construction. Hamadani shared:

> We built a complete in-house application, which is basically a document interface management system that connects to the digital 3D models, where I can monitor various building elements and associate them with every change either happening in design or construction, let's say up to construction. I received on a daily basis tons of changes that exceeded 3,000 or 7,000 drawings.

A plus point in Hamadani's daily routine as manager of the digital information in the NATB project was that, with the help of the automated system, she could leave the information to be consolidated from all different departments and partners overnight, then she and the BIM team received the changes report in less than 24 hours. The changes were highlighted in red, green or grey, depending on their importance. Later manager of the process, Hamadani would monitor all the changes, decide on the important elements to focus on, quantify the changes and report them to the other departments as needed. These systems helped make informed decisions and also served as a basis for communication with other collaborators.

Due to the enormous scale of the NATB project, this system gave the team visibility into the project. There were more than 2.5 billion different elements completely tagged and thoroughly monitored, starting from the design, going through the procurement up to execution and until the handover. In addition to the digital models that helped to visualize and design the work to be implemented on site, MCC created a system to monitor the construction site as it was developing. According to Hamadani: "We built a complete BIM-driven system to monitor disruption on site – any kind of disruption, coming from design, environmental or whatever – and to scale it on a digital dashboard that was connected to our BIM models."

The connection between the construction site and the digital models was made possible through sensors and actuators of the Internet of Things (IoT). IoT devices expand internet connectivity beyond the usual standard devices like computers, laptops, smartphones and so on that can be used on the construction site. Devices such as smart fire alarms, smart locks and smart security systems can communicate or interact over the internet smoothly and also be controlled remotely and wirelessly, providing information about parts of the construction site. These systems used technologies such as low-energy wireless, Bluetooth and near-field communication (NFC) protocol, as well as older technologies such as radio frequency identification (RFID). These systems allowed every site engineer involved in this complex project to be quickly in a position to check whether the digital models complied with the on-site model. At the same time, they made the most of less sophisticated technologies such as QR codes and included them in every maintainable asset on site, which gave the facility management team quick access to all kinds of information regarding those erected assets in order to track defects or liabilities.

With its robust network and in-house document management applications, MCC had a smooth transition on the NATB project. Alongside its internal system innovations, it created the i-Room to achieve better visibility and transparency within the BIM environment by opening it up to the rest of the joint venture partners and collaborators. Aligning with international standards such as the Industry Foundation Classes (IFC) and use of digital ground/terrain models was a priority for the i-Room platform. For each of MCC's 65 different subcontractors, it had to communicate in a different electronic data interchange (EDI) manner. Hamadani explained: "Like every subcontractor, they had their own booklets, abbreviations and levels of detail. We gave them a kind of space to use any kind of platform they wanted, and then we assembled within international standard formats to consolidate their models."

Thus the digital platform provided a basis for MCC's communication and negotiation among all the site's partners. Hamadani recalled:

> We were obliged to have a kind of centralized database to manage all that amount of knowledge and information, either static or dynamic coming from the site, or coming from the designer in one port that is accessible to over 65 different joint subcontractors, more than 35 different consultants spread all over the world, and more than 170 vendors. But, what happened actually, with the common environment platform and the model, with our technical reviews, we discovered a lot of design errors, a lot of clashes – a lot of nonsense, let's say, set-ups that forced the designer to continue with further changes, plus, of course, there were market changes and the client's input. The client got more ambitious and raised the demands, asking for more and more changes to the original brief.

The i-Room as a digital platform also provided a basis for more digital technologies to connect and share data and information, not only within the NATB project but also outside, for example linking to digital libraries. Later, this even encouraged MCC to be more ambitious in further developing and enhancing its work style. With further standardization, more flexible logistics and more modularization, MCC also integrated its digital procurement system – e-Proc. This was used to reinforce the local supply chain to avoid delays in importing materials or fabricated parts.

The number of contractors and subcontractors involved created a challenge in addressing the nature of the work with a digital approach. While everyone agreed that digital delivery was the best way forward, it was hard to satisfy all the different types of partners, each with their own capabilities. Al-Zubi explained the contractual side of MCC's digital strategy:

> We came up with a contract that consists of three main requirements. First of all, if they were capable of delivering information as per the quality procedure, following the digital delivery process, then there was no contractual obligation. If they were not digitally capable, then they had a contractual obligation to fulfil this requirement in three ways. They had to either consult one of MCC's preferred suppliers for BIM and digital services, or MCC would teach them in the BIM centres for a period of time agreed in advance, or they would pay MCC to deliver digitally on their behalf.

MCC also invested in sharing knowledge with its project collaborators through human–computer co-location in the form of the i-Room or War Room (Figure A14.12). This was inspired by NASA's control room,[7] and would help to bring together the multicultural and geographically dispersed team of the NATB project. The War Room helped the team to innovate, identify bottlenecks, negotiate solutions and meet project goals. Al-Zubi recalled:

> In the construction process, there is really a tremendous amount of time wasted in solving problems. So, we came up with a creative idea at that time to create this i-Room where people can sit together, visualize in a nice way the issues and the problems. This is very common now, but back then it was a novel and creative idea.

Representatives of all the stakeholders, subcontractors, contractors, designers and clients would sometimes sit in the same room and not leave until most of the issues, or at least the big issues, were solved. This helped MCC reduce its project review cycle from 28 days to seven days or sometimes even two days.

Apart from timely decision-making, the War Room changed the culture of how people working on projects dealt with mistakes and errors, which had typically been through litigation. The War Room instilled a more visual and transparent culture to encourage and invite people from all over the world to sit in the same space at the same table (with interactive computers), consulting on their problems. "Inviting various specialists and decision-makers to make on-the-spot decisions is counter-intuitive, but with the War Room it worked well as they had full insight on any event with the related capsules of knowledge to take an instant decision," explained Hamadani, who continued that now people did not have to point fingers anymore. Hamadani described how this has changed the culture:

> On a daily basis, it was always the black hole waiting for you at the corner, with a hell of challenges. But with the digital opportunities we took, of course, we learned, and we are still learning. We learned how to talk to the engineering department, understand their language and how they think practically. Also, how to talk to people on the site, to the procurers, even the top management.

The NATB project's complexity and scale required extensive use of digital technologies, including BIM. MCC's experience in digital methods was invaluable in winning the bid and executing the project. As MCC trained its engineers and partners in digital methods, this was a conscious strategy in investing in innovation resources, processes and capabilities that extended beyond the NATB project boundaries.

CONCLUSION

MCC's digital innovation strategy provides an example of how a project-based firm in a traditional industry like construction can embrace digital technologies to enhance efficiency, quality and competitiveness. It also illustrates the importance of business acumen, leadership, strategy, investment in technology and training and a clear vision in driving digital transformation. It underscores the challenges and complexities of implementing such a strategy in a fragmented and often resistant industry. The construction sector is project-based, with businesses developing their models around projects, typically their only source of income. This temporary nature of projects results in fragmentation in resources, social capital, knowledge and finances for R&D and innovation. However, MCC invested various types of resources in being an innovative company, recognizing the benefits of digital technologies in managing changes in design. Nonetheless, MCC's digital innovation strategy faced challenges. The board's scepticism and the industry's slow adoption of digital technologies posed risks. Despite MCC's clear innovation strategy, there were daily challenges in managing digital information in a large-scale project like the NATB. To this end, the dilemma for Shalhoub on being asked by the board to make concessions in the innovation strategy since the NATB project was struggling with various emerging uncertainties and MCC was losing money had important implications for MCC's future business.

On the morning of July 30, 2019, Shalhoub entered the large meeting room overlooking Kifissia's ring road, the busiest intersection in north Athens, to meet with the board. He barely slept the previous night, knowing that he would be asked to lose or give back some of his department's resources, but he had spent the previous weeks preparing by discussing the situation with his closest colleagues like Al-Zubi and Hamadani and his digital innovation team. Together, they had explored different scenarios of how to adjust the digital strategy by sacrificing certain key resources or processes. Given that MCC had developed mature digital capabilities over the last few years, mainly due to the NATB project that trained and created the bedrock of digitalization in MCC, Shalhoub decided with a heavy heart to let some of his people be redeployed in the company. MCC was ready for the change as he had created all the necessary capabilities by combining their skills, processes, technologies and human capital to differentiate MCC. He knew that he could do it again with new people when the times would be more welcoming for innovation investment. Shalhoub explained: "Actually, I believe in the coming generation. The coming generation are so aggressive, so hyper, so intelligent, and they are more than ready."

DISCUSSION QUESTIONS

1. What are the differences between innovation in a firm that is project-based, such as MCC, and other service or product development firms?
2. How does MCC explore and exploit digital innovations?
3. What are the challenges of Shalhoub's digital innovation strategy developed in the NATB project and MCC's business strategy?
4. What were the effects of MCC's digital innovation strategy, based on key elements of (digital) innovation, namely resources for innovation, innovation processes and innovative capabilities?
5. Do you agree with Shalhoub's concessions decision, and why?
6. Is Shalhoub a good leader, and why?

NOTES

1. www.mckinsey.com/business-functions/operations/our-insights/imagining-constructions-digital-future
2. Project-based firms are firms in different market sectors (e.g., film, media, research, construction) whose main business depends upon delivering projects that are usually temporary and inter-organizational. Their economic activity is organized through the delivery and execution of projects (Gann & Salter, 2000).
3. McKinsey Global Institute report *Reinventing construction through a productivity revolution*, February 2017, p. 64, available at: www.mckinsey.com/industries/capital-projects-and-infrastructure/our-insights/reinventing-construction-through-a-productivity-revolution
4. Government Construction Client Group: *BIM Working Party Strategy Paper*, 2011:www.cdbb.cam.ac.uk/Resources/ResoucePublications/BISBIMstrategyReport.pdf (Accessed January 2021).
5. The UK BIM Framework is an overarching approach to implementing BIM in the UK: https://ukbim-framework.org/faq
6. The UK Government Construction Strategy was published in May 2011 and publicly launched by the Cabinet Office in July 2011: www.gov.uk/government/publications/government-construction-strategy
7. Mission Control, Houston: www.nasa.gov/wp-content/uploads/2015/05/160406main_mission_control_fact_sheet.pdf

REFERENCES AND FURTHER READING

Artto, K. A., & Wikström, K. (2005). What is project business? *International Journal of Project Management*, *23*(5), 343–353.

Birkinshaw, J., & Gibson, C. (2004). Building ambidexterity into an organization. *MIT Sloan Management Review*, *45*(4).

Boland, R. J., Lyytinen, K., & Yoo, Y. (2007). Wakes of innovation in project networks: The case of digital 3-d representations in architecture, engineering, and construction. *Organization Science*, *18*(4), 631–647.

Dodgson, M., Gann, D., & Salter, A. (2008). Innovation strategy. In *The management of technological innovation: Strategy and practice* (pp. 94–132). Oxford University Press.

Gann, D. M., & Salter, A. J. (2000). Innovation in project-based, service-enhanced firms: The construction of complex products and systems. *Research Policy*, *29*(7–8), 955–972.

Nambisan, S., Lyytinen, K., Majchrzak, A., & Song, M. (2017). Digital innovation management: Reinventing innovation management research in a digital world. *MIS Quarterly*, *41*(1).

Svahn, F., Mathiassen, L., Lindgren, R., & Kane, G. C. (2017). Mastering the digital innovation challenge. *MIT Sloan Management Review*, *58*(3), 14.

O'Reilly, C. A., & Tushman, M. L. (2004). The ambidextrous organization. *Harvard Business Review*, *82*(4), 74–83.

Tidd, J., Bessant, J., & Pavitt, K. (2005). Developing an innovation strategy. In *Managing innovation: Integrating technological, market and organizational change* (pp. 115–163). John Wiley & Sons.

Yoo, Y., Henfridsson, O., & Lyytinen, K. (2010). Research commentary – the new organizing logic of digital innovation: An agenda for information systems research. *Information Systems Research*, *21*(4), 724–735.

APPENDIX

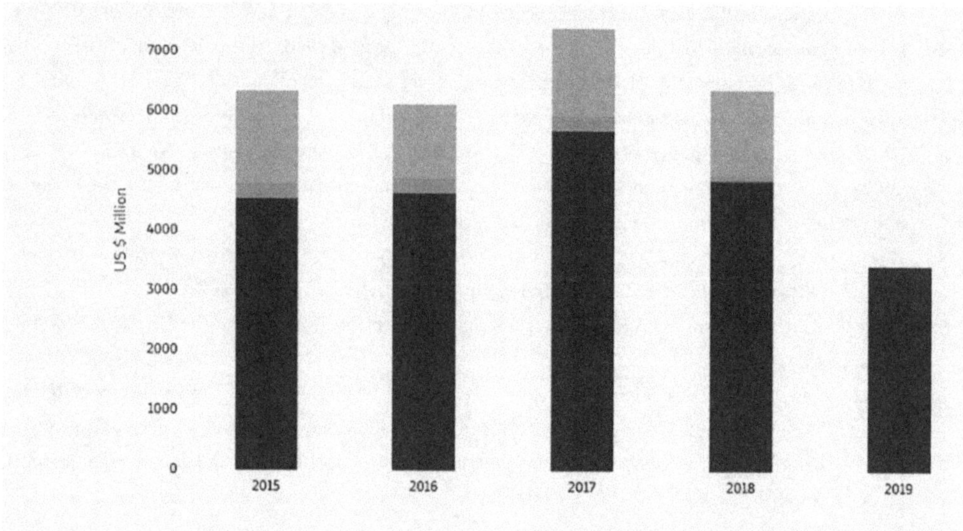

Source: MCC.

Figure A14.1 Total revenue of MCC

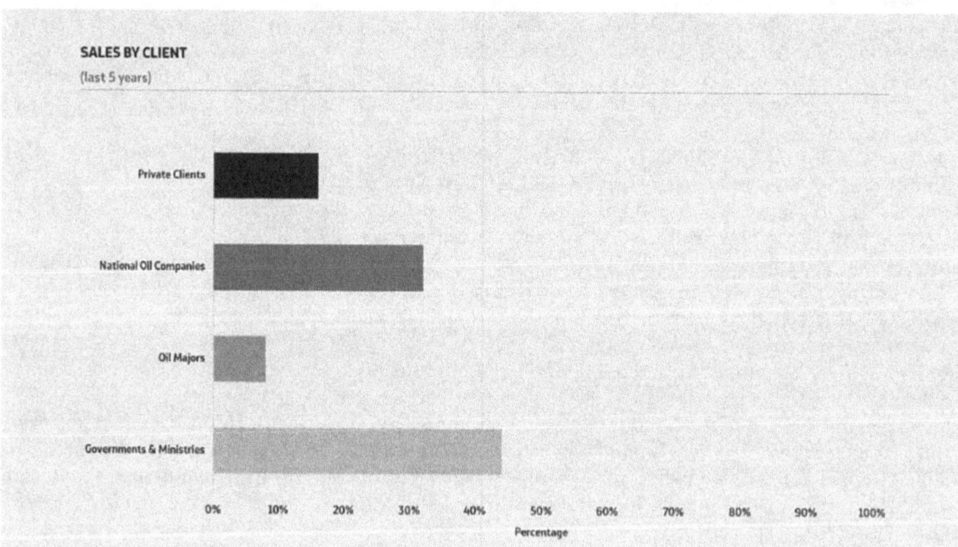

Source: MCC.

Figure A14.2 Sales of MCC by type of client

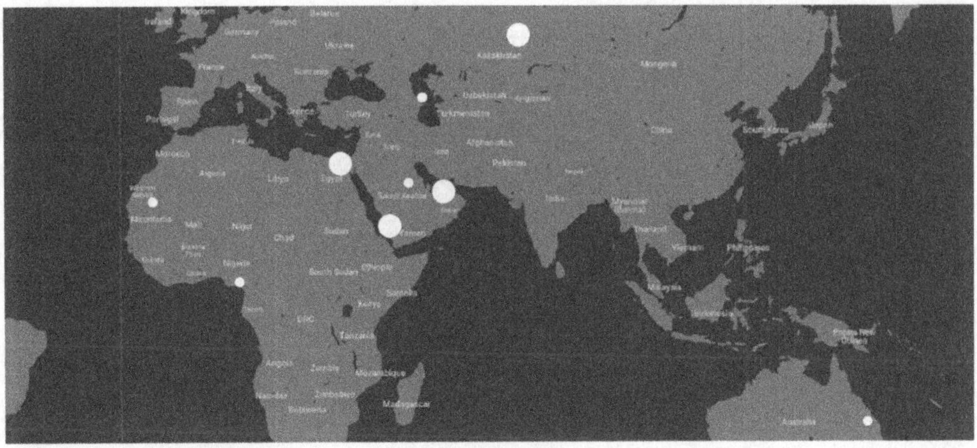

Source: MCC.

Figure A14.3 Major projects of MCC around the world

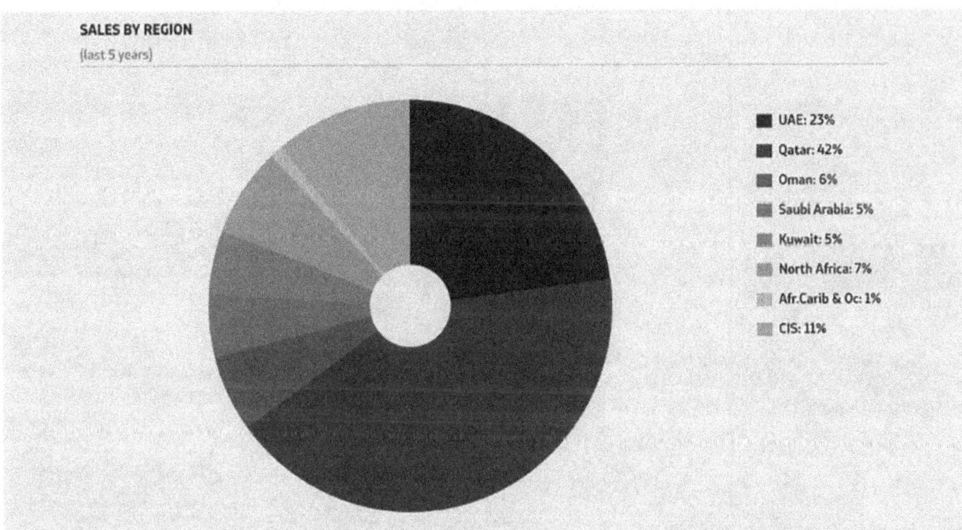

Source: MCC.

Figure A14.4 Sales of MCC per country

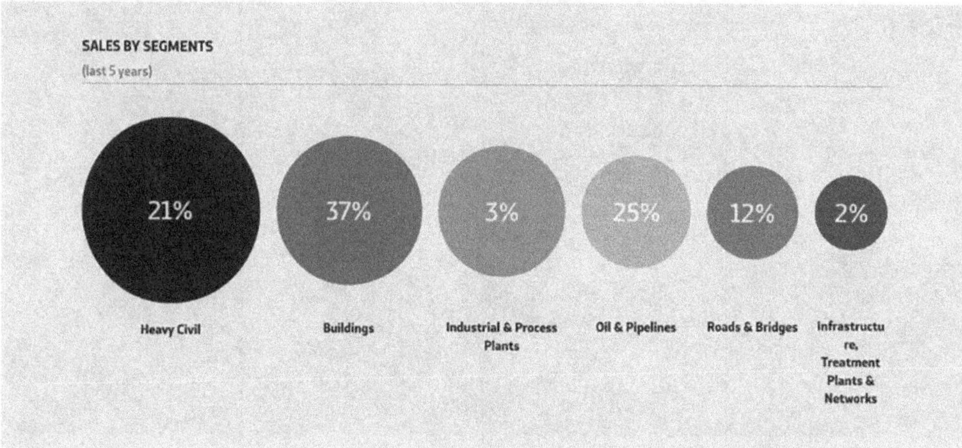

Source: MCC.

Figure A14.5 Types of projects undertaken by MCC

Source: MCC.

Figure A14.6 Overview of the New Airport Terminal Building at Middle East International Airport

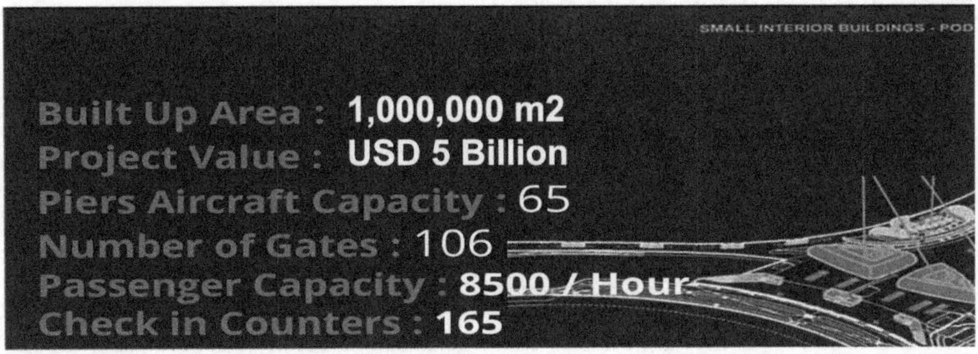

Source: MCC.

Figure A14.7 Basic information about the New Airport Terminal Building project

Source: MCC.

Figure A14.8 Close-up of the New Airport Terminal Building gates

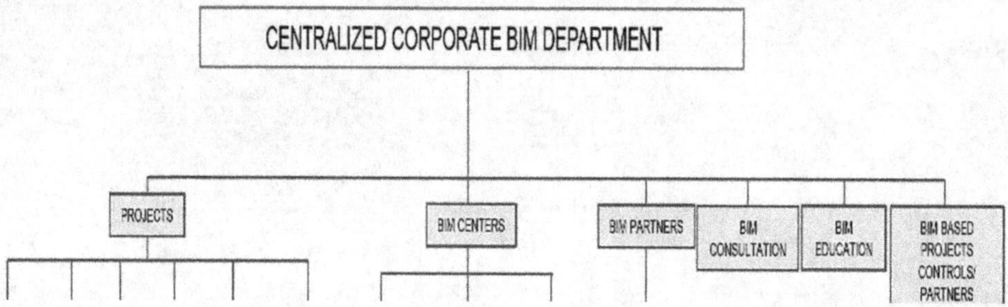

Source: MCC.

Figure A14.9 Organigram of MCC's digital/BIM department

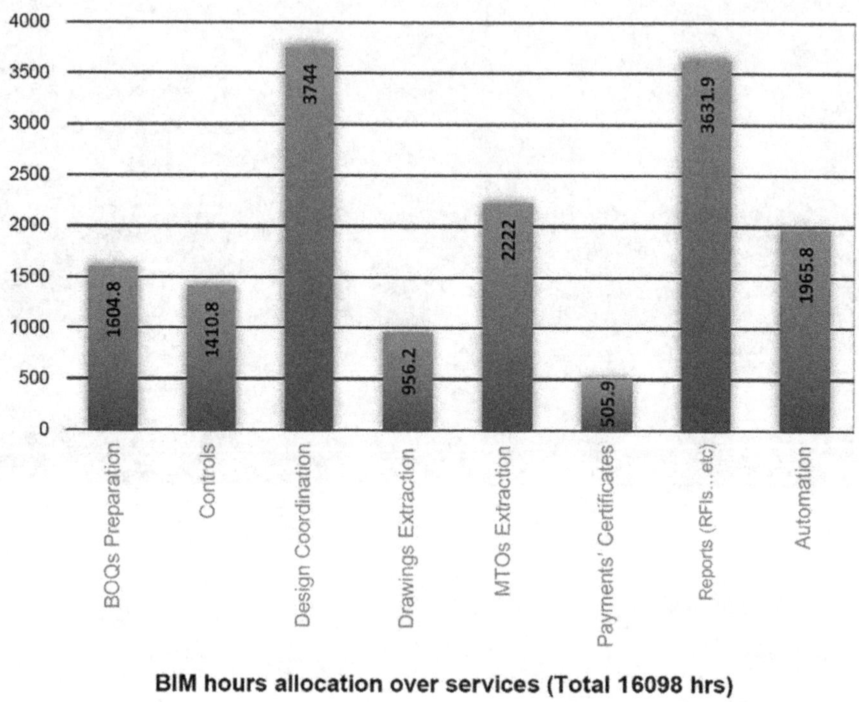

Source: MCC.

Figure A14.10 Types of services from the digital/BIM department

Source: MCC.

Figure A14.11 Laser-scanning and colour-coding of deviations from the design for as-built information

Source: MCC.

Figure A14.12 Aspect and functionality of the i-Room in the New Airport Terminal Building

15
Achieving performance in major public infrastructure projects: the case of road works in Senegal

Mohamed Laye

OPENING PARAGRAPHS

Public infrastructure refers to public facilities having an economic and/or social function in different areas such as energy, hydraulics, transport, agriculture, health, education and so on. For instance, we can cite energy production and distribution systems, water distribution and treatment systems, roads, airports, public transport, irrigation systems, information and communication technologies, public hospitals and public schools.

According to Hansen (1960), public infrastructures are "infrastructures that provide direct support for productive activities and/or the circulation of goods, or those that allow the development of human capital". The United Nations (n.d.-a) includes in its Sustainable Development Goals that "growth in productivity and incomes, and improvements in health and education outcomes require investment in infrastructure". Africa lags significantly behind the rest of the world in all aspects of infrastructure (quantity, quality, cost and access). Therefore, the future of Africa is particularly at stake regarding infrastructure, with annual needs of more than $170 billion in terms of financing, less than half of which is mobilized. This is a huge challenge that calls for a paradigm shift by aiming for excellence to amplify results. To meet this challenge, the Senegalese government developed in 2014 the Emerging Senegal Plan (PSE). The PSE was a ten-year strategy, over the period 2014 to 2023, backed by a vision of an emerging Senegal for 2035 through three strategic axes: (i) the structural transformation of the economy and growth; (ii) human capital, social protection and sustainable development; and (iii) governance, institutions, peace and security. The first axis of the PSE addresses the infrastructure needs considering that "to meet the challenge of growth, Senegal must have structuring infrastructures of the highest standards" (Republic of Senegal, 2014).

Increasing infrastructure capital requires the implementation of massive investments through large public infrastructure projects. However, the implementation of large infrastructure projects often experiences performance problems that result in schedule overruns, cost overruns and quality defects. Indeed, "large public construction projects, in Quebec and elsewhere in the world, often experience significant cost and schedule overruns and are the subject of all the speculation that accompanies this type of problem" (Miller et al., 2006: I). This is confirmed by the French development agency AFD, which indicates that, because of "the repeated failures of very large infrastructure equipment projects, the history of Public Development Assistance (PDA) is that of a relative disappointment of donors" (Jacquet & Charnoz, 2003: 1).

In Senegal, road construction, rehabilitation and maintenance projects in the registered road network are implemented by the Road Works and Management Agency (AGEROUTE). AGEROUTE acts as an executing agency of the ministry responsible for roads. In May 2024, following the election in February of a new president, a large change occurs in the Senegalese government and a new chief executive officer (CEO) is appointed for AGEROUTE. In his mandate, assigned by the minister in charge of the road's infrastructures, the main duty is to improve the execution of the road projects to be implemented by AGEROUTE for the socio-economic development of the nation.

This case study provides a scenario for evaluation. The reader identifies and analyzes the roles that the various road project's stakeholders should assume to make sure the required project performance will be achieved by the new AGEROUTE CEO. The problem is explained and described in the project context, and the implementation of road projects by AGEROUTE over a decade is described. The main point is that the majority (more than 60 percent) of projects finished with cost and schedule overruns, while, regarding the scope, the quality of the road infrastructure was assessed as good for 75 percent of the projects. The main explanations for these mostly undesirable results are the complexity of managing the stakeholders with their sometimes divergent interests and the uncertainties in the context of the project implementation.

An evaluation scenario is proposed to deepen the analysis and explore the managerial recommendations, at each stage of the project cycle, to improve this situation of poor performance in the road projects implementation.

BODY OF THE CASE

AGEROUTE's main duties come from the empirical observation made by the authorities that most of the road projects end up with schedule overruns, cost overruns and, sometimes, quality defects. This observation is confirmed by the diagnosis in a recent investigation,[1] summarized in Figures 15.1, 15.2 and 15.3, which show that the major road projects carried out by AGEROUTE between 2007 and 2016 are marked by:

I. schedule overruns, since the majority of projects (around 60 percent) have a time span greater than 0.6 times the initial contractual schedule
II. cost overruns – 60 percent of projects end with a cost overrun from 16 percent to over 32 percent

III. quality defects, but to a lesser extent, given that at least 16 percent of these projects received maintenance works before their fifth year of commissioning.

This empirical observation confirms what emerges from the literature regarding the performance problems of major public infrastructure projects, of which road projects are an example.

The new CEO wonders what the reasons are for so many failures in major infrastructure projects. Laye (2021) notes that, according to the literature, the answer is in the intrinsic nature of these projects, characterized by their complexity and the uncertainty that surrounds them (Ika & Saint-Macary, 2023). The complexity of public infrastructure projects stems from the interventions by various organizations with objectives which may be divergent, and the difficulty of managing this multiplicity of stakeholders, as well as the projects'

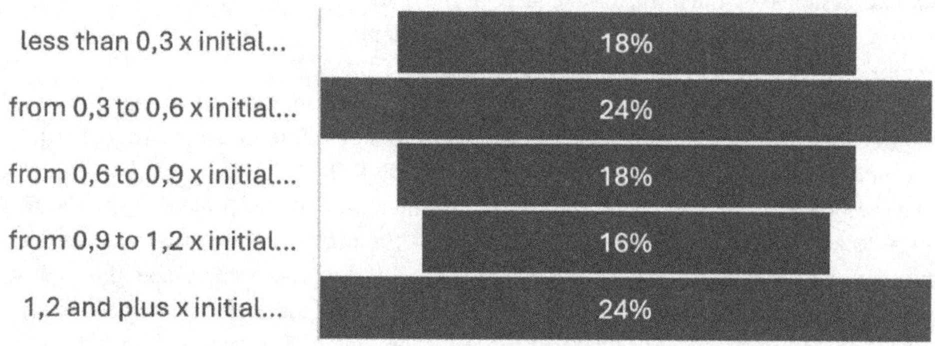

Source: Adapted from Laye, 2021.

Figure 15.1 Schedule overruns in large projects implemented by AGEROUTE from 2007 to 2016

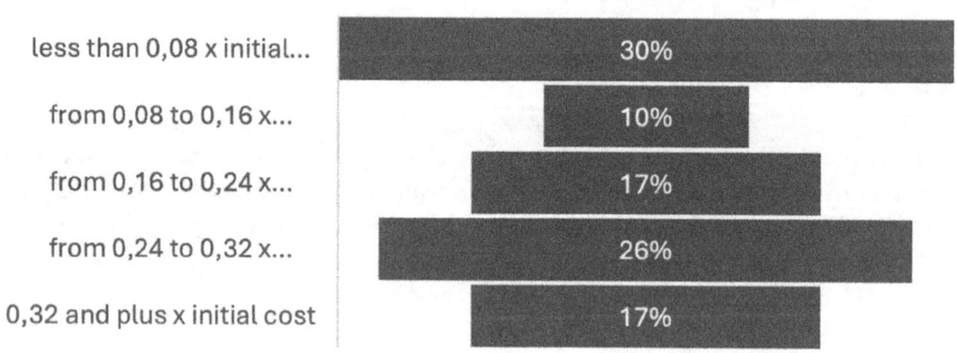

Source: Adapted from Laye, 2021.

Figure 15.2 Cost overruns in large projects implemented by AGEROUTE from 2007 to 2016

Source: Adapted from Laye, 2021.

Figure 15.3 Quality assessment in large projects implemented by AGEROUTE from 2007 to 2016

internal structures and socio-political contexts. As for uncertainty, it is linked with the need to optimize the funding and financing of these large projects, the risks associated and the contractual arrangements to be managed in a changing context. Indeed, to understand the projects' uncertainty, reference should be made to the very definition of the word "project", which etymologically refers to an achievement in the future which is by nature uncertain.

The future is uncertain because the conditions of the physical, political, economic, social and technological environment can change between the moment of intention to take on the project, which implies its preparation, and the actual moment of its implementation. Uncertainty can also arise from an insufficient level of knowledge of the conditions, at the time of project preparation, as illustrated by this example given by Tayeb and Perret (2008: 31) about a project to build an oil refinery: "An additional cost and a delay of a month and a half are attributable to the company responsible for the excavations, which claims that the ground conditions turned out to be different from those specified in the specifications."

Beyond the complexity and the uncertainty, the inadequate consideration of (i) the context in which public infrastructure projects are implemented, (ii) the culture of the actors, and (iii) the involvement of all the stakeholders have also been identified as failure factors.

Project Purpose

Public infrastructures are so important for the socio-economic development of countries that schedule and cost overruns, as well as quality defects, linked to design or construction are problematic to say the least. Country leaders are aware of the importance of public infrastructures. It is for this reason that the member states of the United Nations, within the framework of the 17 Sustainable Development Goals (SDGs), have established Goal 9 (in industry, infrastructure and innovation), which seeks to "build a resilient infrastructure, promote sustainable industrialization and foster innovation."

With a view to achieving Goal 9, many countries are devoting significant public capital to public infrastructure, which gives a significant "leverage effect" to various economic and social activities, notably to business productivity and the development of human capital. The public capital that states devote to infrastructure are investments made through the implementation of public infrastructure projects. Consequently, the performance of the projects is a major issue in the process of socio-economic development of nations. This is corroborated by the first target of SDG 9, which is to "develop quality, reliable, sustainable and resilient infrastructure, including regional and transborder infrastructure, to support economic development and human well-being, with a focus on affordable and equitable access for all" (UN, n.d.-b).

Given the huge investments devoted to public infrastructure and the role they must play in development, schedule overruns, cost overruns and lack of quality, which reflect poor performance of public infrastructure projects, must be avoided. Indeed, these types of results have a negative impact on "the country's budget, the use of the project by the beneficiaries, the reputation of the structures involved in the implementation, the image of the country and on the objectives of the project" (Ndiaye, 2017: 65).

Schedule overruns can have political repercussions because the completion of public infrastructure projects often constitutes a commitment by politicians in response to an expression of need from the population. Missing deadlines often creates a corresponding need to extend the deadline for mobilizing (potentially extra) funds. Additionally, when a project lasts too long, it is rated poorly in the financial institution's project monitoring process. This can negatively impact the disbursement rate as well as the processing of new projects for the country.

Often, cost overruns generate additional financial pressure in a situation of scarcity of public resources and the existence of several priorities in different competing sectors for a country that aspires to greater economic progress and independence, like Senegal.

Quality failing is often the most undesirable result because the intensity of its impact is greater and encompasses all the disadvantages already mentioned. Economic development is delayed in the project area, users are not satisfied, additional financial resources must be sought to try to maintain a certain level of service. The image of the main stakeholders involved in the project is tarnished.

The new AGEROUTE CEO, as a knowledgeable man, sought to discover how similar performance problems of road infrastructure projects had been resolved in other countries. This would capitalize on the experience of good practices in the management of road projects with a view to adapting them to the context in Senegal. He interrogated Laye's literature review (2021) to explore the different literary fields related to the subject: project management, governance of public infrastructures and management of organizations. The purpose was to explore the theories developed in project management to improve performance in large infrastructure projects through schedule, scope and cost criteria. Three main gaps were identified:

- The theories are essentially oriented towards the project manager, to whom different management tools are offered to achieve project performance. Certainly, the project manager has a central role to play since they represents the project owner, who is the promoter of the project. However, the other project stakeholders also have important roles, since they can influence the results of the project and therefore its performance. In the context of road projects, for example, are the important roles of the consultant responsible for pre-project studies, the company in charge of carrying out the works, the project engineer responsible for supervision and control of the works, the donor responsible for mobilizing the budget and finance to fund the project, as well as users, local residents and the physical environment, which may be affected by the achievement of the project objectives.

- The theories have been developed to produce meta-rules (Poulingue, 2007) with regard to the problem of performance faced by all projects around the world and therefore often not appropriate to the context of Senegalese road projects. Indeed, even if the projects were undertaken by a wide variety of companies, they were mainly carried out in North America and Europe, and rarely in Africa or Asia (Ika, 2012). Thus, even if the problem is general, the solution can only be local, inclusive and participatory. Consequently, to adapt the meta-rules to the context of this project, there is a need to consider the environment of the project, its contingencies and the culture of its actors. To this end, Rodrigues et al. (2014: 1048) emphasize that "management is carried out by people imbued with the values and beliefs of the context to which they belong, therefore it is also influenced by culture". This is the second gap which makes it necessary to integrate cultural, political, economic, social, technological, environmental and legal realities in the search for solutions adapted to the specific context of road projects in Senegal.
- In project management generally, the three main performance criteria dealt with are scope, schedule and cost (SSC), and "a certain consensus between the authors on the criteria of respect for time, budget and quality [is an] essential element for evaluating the success of a project" Rodrigues et al. (2014:1048). Whereas, by distinguishing the success of project *management* from the success of the project, other success criteria will emerge. To this end, Perret and Tayeb (2008: 2) emphasize:

> any observation studies in the field have revealed that the assessment of the success of the project after the delivery phase is based not only on the degree of achievement of the objectives set at the outset, but also on the consequences, often unforeseen and sometimes considerable, for the stakeholders. These consequences can ultimately be beneficial or disastrous, even if the performance objectives as initially set have been achieved or not.

Thus, it seems important to evolve from the "iron triangle" of SSC towards a "pentagon" by seeking to achieve, in addition, the criteria relating to the satisfaction of users and residents and the safeguarding of the project's environment.

After understanding the gaps in the literature as explained by Laye (2021), the new CEO asks himself the following research question: "How can we achieve project performance within the framework of a broader vision of stakeholders in the particular case of road projects implemented by AGEROUTE in Senegal?"

Objectives

One of the strategic goals assigned to the new CEO in his mandate is to maximize the value for the Senegalese developing nation of the huge public money dedicated to the road sector. This strategy places sustainable development as a key principle of the new ruling government's policy "to empower people for a sustainable future by driving innovation, developing innovative partnerships, and scaling-up funding to deliver better value for money for the country" Soumare (2023). In this regard, the outcome of any investment for road projects should be to obtain optimal benefits through effective, efficient and economic use of resources, taking into consideration development objectives and the country's socio-economic and environmental aspects. This includes the social value of the road projects, which refer to the health, education and commercial basic socio-economic infrastructures to be constructed or improved for the benefit of the people living around the project's area of influence.

To fill the identified literature's gaps and seek to answer the new CEO research question, with a view to maximizing the value for the nation of public investments in roads, the general objective pursued through this case study is to provide tools to improve the performance of road infrastructure projects in Senegal through understanding the roles of stakeholders. Throughout, is the awareness that the performance of the road project is linked to the roles played by the stakeholders involved at each stage of the project cycle.

The specific objectives of this case study are to determine and analyze the roles of:

- the contracting authority or the project owner
- the service providers (consultant, company, engineer)
- the donor
- other stakeholders (users, residents, public, the environment), and to
- give to the new CEO the capacity to achieve the road project's performance.

To achieve this goal, the "scientific research work will have the specificity of articulating theoretical design and empirical observation", following the example of Popper (1962), cited by Moscarola (2018: 20). In a practical way, ideas from the world of knowledge, concepts, theories and models will be confronted with the empirical world of facts, phenomena and behaviors, using techniques and methods of observation and analysis to produce new managerial knowledge with scientific intent.

This new knowledge will lead to managerial recommendations whose application should have a significant positive impact on the performance of road projects. The goal is to provide solutions that avoid schedule and cost overruns and quality defects and to improve social acceptability while safeguarding the environment.

Conceptual Framework for the Strategic Analysis of the Performance of a Road Project

The main concepts of this case study are the road infrastructure project or road project, stakeholders and performance. What meaning does literature give them and what meaning do we give them?

What is a road project?

Etymologically, "the word project comes from the Latin projectum de projicere which means 'to throw forward'. It thus covers three distinct meanings: an intention to do, preparatory work, an achievement" (Aïm, 2011: 4). Its adaptation in the field of management sciences has led to several standardized definitions. Indeed, the French Standardization Association defines a project as "a specific approach which makes it possible to methodically and progressively structure a future reality" (Afnor, 2002). This rather general definition does not allow us to see certain aspects specific to projects in management.

The International Standard Organization through ISO 10006 defines a project as: "a single process, which consists of a set of coordinated and controlled activities with start and end dates, undertaken with the aim to achieve an objective consistent with specific requirements, including schedule, cost and resource constraints" (Froman & Gourdon, 2003: 149). This definition has the advantage of establishing at first glance,the triangle of scope (specific requirements), schedule (start and end date) and cost (costs and resources) that constitutes the constraint framing the project. This triptych is also at the heart of the problem of road project performance.

Meanwhile, the Project Management Institute (PMI), in its *PMBOK Guide*, presents a project as being "a temporary effort undertaken to create a unique product, service or result. It is temporary because it has a beginning and an end, and it is unique because the product or service is, in some way, different from existing products and services" (PMI, 2017: 4).

These relatively similar definitions mainly emphasize the uniqueness and temporal characteristics of a project as well as the SSC constraints. This distinguishes the project from operations, which are activities carried out by repetitive and continuous processes. However, these definitions do not clearly highlight either the actors involved in the implementation of the project, who can influence its results, nor the environment in which the project is implemented. Therefore, in this case study, the road project is defined as in Box 15.1.

BOX 15.1

The road project is a unique set of activities carried out by stakeholders, and coordinated by a project owner, with a view to carrying out a work (road, including hydraulic works and engineering structures for sanitation and crossing). The project mobilizes resources (means) which are defined, combined and deployed according to the final objective, with a view to producing a result (the infrastructure) that conforms to the specified quality, as quickly as possible, at the lowest cost and safeguarding the environment.

The road project as it is defined, with activities that are carried out with a view to producing a road infrastructure, necessarily involves a process, called the road project cycle, which can be summarized in four main stages shown in Figure 15.4.

Identification: At this stage, the objectives of the project are defined according to the need(s) to be satisfied, the problem to be resolved, the opportunity to be seized or the situation to be changed, as well as the constraints and quality requirements of the social, functional, technical, urban planning and economic elements and safeguarding the human and physical environment.

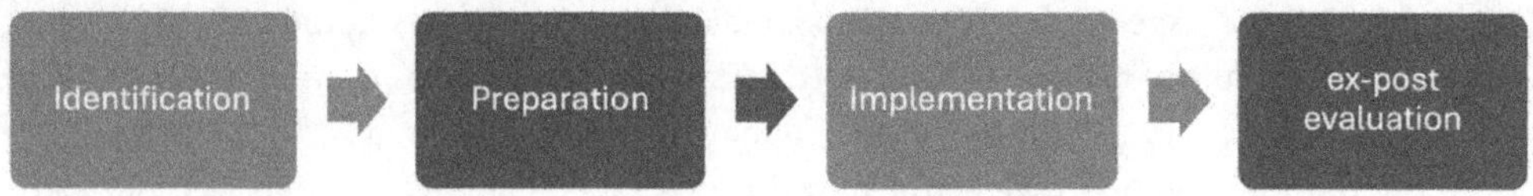

Source: Author.

Figure 15.4 Road project implementation process

Preparation: This stage includes summary pre-project studies, which makes it possible to clarify the problem and the context of the project, and to compare options by exposing advantages and disadvantages realistically, to help the decision-maker in their choice. Subsequently, for the chosen option, the detailed preliminary project studies – environmental, social, economic, hydraulic, hydrogeological, geotechnical, topographical, urban planning and traffic – will be in-depth. These studies thus provide sufficient quantitative elements to enable estimations of the cost and schedule of the project. These elements make it possible to initiate the search for financing, which begins with an ex-ante evaluation to determine the relevance and expected profitability, and provide supporting documents, description, expected results and evaluation indicators of the project. Once the financing has been acquired, it remains to launch the various processes of selecting the service providers responsible for carrying out and supervising the works.

Implementation: This is the phase of transformation, execution of the works, monitoring and control of the implementation. After the detailed execution studies carried out by the company in charge of the work, the construction of a road goes through different phases: preparatory work (clearing and cleaning of the right-of-way), earthworks (excavation and embankment), transverse sanitation works (hydraulic works, box culverts, engineering structures) and longitudinal drainage (masonry ditches, earthen ditches, gutters and so on). These initial works often aim to ensure the road will not flood. This is followed by work on the road structure, made up of several layers with different thicknesses and bearing capacities depending on the traffic to be supported during the road's life cycle (usually 20 years in Senegal) and the bearing capacity of the supporting platform. After the roadworks, the road must be protected with protective works (for the embankments and heads of hydraulic structures) and ensure the safety and comfort of users and residents through adequate vertical and horizontal signage as well as appropriate road safety equipment.

Ex-post evaluation: This stage involves evaluating the results of the project with reference to the objectives set at the start, in the ex-ante identification. It will determine the project's impacts through its direct and indirect effects from macroeconomic, social and environmental points of view. Sustainability is also examined through the medium- and long-term viability of the project's effects. This evaluation includes, among other things, the evolution, from the referral stage to the situation after the project, of traffic conditions (average travel time, average vehicle operating cost, average access index to main basic social services and so on) of people and goods, the increase in traffic, and the economic and social living conditions of the populations in the project's area of influence. The results of the ex-post evaluation are also used to improve the preparation and implementation of new projects.

Who are the Stakeholders in the Road Project?

According to Freeman (2010, p. 1), "the stakeholder approach concerns the groups and individuals who can affect or be affected by the achievement of the organization's objectives, as well as the appropriate managerial behavior in response to these groups and individuals". By adapting Freeman's approach to the context of the road project, we can identify the stakeholders who might influence or be influenced by the realization of the project.

The strategic stakeholders who can influence the performance of the project are the contracting authority (client), the donor, the consultant, the company and the engineer. The "moral" stakeholders who are affected by the realization of the project are the users or beneficiaries, local residents and the physical environment.

The client

The contracting authority, or the client, is the entity that has "an intention to do" the "project". It initiates and is responsible for carrying out the project; it is its promoter. Through the pre-project studies, the client sets the objective, the schedule and the technical specifications, and estimates its cost to satisfy the needs of the end users for whom the project is intended.

In Senegal, in general, the ministry in charge of roads is the client for road projects. AGEROUTE represents the client as the delegated project owner.

To fully understand the place occupied by AGEROUTE in the context of road projects in Senegal, it is necessary to go back to the origins of this executing agency of the ministry, in the 2000s. Indeed:

> After the dark years of the Program of Structural Adjustment (PSA) which was characterized, in the 1980s, by a collapse of investment budgets in transport, the government of President Diouf found, in the 1990s, financial resources which made it possible to reinvest in the area. The Transport Sector Adjustment Program (PAST), running over the period 1991–1995… saw investments increase over five years to 215 million USD (i.e., each year, almost five times more than those spent in 1989–90). (Lombard et al., 2013: 644)

Given the importance of the increasingly high budgets devoted to the sector, at the beginning of the 1990s:

> Various studies were commissioned in order to establish a precise diagnosis of the situation of the transport sector in Senegal and to identify the main existing constraints, in particular an inadequate institutional framework. From 2000, efforts to recover the sector

were further intensified with the overhaul of the institutional system for managing road transport. (Nguessan, 2009: 11).

This institutional reform, intended to correct the dysfunctions of the former Public Works Direction, resulted in the creation of the Autonomous Road Works Agency (AATR). In August 2000, the AATR was given the main mission of the management of the road network under the responsibility of the state as well as the project management of road works on the network. It was put under the supervision of the ministry in charge of roads. In 2004, the missions of the AATR were refocused through another decree, which conferred on the AATR the status of an autonomous public service unit comprising two bodies: the Roads Council – the deliberative body – and the General Management – the executive body. In 2010, the AATR was replaced by the Road Works and Management Agency, designated as AGEROUTE Senegal, a legal entity, endowed with management autonomy and invested with a public service mission. The Agency is an administrative entity placed under the technical supervision of the ministry in charge of roads and under the financial supervision of the ministry in charge of finance. The main mission of AGEROUTE is the implementation of all construction, repair and maintenance works on roads, bridges and other structures as well as the management of the classified road network. The decree (number 2010-430, April 1, 2010) stipulates that AGEROUTE is "responsible, unless otherwise waived, on behalf of the Ministry responsible for roads, for delegated project management of road projects, within the framework of specific financing agreements that may bind the State to donors. In this case, it acts as an executing agency of the Ministry responsible for roads."

The Agency obtained ISO 9001-2008 Certification in June 2016 in the areas of (i) road project management and (ii) management and maintenance of the road network. In 2019, the number of active projects was 49, covering a total length of 2,450 km. The same year, the revised budget of AGEROUTE stood at $628 million, executed at 74 percent, and with human resources of 172 agents of whom 69 percent were executives.

The donor

The donor finances the project. For internal resources, the government through its Consolidated Investment Budget provides the financing. For external resources, there are the technical and financial partners, which are multilateral or bilateral financial institutions such as the World Bank, African Development Bank and the Islamic Development Bank. There is also private financing through public–private partnerships. Indeed, "the limited resources available through government funding sources have led to an increase in interest in private toll roads as an alternative means of meeting road needs" (Fishbein and Babbar, 1997: 2).

These financial institutions are linked to the client by financing agreements. The agreements set the general conditions for the loans or grants and more specific financial conditions, the conditions precedent to entry into force, the disbursement conditions, the closing date and the conditions for the procurement of works and services, as well as various provisions.

The service providers: the consultant, the company and the engineer

In the project preparation phase, the client recruits a consultant responsible for carrying out the preliminary technical, environment and social studies and preparing the tender documents. The same service provider is, usually, also responsible for carrying out the environmental and social impact studies and the action and resettlement plan to mitigate the negative impacts of the project on its physical environment and local population.

Through a procurement process (generally a national or international call for tenders), the client chooses a company that will undertake to carry out the work of the project in return for payment. The client is linked to the company by a contract that sets the fee (cost), the execution time (schedule) and the technical specifications of the work (scope).

Through another procurement process (generally a selection based on quality and cost), the client chooses an engineer in charge of the supervision (monitoring of the implementation process) and control (stop points to be checked) of the works. The engineer is linked to the client by a contract for the provision of intellectual services in return for payment. The engineer represents the client and is responsible for validating the fees to be paid to the company as well as the quality of the works and compliance with the technical specifications. In summary, the engineer "is responsible for the control of the works, the quality of the works, the respect of the financial forecasts as well as the fixed schedule" (Messou, 2017: 22).

Other stakeholders

The moral stakeholders, in the context of the road project, can be split into two groups: the human group, which includes all the beneficiaries and end users such as transporters, residents, the public in general, and the physical environment group, which is made up of the ecosystems of the natural environment (surface and underground water, air, fauna, flora, landscape, soil and subsoil). We call them "other" stakeholders since they externally affect (or are affected by) the road project, unlike the strategic stakeholders who intervene internally in the project. Suitable managerial behavior for the moral stakeholders comes from, in part, the application of the principle of sustainable development, which "meets the needs of present generations without compromising the ability of future generations to meet theirs" (Brundtland, 1987). It is in this sense that the World Bank has established environmental and social policies called safeguard policies. These aim, during the implementation of construction projects, to "ensure the protection of people and the environment against potential negative impacts, through policies that identify, avoid and minimize damage to people and the environment".[2]

Figure 15.5 illustrates the various stakeholders in the road project and the relationships between them.

Road Project Performance

The literature shows us that performance is a polysemous term: it has several meanings relating to the field of employment; it also has several dimensions.

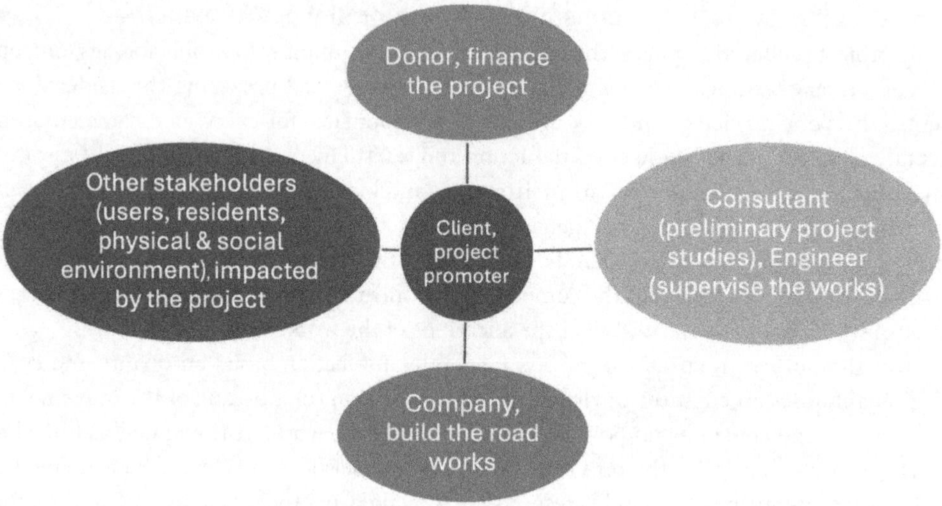

Source: Author.

Figure 15.5 The various stakeholders in the road project

This case study follows the performance model of Moscarola (2018) as it seems consistent with the performance of the road project. The model "describes the performance in a ternary relationship between the objectives (targets, estimates, projections), the means to achieve them (human, material, financial or informational resources) and the results obtained (goods, products, services, etc.)" (Gilbert, 2007, cited in Moscarola, 2018: 39). This definition of performance applies to any ordered system (individual, organization, system and so on) that produces results from basic resources.

The measurement of performance is then carried out on three axes:

- Relevance – the relationship between the objectives and the means acquired to achieve them
- Efficiency – the relationship between the results obtained and the means used
- Effectiveness – the comparison between the results obtained and the objectives set at the start.

Figure 15.6 illustrates Gilbert's performance model.

However, this performance model, being generic, requires adaptation to the context of the road project. Thus, from the client's perspective, which is our center of interest since it is the promoter of the project, the terms of the relationship can be seen as:

- Objectives – the contractual deadline (schedule), the initial cost, the specified quality (scope) and the socio-environmental acceptability of the project
- Results – the duration of the project, the final cost, the quality of the work, the usefulness of the project for the population through its environmental and social impact

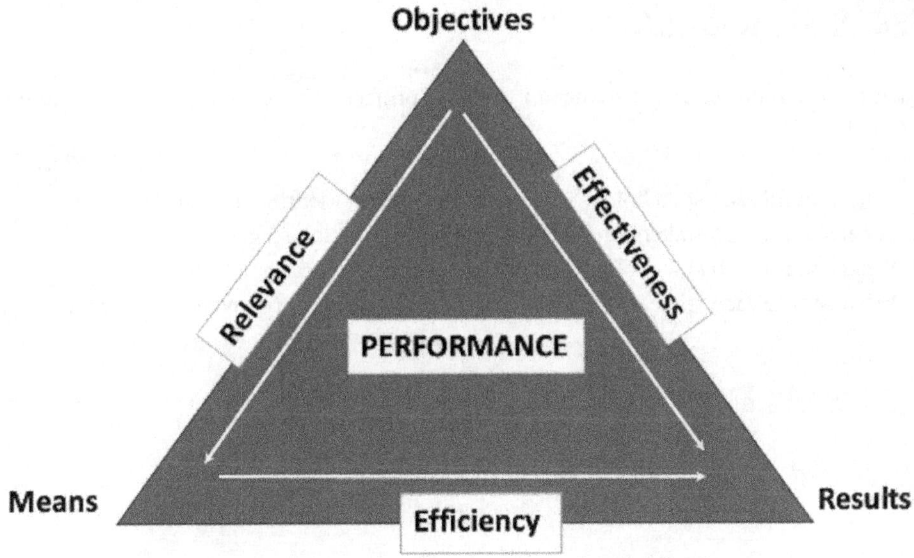

Source: Adapted from Moscarola, 2018.

Figure 15.6 Performance model

- Means – the financial, human and material resources mobilized for the realization of the project.

Thus, in the context of this case study, the performance of the road project can be scored on:

- Effectiveness: The project is carried out with results that correspond to the objectives. The duration of the project does not exceed the contractual schedule, the final cost does not exceed the initial cost, the quality of the work is, at least, in accordance with the technical specifications of the contract. The project has protected its environment (physical and social) and it is useful to the people who accepted it.
- Efficiency: The optimization of the financial resources used to achieve the results of the project. In other words, the best quality of the work is obtained at the lowest cost.
- Relevance: The use of adequate means for the acquisition of the overall objective of the project to meet a need for transport while safeguarding the ecosystem in the physical and social environment. Relevance depends, in part, on the decisions of the political authority, which may consider that such a project should be carried out in place of another for various reasons (territorial development, vision of economic development, satisfaction of social needs, financial profitability and so on). Nevertheless, after the decision to carry out such a road project, certain decisions taken during the different stages of the project implementation process can reinforce the relevance of the political authority's choice.

DISCUSSION QUESTIONS

To achieve the required performance in the road project, the following questions should be answered.

1. What should each stakeholder's role be at the project identification stage?
2. What should each stakeholder's role be at the preparation stage?
3. What should each stakeholder's role be in the implementation phase?
4. What should each stakeholder's role be at the project's ex-post evaluation stage?

NOTES

1. Laye (2021).
2. www.banquemondiale.org/fr/projects-operations/environmental-and-social-policies

REFERENCES AND FURTHER READING

Afnor (2002). *Normes françaises et européenes*, X50-115. Afnor Éditions.

Aïm, R. (2011). *Les fondamentaux de la gestion de projet.* Afnor Éditions.

Brundtland, G. H. (1987). Notre avenir à tous: Rapport de la Commission mondiale sur l'environnement et le développement de l'ONU, présidée par Madame Gro Harlem Brundtland.

Fishbein, G., & Babbar, S. (1997). *Private financing of toll roads.* World Bank.

Freeman, R. E. (2010). *Strategic management: A stakeholder approach.* Cambridge University Press.

Froman, B., & Gourdon, C. (2003). *Dictionnaire de la qualité: Plus de 800 définitions, équivalents anglais, informations normatives commentées.* Afnor.

Hansen, N. M. (1960). Unbalanced growth and regional development. *Economic Inquiry*, *4*(1), 3–14.

Ika, L. A. (2012). Project management for development in Africa: Why projects are failing and what can be done about it. *Project Management Journal*, *43*(4), 27–41.

Ika, L., & Saint-Macary, J. (2023). *Managing fuzzy projects in 3D: A proven, multi-faceted blueprint for overseeing complex projects.* McGraw Hill Professional.

Jacquet, P., & Charnoz, O. (2003). *Infrastructures, croissance et réduction de la pauvreté.* Article pour le forum franco-vietnamien.

Laye, M. (2021). *Optimisation de la performance dans les grands projets d'infrastructures publiques: Le cas ageroute senegal* [Doctorate in Business Administration]. Business Science Institute and IAE Université Lyon.

Lombard, J., Steck, B., & Cissokho, S. (2013). Les transports sénégalais: Ancrages internationaux et dérives locales. *CRES, Karthala*, 643–671.

Messou, M. (2017). Notes sur la pratique du contrôle des travaux routiers, Kamponi Abidjan, Côte d'Ivoire, *210*, 22.

Miller, R., Castonguay, J., & Chebil, F. (2006). *La gouvernance des grands projets d'infrastructure publique: Le processus de révision de la qualité* (Project report 2006rp-23). CIRANO.

Moscarola, J. (2018). *Talking about the data: Quantitative and qualitative methodologies.* EMS Éditions.

Ndiaye, P. M. (2017). *Facteurs de risque dans la gestion des projets de développement au Sénégal.* EMS Éditions.

Nguessan, L., & Privé, E. S. (2009). Le secteur des transports au Sénégal: Enjeux et défis pour la réalisation des objectifs de croissance durable et de réduction de la pauvreté. PFANE-GT Transports.

PMI (2017). *PMBOK: A Guide to the Project Management Body of Knowledge* (6th ed.) Project Management Institute.

Poulingue, G. (2007). Have the members of the Montreal Club influenced project management research? *Future Management*, *2*, 89–104.

Rodrigues, J. S., Costa, A. R., & Gestoso, C. G. (2014). Project planning and control: Does national culture influence project success? *Procedia Technology*, *16*, 1047–1056.

Republic of Senegal. (2014). Emerging Senegal Plan. Plan Sénégal Émergent. https://plandev.sn/index.php?option=com_content&view=article&id=13:plan-senegal-emergent&catid=16&Itemid=166

Soumare, M. (2023). *Challenges of contractors and consultants' performance to achieve sustainable development projects, International Colloque "performance-based asset management of land transport infrastructures and services for sustainable development"* [Seminar]. Dakar.

Tayeb, L., & Perret, F. L. (2008). *Créativité et innovation: L'intelligence collective au service du management de projet*. Presses Polytechniques et Universitaires Romandes.

UN (n.d.-a). *Academic impact: Industry, innovation and infrastructure*. www.un.org/en/academic-impact/page/industry-innovation-and-infrastructure

UN (n.d.-b). *The Global Goals: 9: Industry, innovation and infrastructure*. www.globalgoals.org/goals/9-industry-innovation-and-infrastructure

16

Developing systems thinking competencies in project managers

Shankar Sankaran

OPENING PARAGRAPHS

This case study is a simulation using role play. It teaches systems thinking concepts to project management students or other participants who want to apply systems thinking in their work. Learning these principles will empower project managers to apply the concepts in practice when problems they face require stepping away from a reductionist approach to using a holistic approach.

Project managers are trained to break down the tasks of a project and manage them within constraints such as time, cost, scope, or quality to complete a project. A work breakdown structure (WBS) is a hierarchical breakdown of tasks to be done in a project based on the deliverables of the project with the aim of efficiently managing the project. However, it is also important for project managers to stand back and look at a project as a whole when needed. Learning to adopt a systems perspective helps to 'see the forest and the trees' to address tensions that can arise in complex projects (Schad & Bansal, 2018).

Why Systems Thinking is Useful in Projects

Systems thinking enables project managers to take a holistic perspective towards a project:

> Systems thinking is a way of looking at (and making sense of) the world. It is based on an understanding that if one considers the situation as a whole, rather than focusing on its component parts, then there are properties that can be observed which cannot be found simply from the properties of the component parts. (Reynolds & Holwell, 2020, p. 8).

An ability to adopt a systems thinking perspective is useful when dealing with a project that has multiple stakeholders who may have different viewpoints of the situation being addressed and ways to deal with it, thus rendering a project complex. By taking a holistic view, project managers can study the interrelationships between tasks in a project that could create unanticipated issues due to a property of systems called *emergence*. The emergent properties of a system 'are novel in the sense that they are not present in the parts; they emerge from the specific relationships and interactions among the parts in the organized ensemble' (Capra & Luisi, 2014, p. 155): think about how a symphony orchestra comes together to produce a melodious piece of music. A few examples of applications of systems thinking are: business (new product development, decision making, inventory management); healthcare (improving safety, disease prevention); government (policy development, modelling); high-technology organisations (embedding technology and data science into products); sustainable development (adopting circular economy principles, waste reduction).

BODY OF THE CASE

This case study was developed at a university of technology's master of project management course accredited by the PMI Global Accreditation Center (GAC). Thesubject was 'Systems Thinking for Managers', and it has been taught since 2010. It was developed in its current form by Tim Haslett, Jeffrey Scales, and the author through their years of reflecting on teaching and finding the best way to teach the subject to students. They found that exposing participants to a real-life complex situation using a role-play simulation worked well to meet their aspirations.

While the subject is taught in a four-day block workshop in the project management course, it can be tailored to a weekly teaching mode or to be delivered in one or two days. The author has delivered it as a one-day workshop with doctoral students (Ninan et al., 2019).

To decide on the systems approaches to be taught, Tim and the author used the 'system of systems methodologies' proposed by Michael Jackson (Jackson, 2004, p. 24) which classifies systems methodologies according to the different situations in which they are applicable. Hard systems are useful for addressing simple and complex situations where participants shared a common purpose. An example is developing weapons or building a bridge. Examples of such methodologies in complex problems are system dynamics (Sterman, 2002) and the viable system model (VSM) (Beer, 1985). Soft systems approaches such as soft systems methodology (SSM) (Checkland, 1999) were found to be more useful in complex problems where stakeholders had different values and beliefs and their views could be accommodated through dialogue and debate. Such situations can be found when different functions in an organisation have different views on the organisation's strategy. However, in coercive situations where participants have few interests in common as power and politics play an influential role, approaches like critical systems heuristics (CSH) (Ulrich, 1983), a framework for reflective practice based on practical philosophy and systems thinking, are needed.

In the course taught at the author's university, system dynamics (a modelling technique to frame and understand complex issues), SSM, VSM and CSH were selected to be taught and applied to a case study. You are welcome to choose other methodologies (Jackson, 2019), but we believe it is best to expose students to a variety of methodologies used in different contexts to learn to address complex situations.

Learning Objectives of this Simulation

1. Demonstrate a capacity to analyse and effectively communicate a way forward to improve a situation at work by applying systems thinking.
2. Explain the basic concepts of systems thinking as applied to management problems.
3. Apply system dynamics, soft systems thinking methodology, VSM and/or CSH to complex problems. (Please change based on which methodology you are teaching.)
4. Use systems thinking and systems diagnosis tools to address issues arising in projects.
5. Demonstrate a capacity to apply computer software to create and analyse causal loop diagrams and build.
6. Demonstrate a systemic thinking approach to practice.

Preparing for the Case Study

The case study requires a complex unstructured problem that needs structuring (Mingers & Rosenhead, 2004) before it is addressed. Such problems are characterised by the presence of multiple actors, multiple perspectives, incommensurable and/or conflicting interests, important intangibles and key uncertainties (Mingers & Rosenhead, 2004). A contemporary problem of national and global interest should lend itself well to students' preparation and participatation. For example, you could discuss the ethical implications of the use of artificial intelligence. The diversity of students should also be considered when selecting the problem to encourage debate from students of different gender, disciplinary and cultural backgrounds and styles of thinking. An assessment tool such as project skills inventory (Elbeik & Thomas, 1998), Hermann's Whole Brain Thinking Model[1] or Myers-Briggs Type Indicator[2] could be used to analyse preferences to help with selecting diverse teams.

Once you have decided on a problem, it will be ideal to identify someone who is facing the problem and can act as a client, whose problem the students will address. You could ask a student to play the role of a client, but they will need to know all the characteristics or views of the role they are playing. If the client can present in the classroom, it will result in better learning outcomes, but they could participate virtually if they are unable to come to the class. Preparatory work by students will also be necessary so that they can participate as stakeholders during the simulation with prior knowledge of the issues and roles they will play.

If possible, ask the prospective client to provide reading resources or links to videos or newspaper articles that students can access before the class. Discuss with the client the key stakeholders who may have an impact on the situation and use this information to select roles for students to play during the simulation. Once the stakeholders are known, decide on the number of teams to act as stakeholders, based on class size. Aim for a team size of between five and eight participants, and merge stakeholders who have similar attitudes if required to fit the class size. While there are several methods of allocating roles, it has been found that asking students to select and rank roles they would like to play contributes to good teamwork.

To help students get used to systems thinking before the class, you might set a preparatory assignment in which you ask them to identify one key issue that has caught their eye while reading up on the problem. You can ask them to put their issue in the centre of a sheet of paper and draw a system map with a boundary and an influence diagram that capture influences on the problem from within and outside the boundary. The article by Lane & Morris (2001) can help students to learn about the systems concepts of the boundary and the environment and how to draw an influence map. An influence map could help them later when they learn about causal loop iagrams (CLD). 'A causal loop diagram consists of four basic elements: the variables, the links between them, the signs on the links (which show how the variables are interconnected), and the sign of the loop (which shows what type of behaviour the system will produce)' (Lannon, 2012).

Case Study Phases

Aim to set up the simulation in phases, interspersed with some lecturing followed by activities, and ending with capturing some lessons learnt that can be presented once the simulation has been completed.

- Phase 1 – Finding out: Developing multiple perspectives of the problematic situation from the viewpoint of stakeholders.
- Phase 2 – Analysing the problematic situation and developing a model to transform the situation from the perspective of different stakeholders.
- Phase 3 – Moving towards accommodation of views of different stakeholders and developing a way forward collaboratively.
- Phase 4 – Developing a viable organisation to implement the way forward, and presenting lessons learnt during the process.

Phase 1

Phase 1 familiarises participants with some basic systems thinking concepts, including CLDs, to get them thinking more systemically. Soft systems methodology is then introduced before the client is invited to present their problem. The focus in Phase 1 is to get students to start role-playing in teams to draw *rich pictures* that capture their view of the problematic situation. A learning process is repeated at the end of each phase to help with capturing the learning each day. Table 16.1 presents an overview.

Phase 2

In Phase 2, participants try to make sense of what they found in their rich pictures in Phase 1 to understand the views of the different stakeholders. They then begin to analyse the situation in detail using SSM tools as well as CLDs and using CSH to ensure that everyone who has a stake in the situation has been considered, with a view to proposing a transformation to improve the situation (Table 16.2). For a shorter workshop, Phase 2 can be the point where the simulation is ended and students make their concluding presentations.

Here you could ask teams to make a 15–20-minute presentation based on all the learning captured from the two phases. They can use photos of artefacts they produced during the phases to support their presentation. After all student teams have presented, the lecturer/

Table 16.1 Scenario for Phase 1

Step	Topic/activity	Purpose/explanation	Time	Resources
1	Welcome and introductions with an overview of the case study	Provide an overview of the case study and its purpose and expectations of students.	15 minutes	-
2	Systems thinking overview	Introduce a basic idea of systems thinking with some short activities as ways to break away from reductionist thinking.	45 minutes	Sweeney & Meadows (2010); Kim (1999); Senge (2006); Meadows (2008)
-	Break	-	-	-
3	Systems thinking concepts including CLDs	Use CLDs to understand systems thinking concepts (relationships, influence, behaviour over time). Help students to draw CLDs manually.	45 minutes	Anderson & Johnson (1997); Sterman (2002); Senge (2006); Maani & Cavana (2007); Sherwood (2011); Dangerfield (2014)
4	SSM 1 (rich pictures)	Introduce SSM and rich pictures (Checkland & Poulter, 2007 is a useful resource).	60 minutes	Checkland (1999); Checkland & Poulter (2007)
5	Announce teams and ask them to prepare a team charter	A good spot to get teams together and ask them to develop a team charter on ways they will work together effectively. Videos can be used as well.	30 minutes	Hunsaker et al. (2011)
6	Presentation by client on selected topic	Invite the client to present the problematic situation (refer to Checkland, 1999, for using this term while applying SSM).	60 minutes	-
-	Break	-	-	-
7	Drawing rich pictures about client's problems	Ask teams to draw rich pictures expressing their problem as the stakeholder they represent. Provide examples of rich pictures and explain what elements are best to include and exclude. Emphasise that, at this stage, they are not analysing, just presenting the problem. Afterwards, organise a walk about to visit each rich picture and allow time for asking questions or clarifications.	90 minutes plus	Lewis (1992); Monk & Howard (1998); Bell et al. (2016); Bronte-Stewart (1999)
8	Learning capture process	Explain the learning capture process to be used at the end of each phase.	30 minutes	Hay et al. (2008)
9	Reflect on what was learnt using concept mapping	Allow time for students to reflect on what they learnt at this phase. Concept mapping is one possible way of distilling the learning.	60 minutes	Hay et al. (2008)

Table 16.2 Scenario for Phase 2

Step	Topic/activity	Purpose/explanation	Time	Resources
1	Reflections	Reflect on the surprises from Phase 1. Taking a poll can be interesting.	15 minutes	-
2	CLDs from rich pictures	Ask teams to find some causal loops in their rich pictures to practice their system dynamics skills. (Vensim software could be use to draw the CLDs).	45 minutes	Tip (2011); Sherwood (2011) Garcia (2018); Garcia & Sterman (2018)
-	Break	-	-	-
3	SSM analysis 2 and 3	You could introduce two more analyses suggested in SSM – Roles–Norms–Values and Power and Influence – before asking the teams to identify the stakeholders' perceptions and values. Explain that, when applying SSM in real life, it will take time to carry out these analyses.	45 minutes	Checkland & Poulter (2007); Checkland (1999)
4	CSH	The 12 questions posed in CSH can be introduced to consider how to deal with a coercive situation. This will allow for the stakeholders they missed during their analysis when they do a CARWOE analysis during SSM 2.	45 minutes	Ulrich (1983)
-	Break	-	-	-
5	SSM 2 (CATWOE)	Teams develop a CATWOE (customer, actor, transformation, worldview, owner, and environment) by identifying a transformation that each group of stakeholders wants to achieve to improve the situation. It is important to spend some time explaining what these terms mean in an SSM context.* Carry out a walkabout after the CATWOEs.	90 minutes	Checkland & Poulter (2007); Bergvall-Kåreborn et al. (2004); Burge (2015); Bergvall-Kåreborn & Grahn (1996)
-	Break	-	-	-
6	SSM 3 (root definitions/HAS – human activity systems – models)	Using the CATWOE outputs, teams develop a 'root definition' for their transformation (a mission statement), which then allows them to develop a HAS as a high-level scope for a project that will help deliver the transformation.** The HAS can then be evaluated using the three Es of efficiency, effectiveness and efficacy to confirm that the transformation will use these attributes.	60 minutes	Checkland & Poulter (2007); Bergvall-Kåreborn et al. (2004); Burge (2015); Bergvall-Kåreborn & Grahn (1996)

Step	Topic/activity	Purpose/explanation	Time	Resources
7	Learning capture	Capture what has been learnt in Phase 2.	60 minutes	-

Note: * For example, transformation fulfils an identified need; world-view is the attitude of the stakeholder groups, such as, 'Ethical values are important'. ** The resources provide guidelines to develop the HAS with around seven activities in a sequence, with provision for monitoring and control.

facilitator should provide feedback. The expected content is: i) title of presentation and team names, ii) revised rich picture, iii) CATWOE and root definition for transformation, iv) HAS (high level scope) and evaluation, and v) reflections from learning captured.

Phase 3

The purpose of Phase 3 is to encourage participants to reconcile their views and work together to move forward. They revisit their rich pictures and make any necessary adjustments based on what they have understood about multiple stakeholder views. Participants then try to move into a more collaborative phase to develop innovative ideas to transform the problematic situation using their collective wisdom. They should prioritise ideas according to desirability and achievability, looking for quick wins that can generate momentum to help improve the situation in the longer term (Table 16.3).

Phase 4

The purpose of Phase 4 is to design, via VSM, a viable organisation that can implement one of the solutions selcted during the town hall process, with all five subsystems identified (Table 16.4). VSM also helps students to think about the governance of the organisation.

The expected content of the presentation is: i) title of presentation and team names, ii) revised rich picture, iii) CATWOE and root definition for transformation, iv) HAS (high level scope) and evaluation, v) team reflections from the town hall process, vi) governance model using VSM for the transformation project, and vii) reflections from learning captured.

Table 16.3 Scenario for Phase 3

Step	Topic/activity	Purpose/explanation	Time	Resources
1	Reflections	Reflect on surprises from Phase 2.	15 minutes	-
2	Systems archetypes	A review of archetypes so that students can recognise some archetypes in the situation.	45 minutes	Senge 2006; Kim (1999); Kim & Anderson (1998)
3	Revisiting rich pictures	Students revisit the rich pictures and collect their thoughts on working together as a community of stakeholders looking for innovations for the town hall meeting that follows.	60 minutes	-
-	Break	-	-	-
4	Town hall meeting: ideation	If students have been working at tables, theatre-style seating will be better to conduct the town hall meeting, with lecturers or client acting as 'mayor' to manage proceedings. Students are now thinking together as stakeholders who have achieved a way forward, and start with some innovative solutions to the problem. Students, in groups, come up with two or three ideas and explain it to the community in the town hall. Each group's ideas are then posted on a flip chart side by side. Some ideas that are similar can be removed, combined and/or renamed.	60 minutes	Rucker (2015)
5	Town hall meeting: voting	All present at the meeting have three green dots and one red dot to vote on the ideas. Green dots are placed on liked ideas. Once the green dots are fixed, everyone stands back and looks at the whole picture. Then they place a red dot on one idea that they think takes priority. They can be asked to evaluate the idea using words such as 'desirable' and 'achievable'.	30 minutes	Rucker (2015)
6	Learning capture	Capture learning from this phase.	60 minutes	-

Table 16.4 Scenario for Phase 4

Step	Topic/activity	Purpose/explanation	Time	Resources
1	Reflections	Reflect on surprises from Phase 3.	15 minutes	-
2	VSM	Introduce VSM as an example of cybernetics.	45 minutes	Beer (1984); Beer (1985);Espejo & Harnden (1989)
-	Break	-	-	-
3	VSM activity	Ask students to apply the VSM as a governance model for an organisation for the transformation project selected from the town hall meeting.	45 minutes	-
-	Break	-	-	-
4	Preparation for presentations	Allow student teams to put together a set of slides to present what they learnt from the simulation.	60 minutes	-
-	Break	-	-	-
5	Class presentations and feedback	Participant teams make a 15–20-minute presentation on all the learning they captured from the phases. They can use photos from artefacts they produced during the phases to support their presentation. After all participants have presented, lecturers can provide feedback.	120 minutes (depending on number of teams)	-
6	Close	Explain the post-workshop task that needs to be submitted as an assessment.	30 minutes	-

DISCUSSION QUESTIONS

Apply systems methodologies discussed during the case study to analyse a problem. To help in choosing a problem, consider:

- Something at your workplace (or a workplace you are familiar with), in a project management context that you are familiar with so that you might improve the situation.
- A problem that has an impact on your life (health, career and so on).
  - If this problem that you have extracted is from a published case study, rather than a real-life situation, provide a reference to the case study.
  - Choose a suitable problem that would benefit from exploration using systems methodologies.

Limit your submission to ten pages, excluding any cover sheet.

1. Describe the context:
   - Provide a brief (three sentences) description of the problem you are analysing.

2. Structuring the problem (about three pages):
   - Draw a behaviour over time graph of the problem and the desired change, and then two more: one for the causes of the problem and one for the effects on the problem because of the change.
   - Provide either a CLD or a rich picture exploring the dynamics and solution to the problem situation.
3. Finding a way forward (about three pages):
   - Provide a VSM or a description of an SSM that would meet the requirements of dealing with the problem.
   - If relevant, ask questions explained under CSH to address any boundary-related issues.
4. Developing activities to implement the solution (about two pages):
   - Provide a HAS to solve the problem.
   - Provide one evaluation criterion for each of efficiency, efficacy and effectiveness of your HAS.
5. Personal learning (about one page):
   - Reflect on what you have learnt from the course.
   - How do you think you can use what you learnt in your work or life?

NOTES

1. www.thinkherrmann.com/whole-brain-thinking-methodology
2. www.myersbriggs.org/my-mbti-personality-type/the-mbti-preferences

REFERENCES AND FURTHER READING

Anderson, V., & Johnson, L. (1997). *System thinking basics: From concepts to causal loops.* Pegasus Communications.

Beer, S. (1984). The viable system model: Its provenance, development, methodology and pathology. *Journal of the operational research society, 35*(1), 7–25.

Beer, S. (1985). *Diagnosing the system for organizations.* John Wiley & Sons.

Bell, S., Berg, T., & Morse, S. (2016). What is a rich picture? In *Rich pictures: Encouraging resilient communities* (pp. 1–36). Routledge.

Bergvall-Kåreborn, B., & Grahn, A. (1996). Expanding the framework for monitor and control in soft systems methodology. *Systems Practice, 9*(5), 469–495.

Bergvall-Kåreborn, B., Mirijamdotter, A., & Basden, A. (2004). Basic principles of SSM modelling: An examination of CATWOE from a soft perspective. *Systemic Practice and Action Research, 17*, 55–73.

Bronte-Stewart, M. (1999). Regarding rich pictures as tools for communication in information systems development. *Computing and Information Systems, 6*, 85–104.

Burge, S. (2015). An overview of the soft systems methodology. *Systems Thinking: Approaches and Methodologies*, 1–14.

Capra, F., & Luisi, P. L. (2014). *The systems view of life: A unifying vision*. Cambridge University Press.

Checkland, P. (1999). *Systems thinking, systems practice: Includes a 30-year perspective*. John Wiley & Sons.

Checkland, P., & Poulter, J. (2007). *Learning for action: A short definitive account of soft systems methodology, and its use for practitioners, teachers, and students*. John Wiley & Sons.

Dangerfield, B. (2014). Systems thinking and system dynamics: A primer. In S. Brailsford, L. Churilov, & B. Dangerfield (Eds), *Discrete-event simulation and system dynamics for management decision making* (pp. 26–51). John Wiley & Sons.

Elbeik, S., & Thomas, M. (1998). *Project skills*. Routledge.

Espejo, R. and Harnden, R. J. (Eds) (1989). *The viable systems model: Interpretations and applications of Stafford Beer's VSM*. John Wiley & Sons.

Garcia, J. M. (2018). System dynamics modelling with Vensim: 2020. Independently published.

Garcia, J. M., & Sterman, J. (2018). Theory and practical exercises of system dynamics: 2020. Independently published.

Hay, D., Kinchin, I., & Lygo-Baker, S. (2008). Making learning visible: The role of concept mapping in higher education. *Studies in Higher Education*, *33*(3), 295–311.

Hindle, G. A. (2011). Case article: Teaching soft systems methodology and a blueprint for a module. *INFORMS Transactions on Education*, *12*(1), 31–40.

Hunsaker, P., Pavett, C., & Hunsaker, J. (2011). Increasing student-learning team effectiveness with team charters. *Journal of Education for Business*, *86*(3), 127–139.

Jackson, M. C. (2004). *Systems Thinking: Creative Holism for Managers*. John Wiley & Sons.

Jackson, M. C. (2019). *Critical systems thinking and the management of complexity*. John Wiley & Sons.

Kim, D. H. (1999). *Introduction to systems thinking*. Pegasus Communications.

Kim, D. H., & Anderson, V. (1998). Systems archetype basics. Pegasus Communications.

Lane, A., & Morris, D. (2001). Teaching diagramming at a distance: Seeing the human wood through the technological trees. *Systemic Practice and Action Research*, *14*(6), 715–734. doi: https://doi.org/10.1023/A:1013178328419

Lannon, C. J. S. T. (2012). Causal loop construction: The basics. *The Systems Thinker*, *23*(8), 7–8.

Lewis, P. J. (1992). Rich picture building in the soft systems methodology. *European Journal of Information Systems*, *1*(5), 351–360.

Maani, K., & Cavana, R. Y. (2007). *Systems thinking, system dynamics: managing change and complexity* (2nd ed.). Pearson Education New Zealand.

Meadows, D. H. (2008). *Thinking in systems: A primer*. Chelsea Green.

Mingers, J., & Rosenhead, J. (2004). Problem structuring methods in action. *European Journal of Operational Research*, *152*(3), 530–554.

Monk, A., & Howard, S. (1998). The rich picture: A tool for reasoning about work context. *Interactions*, March–April, 21–30.

Ninan, J., Phillips, I., Sankaran, S., & Natarajan, S. (2019). Systems thinking using SSM and TRIZ for stakeholder engagement in infrastructure megaprojects. *Systems*, *7*(4), 48.

Reynolds, M., & Holwell, S. (Eds) (2020). *Systems approaches to managing change: A practical guide* (2nd ed.). Springer.

Rucker, D. (2015). Crowdsourcing wisdom: A guide to doing public meetings that actually make your community better (and won't make people wish they hadn't come). Wise Fools Press.

Schad, J., & Bansal, P. (2018). Seeing the forest and the trees: How a systems perspective informs paradox research. *Journal of Management Studies*, *55*(8), 1490–1506.

Senge, P. (2006). *The fifth discipline: The art and practice of the learning organization*. Random House.

Sherwood, D. (2011). *Seeing the forest for the trees: A manager's guide to applying systems thinking*. Nicholas Brealey International.

Sterman, J. (2002). *System dynamics: Systems thinking and modelling for a complex world* [Working Paper Series]. MIT Engineering Systems Division.

Sweeney, L. B., & Meadows, D. (2010). *The systems thinking playbook: exercises to stretch and build learning and systems thinking capabilities*. Chelsea Green Publishing.

Tip, T. (2011). Guidelines for drawing causal loop diagrams. *Systems Thinker*, *22*(1), 5–7.

Ulrich, W. (1983). *Critical heuristics of social planning: A new approach to practical philosophy*. Haupt/Wiley.

INDEX